THE KHOE AND SAN
AN ANNOTATED BIBLIOGRAPHY

VOLUME TWO

Shelagh Willet

*in cooperation with Sidsel Saugestad of
the University of Tromsø, and assisted by
Violet Radiporo and Albertina Motlogi of
the University of Botswana.*

THE KHOE AND SAN: AN ANNOTATED BIBLIOGRAPHY: VOLUME TWO

Published by *LIGHTBOOKS*
a division of
Lentswe La Lesedi (Pty) Ltd
PO Box 2365, Gaborone, Botswana.
Tel: 3903994, Fax: 3914017, E-mail: publisher@lightbooks.net

First published 2003

ISBN 99912-71-32-5

© Copyright University of Botswana/University of Tromsø Collaborative Programme for San/Basarwa Research and Capacity building (NUFU PRO 20/96) 2002

All rights reserved. No part of the work contained in this publication may be reproduced, stored in a retrieval system, or transmitted by any means without the prior permission of the publisher and the copyright holders.

Typesetting and design by *LENTSWE LA LESEDI (PTY) LTD*

Cover design by Paul Melenhorst

Maps by Bjørn Hatteng

Printed by Printing and Publishing Botswana (Pty) Ltd

Contents

Preface to Volume 2 v

Preface to Volume 1 vii

Botswana, Namibia and South Africa: Frequently Mentioned Locations viii

Approximate distribution of Main Khoe and San languages ix

Introduction 1

Abstracts 9

Author Index 113

Subject Index 117

Geographic Index 123

Preface to Volume 2

This second volume of the *Khoe and San Bibliography* has been produced to fulfil several purposes. It extends the scope of the first volume and supplements it with new subject fields and authors that were previously missing. For example, much of the earlier linguistic material by Dorothea F. Bleek, L.F. Maingard and others, which first appeared in *African Studies* and other South African publications, have been included. These studies were of a groundbreaking nature but were probably not well known outside the southern African region. Some articles in Afrikaans relate to the earliest attempts to record the language of the Khoekhoe at the Cape. In addition, new studies carried out by Professor Keyan Tomaselli and his students at the University of Natal's Centre for Cultural and Media Studies bring in information on the way in which San have been portrayed in films. Several recent publications included in the *Bibliography* reflect new insights in areas not previously dealt with, as for example two books based on the Bleek/Lloyd translations of the folklore related by the |Xam informants. The texts reveal their lyrical and imaginative abilities as the hitherto almost incomprehensive originals come back to life. Several other recently published articles refer to San characters who have appeared in literary works such as Margaret in Bessie Head's novel *Maru*. In the context of the New South Africa, it is also interesting to note that the motto on the national coat of arms is in the extinct San language |Xam and means 'People who are different come together' and the two heraldic figures on the coat of arms are based upon a rock painting.

Much recently published material is illustrative of the present status of the San and Khoe peoples as they strive to surmount the challenges they face as marginalized minority groups in their respective countries. Notable among these are the five volumes of the *Regional Assessment of the Current Status of the San in Southern Africa* (Suzman *et al.*), commissioned in 1996 by the European Union. These volumes contain valuable statistical information plus analysis of various aspects of San life in each of the countries covered by the report. One volume deals with gender issues.

There have been several relevant conferences of which the collected papers are now in published form. Most of these conferences took place in Botswana and the following are included in this volume:

- *Proceedings from the Basarwa Research Workshop Gaborone. 2–25 August 1995* (Paul Lane, Janet Hermans and Chadzimula Molebatsi, eds.).

- *Parks, Property and Power; Managing Hunting Practice within State Regimes. Papers presented at the 8th International Conference on Hunting and Gathering Societies (CHAGS). Osaka, 1998* (David G. Anderson and Kazinubu Ikeya, eds.).

- *The State of the Khoesan Languages in Botswana. Mogoditshane, 2000* (Herman M. Batibo and Joseph Tsonope, eds.).

- *Minorities in the Millenium: Perspectives from Botswana. Gaborone, 2000* (Isaac N. Mazonde, ed.).
- *Africa's Indigenous Peoples: 'First Peoples' or 'Marginalized Minorities'? Edinburgh, 2000* (Alan Barnard and Justin Kenrick eds).
- *Education for Remote Area Dwellers in Botswana: Problems and Perspectives. Gaborone, 2001* (Otto Oussoren, ed.).

Research on San and Khoe topics continues to proliferate and reports of advocacy organizations such as the Working Group of Minorities in Southern Africa (WIMSA), the Southern African San Institute (SASI) and the Kuru Development Trust indicate the valuable practical work taking place in various areas of southern Africa. Khoe and San are active participants in this work, and increasingly the reports have Khoe or San authors.

The Khoe and San Collection in the University of Botswana Library

The collection upon which the *Bibliography* is based, contains items not yet abstracted, including antiquarian books, information in French on the Cape Khoe, and much other relevant material. One publication of special interest is the book *Qauqaua*, a folktale in Naro, the first book published in this language. It has colourful illustrations by the Kuru artists. This book has been acquired by such well-known organizations as The Smithsonian Institution, the Library of Congress and the Bodleian at Oxford. The Smithsonian has included it as one of the highlights in an exhibition of rare volumes in their collection. The copy ordered for the University of Botswana Library bound in leather and beautifully printed, will be one of the treasures of the University of Botswana Special Collection.

Acknowledgements

The current volume has largely been compiled by Shelagh Willet with the assistance of Violet Radiporo and Albertina Motlogi, both of whom are currently employed in the Documentation and Special Collection of the University of Botswana Library. Their regular involvement will mean continuity as additional documents are obtained for abstracting, and added to the collection. As for the previous volume, the participation of Motlalepula Peloyame in the data entry has been greatly appreciated while Mr K.N. Rao, Senior Librarian (Systems) has provided invaluable technical assistance in the preparation of the document for the publisher. Thanks are also due to Sidsel Saugestad for her continued interest in and support of the *Bibliography* in spite of her very busy academic schedule in Norway, and to Hazel Hudson at the local office of the Collaborative Programme for San (Basarwa) Research and Capacity Building, for practical support in many ways.

Shelagh Willet
Gaborone June 2003

Preface to Volume 1

The publishing of this book – *The Khoe and San Bibliography* – is a groundbreaking event in the field of Basarwa studies. I first got to know about the bibliography project when it started in 1993, during my tenure as Vice Chancellor of the University of Botswana, and I have followed it with interest ever since. The goal is to bring together into one collection all written material on the Basarwa, or San, of Southern Africa, both published and unpublished, and to provide annotations. Needless to say, this is a daunting task, and the volume presented here representsonly the 'tip of the iceberg'. It is my sincere hope that more will follow, and that this exercise will remain a core activity of our University Library.

The inspiration for this project came from a Norwegian anthropologist from the University of Tromsø, Professor Sidsel Saugestad, who originally came to Botswana in 1992 as a Research Facilitator for the Remote Area Development Programme, on a two-year NORAD contract. Working closely with Stella Monageng, Senior Documentalist of the Documentation Unit of the then National Institute for Development Research and Documentation, the idea was developed and others were brought in to assist. An ongoing collaborative programme for San/Basarwa Research between the University of Tromsø and the University of Botswana, which is funded by the Norwegian Council of Universities' Committee for Development Research and Education (NUFU), has provided financial support for the project since 1996.

This printed volume of the Khoe and San Bibliography can also be accessed through the database at the University of Botswana Library, and all the literature annotated is available for consultation, as part of the Botswana Documentation and Special Collection. The Bibliography will undoubtedly be a valuable resource for scholars, students, and all interested parties. Most particularly it is hoped that this collection will serve the interest of San organisations and individuals. The University of Botswana is fortunate to house such a unique collection in its library, and those who have worked so painstakingly over the years to produce this volume are to be heartily congratulated.

Thomas Tlou

Professor of History, University of Botswana

Gaborone, January 2001

BOTSWANA, NAMIBIA AND SOUTH AFRICA: FREQUENTLY MENTIONED LOCATIONS

Approximate distribution of Main Khoe and San languages

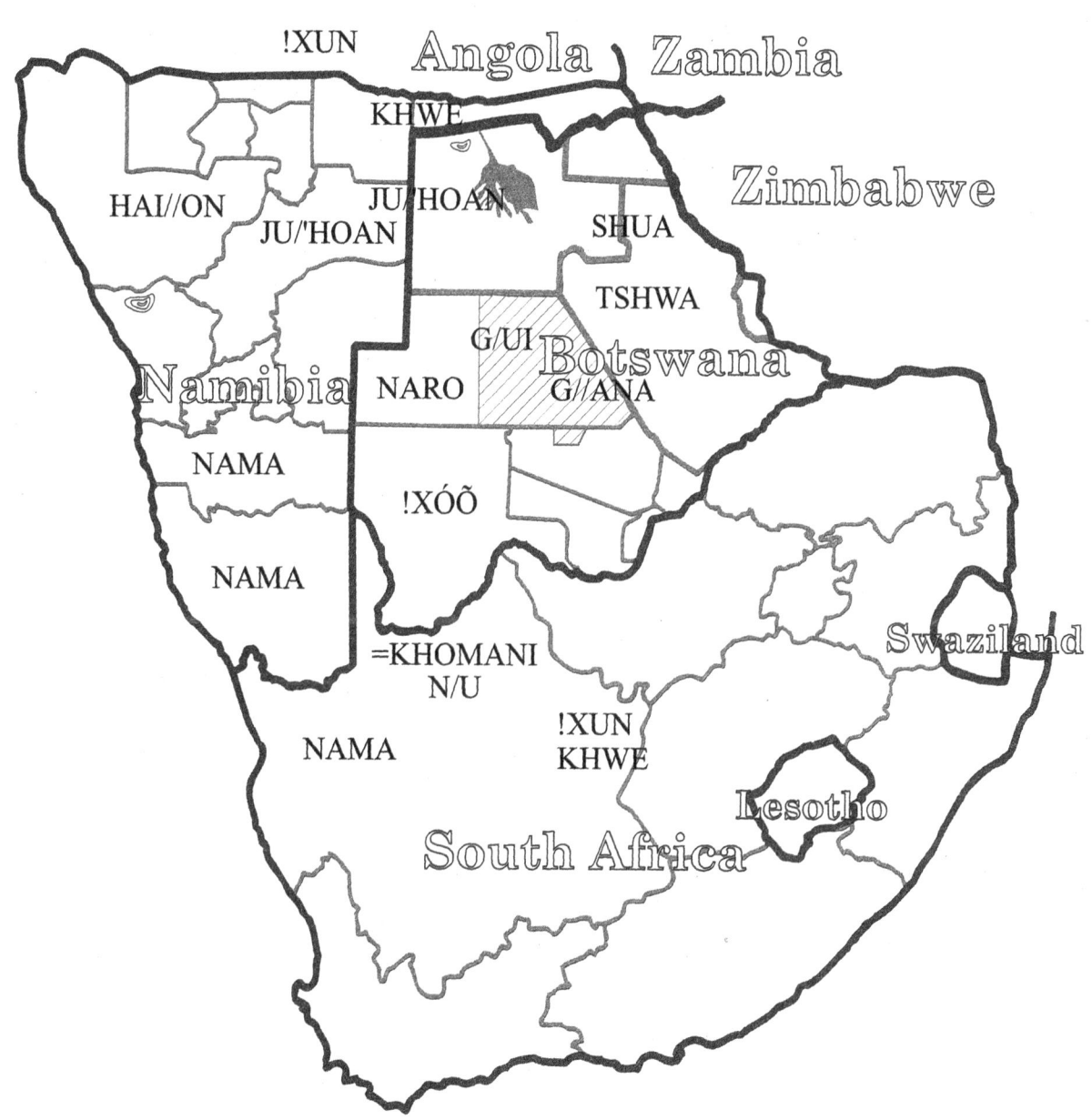

INTRODUCTION

The University of Botswana is presently undertaking a number of activities with the aim of promoting research on, with and by the indigenous minority of Southern Africa, known variously as the Bushmen, Khoesan, San, Basarwa, or N/oakwe. One core activity has so far been known by its working title, "The Basarwa Bibliography Project", which started in 1993. The ultimate objective is for the collection to include all contemporary written material relating to the Khoe and San people of Southern Africa.

It is worth noting that despite the commonly held assertion that the San/Basarwa are among the most researched peoples in the world (an assertion which is only partly true) there is not, anywhere else, to our knowledge, a thematic collection of contemporary literature similar to the Khoe and San Collection in the University of Botswana Library. It is certainly time for such an effort to be launched, and considering the fact that the majority of the Bushmen of Africa are also citizens of Botswana, it is most appropriate that this collection is located at the University of Botswana.

All the titles annotated is this volume can also be accessed in the database at the Botswana Documentation and Special Collection of the University of Botswana Library, and are available on the shelves or in filing cabinets, for consultation.

PROBLEMS OF TERMINOLOGY

One of the problems in recording publications on the people who are the topic of this bibliography, is the lack of an all-embracing generic term that is generally suitable and accepted by all. In Botswana, the official name is Basarwa, but this is not used at all in Namibia or South Africa, where the most common term is San. San representatives in Namibia have adopted San as their preference, and San is favoured in anthropological literature, while Khoesan is increasingly used to denote the broad cultural/linguistic field. The terms Bushmen, or the gender-neutral Bush People, are also widely used. There has been much debate over which of all these appellations has the most derogatory connotation, but this debate has to a large extent focused on the etymological and historical origin of the different labels, not their use. Clearly, *any* terms used to express negative attitudes about a group of people will eventually take on a disparaging meaning, and in this respect, no term is better or worse than the others.

It is the experience from similar situations elsewhere when indigenous populations strive to define their role within the encompassing nation state (or states) that a term for self-appellation must be found with which the members of the group themselves feel comfortable. This requires a process of ethnopolitical conscientization that has not yet run its full course in Southern Africa. Hopefully, over the next few years, this process will bring forward one single term that is acceptable and used by all parties (Saugestad, 2001).

In an early working copy of this bibliography, the problem was evaded by listing as the title the most commonly used names, in historical and present time (Saugestad and Hermans, 1993). We have now selected the terms Khoe and San as the name for the bibliography. This is a construction with which no particular group identifies. However, the two terms reflect properly the comprehensive scope of the bibliographic project. The title chosen alludes to Khoesan as a linguistic term, on the same level of generalization as 'Bantu' and 'Indo-European', referring to categories of language users that are extremely diverse both in time and in space. At the same time the diversity of Khoe and San people is a recurrent topic of debate. However, although not being a clearly defined sociological entity, Khoe and San people have some common characteristics. They are speakers, or descendants of people who have been speaking, Khoesan languages in contrast to Bantu languages, and they share a past as hunter-gatherers or herders, in contrast to Bantu agro-pastoralists. In contemporary society, they share the common experience of being a disadvantaged minority in situations of daily interaction with representatives of the majority.

The regional organisation representing San people, the Working Group of Indigenous Minorities in Southern Africa (WIMSA 2000) recommend that the term is split into two – Khoe and San – to avoid any indication that the one group is before or higher than the other, and we have followed this recommendation. For the purpose of this bibliography we have wanted to use as neutral and abstract terms as possible, leaving it to the reader to determine what they see as the most salient social distinctions.

Although the Bibliography is entitled the *Khoe and San Bibliography*, the focus on the current volume has been on the San, largely because the core collection consists of documents from Botswana dealing with the San people. However, in the linguistic field there are documents dealing with Khoe (Khoi) languages and, in addition, some books on the history and culture of the Khoekhoe (Khoikhoi). In later volumes of the Bibliography, additional material will be added and the balance should thus be adjusted.

THE COLLABORATIVE PROGRAMME FOR SAN/BASARWA RESEARCH AND CAPACITY BUILDING

The activities connected with the bibliography project are part of a broader range of initiatives at the University of Botswana, reflecting a commitment towards the advancement of scholarship in San/Basarwa research. The main objectives of the collaborative programme are –

- To pursue innovative strategies for promoting San access to higher education and capacity building
- To identify ways in which research can make a positive contribution to San development
- To promote and further develop research capacity and competence among University staff and students
- To ensure that capacity is reflected in appropriate teaching and studies within and outside of the University
- To establish a network for San research in the region.

This programme is a collaborative research programme between the University of Botswana and the University of Tromsø, Norway. Norwegian funding has been provided from the Norwegian Council of Universities' Committee for Development Research and Education (NUFU PRO 20/96). Activities include: a number of research projects; international research networking; staff development and training; conferences and workshops; publications; and outreach activities. The Basarwa Bibliography Project, started in 1993 by Stella Monageng, then Senior Documentalist of the then National Institute of Development Research and Documentation (NIR), and Sidsel Saugestad, who at that time was Research Facilitator connected with the Remote Area Development Programme. Saugestad and Monageng later continued as counterparts when the project became part of the NUFU-funded collaborative programme. Since 1996, NUFU funding has financed the abstracting of documents and data entry done by Shelagh Willet.

THE PRESENT STATUS OF THE PROJECT

The design of the project took as its point of departure the ongoing activities of the Unit for Documentation Services at the University of Botswana/NIR. The Unit had developed procedures for collecting, cataloguing, abstracting and publishing material on the economic and social development of Botswana. The collection includes a 'grey zone' of unpublished documents, reports, pamphlets and theses. Thus, the Documentation Unit fills a niche between the 'regular' libraries, focusing on published material, on the one hand, and the National Archives, on the other. When the Documentation Unit was moved to the Main University Library in 1999, the collection of documents became incorporated in the Botswana Documentation and Special Collection.

The collection so far comprises some 1500 titles. All of these are registered in the database, and abstracts have been made. The items are available for consultation, and can be traced by author and a range of main, secondary and geographic descriptors.

The present volume includes just over 1000 titles. The selection of documents to be included in this first volume has been mainly pragmatic: we have started with those items most easily accessible in Gaborone, and those documents that have been donated by helpful authors. In addition, Dr. Richard Rhode went through the Library of the Centre for African Studies at the University of Edinburgh in 1998, and made copies of all material referring to the San/Basarwa. This particular exercise was funded by the European Union, as part of the preparation for a Regional Assessment of the San of Southern Africa.

To some extent, the emphasis on written materials of the non-conventional or fugitive type that otherwise might be difficult to locate, is reflected in the collection. There may be important items that have been left out so far. However, the present volume must be seen as just one stage in an ongoing process. The ambitious long-term objective is to include, ultimately, all relevant contemporary literature. Such literature must be extracted from individuals, organisations, libraries, and other sources in the entire Southern African region, and from libraries in Europe and the USA.

Guidelines for inclusion of items
The following broad guidelines are being followed in the collection of items:

Language

The collection endeavours to include all available documents in English and in or about any Khoesan language. Literature in any other language will be included if an abstract in English can be provided.

Culture

The collection endeavours to include the ethnography of all people known, or previously known, as San/Bushmen and Khoe/KhoeKhoe, including speakers of Nama, the Hadza and Sandawe of Tanzania, and descendants of former Khoesan-speaking groups in South Africa, such as, for example, the Griqua.

Time period

The focus is on contemporary literature. Older literature is included when available. A few antiquarian volumes have been included and are available for inspection upon special request.

Quality

Inclusion in the bibliography *does not* reflect any assessment of the quality of the document. The present collection also includes the unfounded, the racist, the sentimental, the superficial and the stereotyped writings on the Bushmen. However, documents that are clearly in a draft form, i.e., not yet a finished work are as a rule not included. Conference and seminar papers are not included in cases where a full proceeding of papers is promised by the organisers.

Disciplines

All documents that provide information or understanding of the cultural, historical, social, economic, political, linguistic and legal situation of the Khoesan people are included.

Borderline cases are many, and they have to be dealt with on a case-by-case basis. The most typical borderline cases are of the following kinds:

- Books and articles that mainly argue a theoretical (for instance a linguistic or medical) point, and that draw on secondary ethnographic material on Khoesan people only by way of illustration, are sometimes left out.
- In a strict sense, it can be argued that all literature on rock art as well as all archaeology on Stone Age adaptations deals with 'the Bushmen'. We have, however, concentrated on documents and reports that may contribute to an understanding of history and culture.
- Policy papers that have a fairly clear relevance for the Khoesan peoples, such as the Remote Area Development Programme in Botswana, and various development and human rights issues, have been included.

However, many documents covering broad fields of development policies such as nature conservation and wildlife management, may be of obvious relevance for San settlements, but are not exhaustively included in this collection.
- We have not included single articles from newspapers. However, a number of collections of newspaper cuttings have been included.

Authors who have kindly submitted copies of their publications may note that some of these have not been included, because they were obtained after the cut-off date for this volume (which is quite some time back). They will, however, appear in the next volume. In addition, the next volume will give coverage of periodicals and newsletters such as *Kuru News*, and *N=oahn: Newsletter*.

PROBLEMS OF STANDARDIZATION AND ORTHOGRAPHY

In the actual recording of titles and abstract, it has not only been the lack of an appropriate cover term for San people that has represented a problem. As will be abundantly clear in the abstracts, there is a deplorable lack of standardisation in references to languages, speech communities, and place names (Smith, 1998; Treis, 1998; Saugestad, 2000). A main objective of the bibliography is to highlight the variety and the diversification *within* the group of people that outsiders refer to as Bushmen, San or Basarwa. At the same time it is necessary to counteract some of the confusion that is created by the proliferation of spellings devised by explorers and anthropologists.

Accordingly, we have found it necessary to develop a standardised taxonomy that can be used to refer to the different Khoesan languages and speech communities. The taxonomy and orthography used are mainly based on Traill (1994, 1995) and Andersson and Janson (1997). We have also consulted Güldemann (1998), Batibo and Tsonope (eds) (2000), and the *Penduka Declaration* (Government of the Republic of Namibia, 2001).

In order to match the individual entry with this standardised taxonomy we have followed the procedure below.

- In the entry of a title, and in the abstract, we have used the author's choice and spelling of a term. For instance Zu/aosi, Gcui. However, the main descriptor (keyword) to be used in a search for entries are the standardised forms, in this case Ju/'hoansi and G/ui (see list below).
- Depending on the level of precision in the item entered, we use one of the main families of languages as main descriptor (that is to say Ju, Khoe or Southern) or we use the name of the particular language.
- The symbols of the IPA, the International Phonetic Association (/, //,!, =, and ?) are used to denote the click sound. Whenever an IPA symbol comes first in a name, we capitalise the first roman letter. Authors and place names that begin with the same click are alphabetised according to the first roman letter.
- We use the terms Ju for the Northern family of languages, and Khoe for the Central family of languages, while we retain the term Southern for

the third family of languages to include !Xóo (of the Taa dialect cluster) and /'Auni (of the !Kwi language cluster)

The language names used as keywords are the following (sub-divisions that are or may be mainly dialect variations are given in brackets):

JU (Northern)	**Ju/'hoansi** (! Kung, =Kx'au//'ei)
	!Xun (in Angola and Schmidsdrift)
	=Hua
KHOE (Central)	**Naro**
	G/ui (G//ana)
	Tshwa, (Cua, Kua, Tsua, Hietchware)
	Shua (Cara, Danisi, Deti, Ts'ixa, /Xaise)
	Khwe, (//Ani, !Anda, Buga)
	Khoekhoe (Nama, Damara, Hai//om)
SOUTHERN[1]	**!Xóo**
(Taa and !Kwi)	**/'Auni**
	=Khomani
	/Xam (extinct)

OTHER KEYWORDS (MAIN DESCRIPTORS)

All the records in this bibliography have been entered in the database of the University Library, using Micro CDS/ISIS software. In selecting keywords we have not restricted ourselves to the OECD Macro thesaurus, but have developed our own terminology. First and foremost, this refers to names of languages and language groups, as indicated above. In addition we have used keywords that may help to retrieve documents according to the particulars of historical records, subsistence activities (including 'conventional' economic activities), and the multi-faceted aspects of social organisation. Wherever possible, we have noted geographical location (place-name or district) of the study reported on.

The emergence of organisations representing the San people has been a notable feature of developments during the last decade of the 20th century. Written material by and about these organisations, are included in the collection. Due to certain conventions, however, the names of Nyae Nyae Farmers Co-operative (now the Nyae Nyae Conservancy), Nyae Nyae Development Foundation of Namibia (NNDFN), Kuru Development Trust (KDT), First People of the Kalahari (KDT), the !Xu and Kxoe Development Trust, the Working Group of Indigenous Minorities of Southern Africa (WIMSA) and the South African San Institute (SASI) are not listed as keywords in the subject index. It is possible, however, to retrieve them by combining keywords such as 'Non-Governmental Organisations' and 'Advocacy.'

---

[1] Used here as a linguistic term, not a geographical one.

Acknowledgements

A collection like the present one is the outcome of teamwork where many people deserve thanks. First of all the invaluable contribution and commitment of Shelagh Willet should be recognised. Shelagh Willet has done most of the abstracts and has also liaised with public offices, NGOs and libraries to expand the collection. Janet Hermans, of Logistics Consultancy, did most of the earlier abstracts and has continued as a valuable supporter and proof-reader.

The project has been warmly supported by the University of Botswana, particularly by Professor Ansu Datta, then Director of NIR, Professor Thomas Tlou who was Vice-Chancellor when the project started, the present Vice-Chancellor, Professor Sharon Siverts, and Dr. Joseph Tsonope, Botswana coordinator of the NUFU Collaborative programme and Dean of Humanities.

Data entry has been ably provided by Keletso Ranku, Motlalepula Peloyame, Keletso Ndebele, and the late Florence Obakeng.

Last but not least, thanks to Charles Bewlay for extremely efficient and competent copy editing and proofreading.

Sidsel Saugestad   *Stella Monageng*

Gaborone, November 2001

References

Andersson, L. and Janson, T. 1997: *Languages in Botswana*. Longman Botswana.

Batibo, H. and Tsonope, J. (eds): 2000: *The State of Khoesan Language Studies in Botswana*. Mogoditshane: Tasalls Publishing.

Government of the Republic of Namibia, 2001. *Report on the First Regional San Education Conference*. Windhoek: Governmment of the Republic of Namibia.

Güldemann, T. 1998: San Languages for Education: A Linguistic Short Survey and Proposal. Okahandja: National Institute of Educational Development.

Saugestad, S. and Hermans, J. 1993: The Bushmen / Khoisan / San / Basarwa / Ju/'hoan / N/oakhwe: An Annotated Bibliography, A Working Copy. University of Botswana/NIR.

Saugestad, S. 2001: *The Inconvenient Indigenous. Remote Area Development in Botswana, Donor Assistance and the First People of the Kalahari*. Uppsala: Nordic Africa Institute.

Saugestad, S. 2000: "The Need for Standardisation of References to Khoesan Languages – A User's Perspective". In Batibo, H. and Tsonope, J. (eds), 2000: *The State of Khoesan Language Studies in Botswana*. Gaborone: Tasalls Publishing.

Smith, A. 1998: "Khoesaan Orthography". *South African Archaeological Bulletin* 53:37–38.

Traill, A. 1994: "Khoesan Languages: An overview". In Saugestad, S. and Tsonope, J. (eds) *Developing Basarwa Research and Research for Basarwa Development*. University of Botswana/NIR.

Traill, A. 1995: "The Khoesan Languages of South Africa". In Mesthrie, R. (ed): *Language and Social History: Studies in South African Sociolinguistics*. Cape Town: David Philip.

Treis, Y. 1998: "Names of Khoisan Languages and Their Variants". In Schladt, M. (ed), *Language, Identity and Conceptualisation among the Khoisan*. Cologne: Rüdiger Köppe Verlag.

Working Group of Indigenous Minorities in Southern Africa (WIMSA). 2000: *Report on Activities April 1999 to March 2000*. Windhoek: WIMSA.

ABSTRACTS

0001 Adams, F.; Werner, W.
THE LAND ISSUE IN NAMIBIA: AN INQUIRY
Windhoek: Namibia Institute for Social and Economic Research, July 1990. 92pp.
The report on the land issue in Namibia deals mainly with the politics of land policies during both the German period and during the South African jurisdiction of the country and is primary concerned with agricultural issues. Examines each geographical area of Namibia in turn and, in the sections dealing with Caprivi and Bushmanland, describes the problems faced by the Bushman inhabitants and the effect upon them of Government policies and the activities of the South African Defence Force. The section entitled "Bushmanland: Ju/Wa farms in Eastern Bushmanland, 1986" gives details of the establishment of the Nyae Nyae Farmers' Cooperative and its aims and achievements. Outlines the traditional land use system of the Ju/Wa and how this has been adapted to allow a form of mixed land utilization involving both cattle-rearing and traditional use of veld products and game. Highlights the tensions between Ju/Wa and the Department of Nature Conservation which wished to proclaim a Game Reserve in the area.
NAMIBIA; NYAE NYAE; AGRICULTURE; COMMUNAL LAND; COOPERATIVES; FARMING; GAME RESERVES; LAND RIGHTS; LAND USE; SELF-DETERMINATION
92/182

0002 Akira, Takada
THE !XU SAN: POVERTY AND TENSION
Cultural Survival Quarterly, Vol.26 No.1, 2002. pp.18–19.
The article reports on the history of !Xu San in north-central Namibia (formerly Ovamboland) and the social changes that have occurred as a result of Namibia's independence struggle and of the former influence of Finnish Lutheran missionaries. Reports on the existence of tensions between San and their Ovambo neighbours which require active intervention by government, churches and non-governmental organizations.
NAMIBIA; !XUN; MISSIONARIES; NON-GOVERNMENTAL ORGANISATIONS; POVERTY; OVAMBO; SOCIAL CHANGE
R/B 305.8096872 CUL

0003 Amadi, Elechi
//ATARAS
Windhoek: Gamsberg Macmillan, 1997. 282pp.
The novel translated from English into Khoekhoegowab includes a synopsis of the story and is included to demonstrate the orthography employed for the writing of this language in Namibia.
NAMIBIA; KHOEKHOEGOWAB; LANGUAGES; LINGUISTICS; LITERATURE
R/B 496.1 AMA

0004 Anon
THE "STRANDLOPER" SITES OF THE SOUTH AFRICAN COAST
Sampson, C. Garth. The stone age archaeology of southern Africa, Academic Press, 1974. pp.403–438.
The paper looks at the results of investigations of "Strandloper" and other Stone Age sites along the coast of South Africa from the Atlantic coast to the Natal coast. Comments that Van Riebeeck, in his journal, refers to Bushmen from the mountains and Strandlopers who lived on the coast. Considers that these Bushmen probably belonged to the Wilton technical tradition while the Strandlopers were part of an older tradition rooted in the Oakhurst complex. Concludes that the Strandlopers therefore represented an ancient and isolated Stone Age culture which was influenced by bearers of the Wilton culture.
CAPE; SOUTH AFRICA; ARCHAEOLOGY; HISTORY
98/1174

0005 Argyle, W.J.
THE EXTENT AND NATURE OF KHOISAN INFLUENCE ON ZULU
Bernd Heine Sprache und Geschichte in Afrika, Vol.7 No.1, Helmut Buske, Hamburg, 1986. 465pp. pp.43–71. ISBN 3871187607.
The paper examines the attempt by W. Bourquin to estimate the degree of Khoesan influence on Zulu by simply counting the number of pages in the Zulu-English Dictionary which list stems with initial clicks and then giving this number as a factor of the total number of pages in the dictionary. Discusses three major faults which render this method ineffectual: a) the method does not discriminate between the substantive minority of items with clicks which are marked as originating from the uku-hlonipa custom and the majority not so marked; b) ignores the possibility that many items with clicks may be of Bantu origin and so the extent of Khoesan lexical influence may be overestimated; c) there may be many Zulu stems in which non-click consonants have been substituted for the original clicks borrowed from Khoisan languages.
ZULU; SOUTH AFRICA; CLICKS; KHOESAN; LANGUAGES; LINGUISTICS
95/824

0006 Bain, Donald
THE BUSHMEN OF THE KGALAGADI
Empire Exhibition, 1936. 14pp.
The booklet contains a number of photographs of Kalahari Bushmen described as "the last living remnants of a dying race". Makes a plea for the establishment of a reserve in which these "simple, loveable people, unfortunately unable to assimilate the methods of modern civilization" might live in their own way. Notes that the author intends to donate 50% of the income derived from the exhibition of the Bushmen at the Em-

pire Exhibition, to the establishment of a fund to preserve the "aboriginal denizens of the Kalahari Desert".
BOTSWANA; CULTURE; DANCE; PHOTOS; SOCIAL ORGANISATION
99/154

0007 Barnard, Alan
NHARO BUSHMAN KINSHIP AND THE TRANSFORMATION OF KHOI KIN CATEGORIES
Thesis (PhD): University London, Department of Anthropology, London, 1976. 249pp.
The thesis concerns Nharo kinship and its explanation in terms of the general terms of Khoi kinship. The thesis is divided into two parts. Part I includes a brief description and analysis of Nharo culture followed by a descriptive analysis of the kinship system. Considers the method and significance of kin categorization which is extended universally throughout society by means of the naming system. Also looks at social conventions and socio-territorial organization. Provides comparative data on other Khoisan groups. Part II, based partly on the author's fieldwork among several other Khoi peoples and partly on published sources, concerns the unity of Khoi kinship and the structural and probable historical relationship amongst the various kinship systems. Views the Nharo system as a "Khoi" rather than a "San" one. Postulates three types of Khoi system in order of probable historical development; Khoikhoi (e.g. Nama), Central Khoi Bushman (e.g. G/wikhwe) and Western Khoi Bushman (e.g. Nharo). Includes a theoretical and comparative discussion on universal systems of kin categorization in which every member of society is classified as a member of some kin category. Concludes that the Nharo system represents Khoi kinship in its simplest form and that the notion of deep structure is an important key to its understanding.
BOTSWANA; NAMIBIA; BELIEFS; G/UI; KINSHIP; NAMA; NARO; RELIGION; RESEARCH; SOCIAL ORGANISATION
TH 301.296872 BAR

0008 Barnard, Alan
STATE OF THE ART IN ANTHROPOLOGY AND SOCIOLOGY: KEYNOTE ADDRESS
Lane, Paul; Hermans, Janet; Molebatsi, Chadzimula, Proceedings from the Basarwa Research Workshop, Gaborone, 24–25 August, 1995. Refs, 106pp, 2001. pp.3–20.
The keynote address from the Basarwa Research Workshop held in the University of Botswana in August 1995 provides information on research already carried, among the Basarwa. Lists the names of the researchers and gives details of the groups they studied and the main area of specialization or interest. Sets out these details in the context of his own research background. Reveals how work on settlement and kinship developed and became the main thrust of further investigation and suggests how the results might be of practical value. Examines the three major types of research: empirical, theoretical and applied, and shows how they relate to each other. Points out that applied research has two aspects, namely research on behalf of the community at the source of the data, and research on behalf of the community receiving the data. Concludes that good, empirical research with a clear theoretical background may be applicable both locally and internationally.
BOTSWANA; NAMIBIA; !XOO; =KHOMANI; =HUA; CONFERENCE PAPERS; CULTURE; G/UI; G//ANA; NARO; RESEARCH; TERRITORIALITY
R/B 305.8096872 PRO

0009 Barnard, Alan; Widlok, T.
NHARO AND HAI//OM: SETTLEMENT PATTERNS IN COMPARATIVE PERSPECTIVE
Kent, Susan. Cultural diversity among twentieth-century foragers: an African perspective. Cambridge, Cambridge University Press, ill., maps, 1996. xiii, 344pp. pp.87–107. ISBN 0521482372.
The chapter uses the method of regional comparison to examine settlement patterns among several groups of Nharo in Botswana and of Hai//om in Namibia. Justifies the methodology employed. Examines the factors which influence the effects on the Nharo and Hai//om of establishment of commercial farms in their former hunting and gathering areas. Shows, by means of case studies, that both groups display a variety of settlement patterns. Considers it significant that an individual can move from one settlement to another and therefore from one settlement type to another. Notes, as an important factor, the persistent foraging ethos common to both groups studied, and suggests that the new structures are treated as something to be foraged as was previously the case with the natural environment. Suggests further topics for research which might employ methodological tools from such diverse disciplines as genealogy, ecology and diplomacy.
BOTSWANA; NAMIBIA; FARM WORKERS; FORAGING; HAI//OM; NARO; SEDENTISM; SETTLEMENTS; SOCIAL ORGANIZATION
306.346 CUL

0010 Barnard, Alan; Kenrick, Justin
AFRICA'S INDIGENOUS PEOPLES: 'FIRST PEOPLES' OR 'MARGINALISED MINORITIES'?
Edinburgh: University of Edinburgh, Centre of African Studies, 2001. xv, 322pp.
The book is based on a conference held on May 24 and 25 2000 and focuses on the indigenous peoples living in modern African states. Notes that one purpose of the conference was to draw attention to the plight of some of the most economically disadvantaged groups on the continent. Comments that

such people are also among the world's most culturally resilient populations. The preface examines definitions of the term "indigenous". Notes that according to one definition the term denotes peoples who are differentiated from others by virtue of: a) their origin in a territory; b) subjugation by external political structures such as those of nation states; c) self-definition as indigenous or "first people". Shows how this definition may be problematic for African governments which consider that all their citizens are indigenous while often regarding those claiming to be "first people" as "backward" or "primitive". Looks briefly at the concept of "marginalised minorities" appearing in the title of this volume, a description which evokes the revisionist position in which indigenous populations were seen as subjugated groups or minorities. Chapters dealing with the southern African San are separately abstracted under authors in this bibliography.
BOTSWANA; SOUTHERN AFRICA; CONFERENCE REPORTS; INDIGENOUS PEOPLES; INTERACTION; POLITICS; REVISIONISM
R/B 305.80968 AFR

0011 Batibo, Herman M.; Tsonope, Joseph
LANGUAGE VITALITY AMONG THE NAMA OF TSABONG
Batibo, Herman M.; Tsonope, Joseph. The state of Khoesan languages in Botswana. Mogoditshane: Tasalls, ill., 2000. viii, 169pp., pp.47–56. ISBN 9991295208.
The chapter describes the extent to which the Nama of Matlhatlaganye Ward in Tshabong, south-western Botswana, have succeeded in keeping their language as a viable communication medium. Notes that they arrived in what is now Botswana from 1904–1907 having fled from Namibia during the war between the Germans and Herero. Shows the positive attitude of Nama speakers towards their language. Notes that they wish their children to acquire their mother-tongue and use it correctly. Provides information on the use and knowledge of other languages among the Tshabong Nama. Finds that most Nama, while wishing to integrate into Tswana society, also wished to retain their ethnic identity as Nama. Notes, however, that for the Nama language to survive in Tshabong it would have to provide socio-economic advantages if it was to be attractive to younger Nama. Concludes that eventually language shift and possibly language death will overtake Nama in Tshabong.
BOTSWANA; TSHABONG; INTERGROUP RELATIONS; KHOEKHOEGOWAB; LANGUAGES; LINGUISTICS; SETSWANA
R/B 496.1 STA

0012 Batibo, Herman M.; Tsonope, Joseph
PATTERNS OF CULTURAL EXCHANGE BETWEEN BANTU AND KHOESAN LANGUAGES: LINGUISTIC EVIDENCE FROM G/WI, NARO, SETSWANA AND SEKGALAGADI
Lane, Paul; Hermans, Janet; Molebatsi, Chadzimula. Proceedings from the Basarwa Research Workshop, Gaborone, 24–25 August, 1995. 106pp. 2001. pp.88–97.
The paper presented at the Basarwa Research Workshop held 24–25 August 1995, uses linguistic information to deduce the degree of cultural interaction which has taken place between Bantu and Khoesan-speaking peoples in the Kalahari region of southern Africa. Presents four possible theories regarding cultural exchange between Khoe-speaking Bushmen and Bantu-speakers and suggests that all four theories may be relevant in varying degrees depending on the Khoesan languages in question. Examines data from the Bantu languages Setswana and Sekgalagadi and from the Khoesan Languages Naro and G/wi. Concludes that the data suggests that when comparing Naro and G/wi few Bantu loan words were found, which suggests the two groups had few contacts with Bantu-speaking groups until the recent past and that many loan words in these languages represent modern socio-economic and political terms. Contends that the study shows that while some groups may have been in contact with non-Khoesan groups in the past, linguistic studies point to the fact that others remained isolated until recently. Concludes that the study demonstrated the value of linguistic approaches to studies of prehistory.
BOTSWANA; G/UI; LANGUAGES; LINGUISTICS; NARO; SEKGALAGADI; SETSWANA
R/B 305.8096872 PRO

0013 Batibo, Herman M.; Tsonope, Joseph
THE STATE OF KHOESAN LANGUAGES IN BOTSWANA
Mogoditshane: Tasalls, 2000. xxi, 169pp. ISBN 9991295208
The book supercedes the collected proceedings of the International Workshop on Khoesan Language Studies held in Gaborone in 1999 (Vol.1 No.0056). The Introduction gives the aims of the Workshop as follows: review of the current state of Khoesan studies in southern Africa and particularly in Botswana by the identification of gaps in the knowledge of the number and location of these languages; examination of the present state of their classification; the level of linguistic and literary documentation; strategies for preparing orthographies, dictionaries, grammar books and other reference materials; patterns of language use and transmission among the Khoesan speakers, and factors determining language shift/ death or maintenance. Explains that the Workshop contributions were rewritten or revised to form the current volume. Notes that the book contains two main sections: Part 1 deals with the descriptive and comparative aspects of the Khoesan languages and Part 2 is concerned with sociolinguistic and educational issues. Lists recommendations aimed at establishing common working procedures among Khoesan language specialists and at facilitating the promotion of these languages for practical use. Notes that the recommendations are to be facilitated through the establishment of an International Re-

source Committee composed of scholars from Botswana, Namibia, South Africa and elsehere. Sets out the proposed functions of the committee and suggests areas requiring special attention from researchers. Papers dealing with the San are abstracted under names of authors in this bibliography.
BOTSWANA; NAMIBIA; KUA; G/UI; JU/'HOANSI; KHWEDAM; LANGUAGES; LINGUISTICS; ORTHOGRAPHY; RESEARCH; TSHWA
R/B 496.1 STA

0014 Beake, Lesley
SONG OF BE
Young African Series, Cape Town: Maskew Miller Longman, refs., 1991, 76pp.
The novel tells the story of Be, a young Bushman girl living on a farm in Namibia. Told at the time of Namibia's first democratic elections after independence, it describes a life of poverty and despair but ends on a note of hope. The setting is Eastern Namibia near Tsumkwe and the old hunting and gathering life of the Bushmen is described and contrasted with that lived in the settlement at Tsumkwe and on the white-owned farm where the lives of all concerned are curiously intertwined in spite of their apparent antagonism. The book is written for younger readers.
NAMIBIA; TSHUMKWE; LITERATURE; POLITICS; SELF-DETERMINATION
398.20968 BEA

0015 Bennett, Bruce S.
SOME HISTORICAL BACKGROUND ON MINORITIES IN BOTSWANA
Mazonde, Isaac N. Minorities in the millennium: perspectives from Botswana. Gaborone: Lightbooks, 2002. vii, 136pp. pp.5–15. ISBN 9991271244.
The paper presents the historical background of the different tribes and ethnic groups of Botswana with regard to their settlement in the country from colonial times until independence in 1966. Concentrates on the situation in the reserves which succeeded the pre-colonial proto-states and which were each ruled over by a paramount chief. Notes that the history of minorities follows a pattern of incorporation within the multi-ethnic societies in the various reserves. Analyses the term "tribe" and shows that it can mean "a multi-ethnic political unit" or "an ethnic identity". Shows that colonial thinking on what constituted a tribe was confused and the independent state did nothing to correct the confusion. Emphasises the fact that the independence constitution refers to territorial units rather than to the ethnic identity of groups. Considers that it is essential for the current debate on the constitution and the representation of minorities escape this confusion and become based on a more historically oriented understanding of Botswana's complex and changing situation.
BOTSWANA; CONFERENCE PAPERS; CONSTITUTIONS; ETHNICITY; HISTORY; MINORITY RIGHTS; POLITICAL SYSTEMS
R/B 968.72 MIN

0016 Bertin, G.
THE BUSHMEN AND THEIR LANGUAGE
Journal of the Royal Asiatic Society, Vol.15, 1883. pp.1–31.
The article deals with the physical and moral characteristics of the Bushmen, their possible ethnic origins, rock art and language. Bases the language information on the work of W.H.I. Bleek and other early writers. Gives an outline of grammar and phonetics, and emphasises the potential value of a thorough study of Bushman languages by competent philologists. Outlines the nature of the hitherto unpublished Bleek collection of Bushman folklore, personal histories and customs, revealing its unique nature and regretting that the material remained unpublished. This article is probably one of the earliest dealing with the Bushman language and culture in a scientific and objective fashion.
SOUTH AFRICA; FOLKLORE; LANGUAGES; LINGUISTICS; RESEARCH; ROCK ART
PH/B 496.27 BER

0017 Bible Society of Botswana, Gaborone
MAREKO: THE GOSPEL OF MARK IN THE NARO LANGUAGE
Gaborone, n.d. 57pp.
The translation of the Gospel of Mark in the Naro language is the first book of the New Testament in this language. The orthography is that employed by the Naro Language Trust in which the clicks are represented by Roman letters rather than International Phonetic Alphabet signs.
BOTSWANA; BIBLE; LANGUAGES; LINGUISTICS; NARO
99/743

0018 Biesele, Megan
A NOTE ON THE BELIEFS OF MODERN BUSHMEN CONCERNING THE TSODILO HILLS
South West Africa Scientific Society Newsletter, Vol.15 No.3/4, June 1974.
The paper deals with the beliefs of !Kung living in the vicinity of the Tsodilo Hills about the paintings at this rock art site in north-western Botswana. Reports that all those interviewed agreed that the paintings were made, not by human beings but by the great god Gaoxa for a variety of reasons. Notes that the beliefs concerning the origin of the hills themselves are associated with another sacred spot, a spring in a depression at a place called N!aha from which the Hills were believed to have emerged and then travelled to their current location along a dry river bed. Gives details about the beliefs concerning the spring, which is believed to possess supernatural power (n/um) as do the Tsodilo Hills. Notes that the Hills are associated with

rain and weather. Concludes that the beliefs of contemporary Bushman indicate that Tsodilo has been inhabited for a long period of time.
BOTSWANA; TSODILO HILLS; !KUNG; BELIEFS; FOLKLORE; RELIGION; ROCK ART
99/713

0019 Biesele, Megan
'BUSHMAN FOLKTALES' BY MATHIAS G. GUENTHER: A REVIEW
African Studies, Vol.49 No.1, 1990. p.180.
The review commends the book for its interest and readability. Notes the creative format by means of which texts from the now extinct /Xam Bushmen collected in the late 1800s and early 1900s are juxtaposed with texts from contemporary Nharo in Botswana. Notes that this method of presentation allows similarities between two traditions of story-telling, separated by vast differences in time, space and language to be revealed. Notes the organization of the book under broad headings each one prefaced by revelations about the cultural content to which the tales refer, the sociology of knowledge among Bushman peoples, their customs and manners, methods of communication and oral life. Also provides details for each tale, the conditions under which it was performed based on the author's own field notes for the Nharo, and from those of earlier writers where available, for the /Xam. Notes that the book will be of value not only to the researchers but to the Bushmen themselves as they attempt to preserve their own heritage.
BOTSWANA; CAPE; SOUTH AFRICA; /XAM; BELIEFS; BOOK REVIEWS; CULTURE; FOLKLORE; NARO
P 960.05 AST

0020 Biesele, Megan; Royal-/o/oo, Kxao
JU/'HOANSI
Lee, Richard; Daly, Richard. *The Cambridge encyclopedia of hunters and gatherers, Cambridge, Cambridge University Press, ill, maps, xx, 511pp., 1999. pp.205–210. ISBN 052157109X*
The article deals with the Ju/'hoansi, a !Kung-speaking group living in both Botswana and Namibia. Notes that while Ju/'hoansi of the Dobe area in Botswana and the Nyae Nyae area in Namibia had lived in close contact with both black and white outsiders since 1900, until the 1950s their foraging lifestyle had remained intact. Provides details of their history, ecological setting, economy, settlement patterns, domestic and political organization, religion and spirituality. Outlines the current situation of Ju/'hoansi who have in common the loss of their traditional foraging areas, the need to adapt to changes brought about by modernization and the intervention of the governments of the nation states in which they live. Outlines the activities of the Nyae Nyae Farmer's Cooperative, an indigenous self-help organization.
BOTSWANA; DOBE; NAMIBIA; NYAE NYAE; BELIEFS; ECONOMY; GOVERNMENT POLICY; HISTORY; HUNTING-GATHERING; JU/'HOANSI; NON-GOVERNMENTAL ORGANISATIONS; RELIGION; SEDENTISM; SELF-DEVELOPMENT; SETTLEMENTS
R 306.36403 CAM

0021 Bikeur, A.C.
KÒ-OA TA GE RA: HAIRAREB 1
Khoekhoegowab; Windhoek: Gamsberg Macmillan, n.d.137pp.
This drama in Khoekhoegowab includes a synopsis of the story in English and is included in the bibliography to demonstrate the orthography employed for the writing of this language in Namibia.
NAMIBIA; KHOEKHOEGOWAB; LANGUAGES; LINGUISTICS; LITERATURE
R/B 496.1 BIK

0022 Bikeur, A.C.
KHAU!GAU HÀ !GURI!GAOB: HAIRAREB 2
Khoekhoegowab;Windhoek: Gamsberg Macmillan, 1997. 169pp.
This drama in Khoekhoegowab includes a short synopsis of the story in English and is included in the bibliography to demonstrate the orthography employed for the writing of this language in Namibia.
NAMIBIA; KHOEKHOEGOWAB; LANGUAGES; LINGUISTICS; LITERATURE
R/B 496.1 BIK

0023 Binford, L.R.
MOBILITY, HOUSING AND ENVIRONMENT: A COMPARATIVE STUDY
Journal of Anthropological Research, Vol. 46, 1990. pp.119–152.
The paper provides a cross-cultural survey of hunter-gatherers with particular emphasis on housing, mobility and subsistence, as these features vary with ecological settings and particular environmental variables. Draws implications for investigation of variability as documented archaeologically. Gives particular emphasis to the features listed above and to arguments in the literature that cite these variables, and seeks to evaluate the relative "complexity" of ancient sociocultural systems known from archaeological materials.
ARCHAEOLOGY; FOOD; LIVING CONDITIONS; PREHISTORY; RESEARCH; SOCIAL ORGANIZATION
98/1162

0024 Bird-David, Nurit
HUNTER-GATHERER RESEARCH AND CULTURAL DIVERSITY
Kent, Susan. Cultural diversity among twentieth-century for-

agers: an African perspective. Cambridge, Cambridge University Press, ill., maps, xiii, 344pp. 1996. pp.297–304. ISBN 0521482372.

The chapter comments on the history of hunter-gatherer research which originated with the two conferences in the 1960s entitled "Band Societies" and "Man the Hunter". Notes that the latter conference changed the direction of hunter-gatherer studies in the attempt to use common patterns revealed in modern band societies to understand early human behaviour. Shows however that subsequent research has revealed great variations between and within hunter-gatherer groups. Notes that some researchers have come to regard the concept of "hunter-gatherer" as invalid and have suggested abandoning the project. Notes that the present book continues the project but focuses on variations within single groups, some culturally close and others more distant. Suggests that intracultural diversity may be inherent in band societies world wide. Looks at possible new directions for the comparative project which may arise from the findings indicated in this book.
BOTSWANA; !KUNG; HUNTING-GATHERING; RESEARCH
306.364 CUL

0025 Bjerre, Jens
KALAHARI
New York: Hill and Wang, 1960. 227pp.
The book is an account of the author's travels in the Kalahari and his stay with a group of !Kung Bushmen in Namibia. Describes daily activities, customs, folklore, healing dances, boys' and girls' initiation. Questions the future of the Bushmen in the face of modernization of the country and their displacement by other races.
NAMIBIA; !KUNG; CULTURE; DANCE; FOLKLORE; SOCIAL CHANGE; SOCIAL ORGANIZATION; TRANCE
R/B 309.1688 BJE

0026 Bleek, Dorothea F.
THE DISTRIBUTION OF BUSHMAN LANGUAGES IN SOUTH AFRICA
Festschrift Meinhof: Sprachwissenscaftlich und andere Studien. Hamburg, 1927. pp.55–64.
The paper sets out the classification of Bushman languages in three groups: Southern, Northern and Central, and names some of the distinct languages found in each group, as well as indicating their geographic location. Notes the similarities between the languages of the Central group and those of the Hottentots, and surmises that they had a common root. Points out the linguistic features pertaining to the three groups such as the number of clicks and various grammatical aspects which distinguish them.
BOTSWANA; NAMIBIA; SOUTH AFRICA; !KUNG; !UI; /XAM; HAI//OM; CLICKS; GRAMMAR; JU; KHOE; KHOEKHOEGOWAB;
LANGUAGES; LINGUISTICS; RESEARCH; NARO; SOUTHERN
PH/B 496.27 BLE

0027 Bleek, Dorothea F.
BUSHMAN FOLKLORE
Africa, Vol.2 No.3, 1929. pp.302–313.
The article retells several of the folktales of the now extinct /Xam Bushmen of the Cape and records prayers to the moon and stars thus providing a picture of Bushman religious beliefs. Points out that story-telling and talking were of paramount importance in the traditional Bushman life-style. Notes, however that within 50 years all knowledge of the folklore was lost when the people were taken into service and families broken up.
CAPE; SOUTH AFRICA; /XAM; FOLKLORE; RELIGION
P 960.05 AJI

0028 Bleek, Dorothea F.
CUSTOMS AND BELIEFS OF THE /XAM BUSHMAN: PART I: BABOONS
Bantu Studies, Vol.5, 1931. pp.167–179.
The article recounts /Xam Bushman beliefs relating to baboons and is taken from material collected by W.H.I. Bleek and L.C. Lloyd between 1870 and 1880. The text is in the /Xam language with an English translation. The information was provided by Dia!kwain. Shows that the Bushmen regarded baboons as very like humans, even able to speak Bushman, sing, dance and understand certain Bushman customs and beliefs.
CAPE; SOUTH AFRICA; /XAM; ANIMALS; ANTHROPOLOGY; BELIEFS; FOLKLORE; LANGUAGES; LINGUISTICS; RESEARCH
P 960.05 AST

0029 Bleek, Dorothea F.
CUSTOMS AND BELIEFS OF THE /XAM BUSHMEN: PART II: THE LION
Bantu Studies, Vol.6, 1932. pp.47–63.
The article records /Xam Bushman beliefs and customs relating to lions and is from material collected by W.H.I. Bleek and L.C. Lloyd between 1870 and 1880. The information was provided by Dia!kwain and includes a story related to him by his elder sister about a lion encounter and various beliefs handed on by other older relatives. The text is in the /Xam language with an English translation and indicates clearly the relationships believed to exist between people and lions.
CAPE; SOUTH AFRICA; /XAM; ANIMALS; ANTHROPOLOGY; BELIEFS; FOLKLORE; LANGUAGES; LINGUISTICS; RESEARCH
P 960.05 AST

0030 Bleek, Dorothea F.
CUSTOMS AND BELIEFS OF THE /XAM BUSHMEN: PART III: GAME ANIMALS

Bantu Studies, Vol.6, 1932. pp.233–249.
The article relates to the beliefs of /Xam Bushmen regarding eland, gemsbok and springbok and is taken from material collected by W.H.I. Bleek and L.C. Lloyd between 1870 and 1880. The informants for this article were Dia!kwain and /Han!kasso. The text is in the /Xam language with an English translation. Explains the beliefs concerning relationships between the hunter and his eland prey and the behaviour required of him in this regard. Records the belief that springbok and gemsbok may foretell the death of a person.
CAPE; SOUTH AFRICA; /XAM; ANIMALS; ANTHROPOLOGY; BELIEFS; FOLKLORE; HUNTING; LANGUAGES; LINGUISTICS; RESEARCH
p 960.05 AST

0031 Bleek, Dorothea F.
CUSTOMS AND BELIEFS OF THE /XAM BUSHMEN: PART IV: OMENS, WIND-MAKING, CLOUDS
Bantu Studies, Vol.6, 1932. pp.321–342.
The article records /Xam Bushman beliefs about the dreams of individuals foretelling death and their ideas about the four winds and clouds, and how humans can influence them. The material was collected by W.H.I. Bleek and L.C. Lloyd between 1870 and 1880 and is in the /Xam language with an English translation. The information was dictated by /Han/kasso and Dia!kwain.
CAPE; SOUTH AFRICA; /XAM; ANTHROPOLOGY; BELIEFS; FOLKLORE; LANGUAGES; LINGUISTICS; RESEARCH
p 960.05 AST

0032 Bleek, Dorothea F.
CUSTOMS AND BELIEFS OF THE /XAM BUSHMEN: PART V: THE RAIN
Bantu Studies, Vol.7, 1933. pp.297–312.
The article records /Xam Bushman beliefs and customs about the rain and is taken from material collected by W.H.I. Bleek and L.C. Lloyd between 1870 and 1880. The information in the article was dictated by Dia!kwain, /Han/kasso and //Kabbo. The text is in the /Xam language with an English translation and makes it clear that the /Xam regarded the rain as a living being which could interact with humans and which became angry if they behaved towards it in inappropriate ways. Mentions the belief that rain-makers would milk the rain animal to make rain and cut it so that its blood would flow and cause rain to fall. Names animals which are sacred to the rain and taboo as food, especially to young girls and unmarried men.
CAPE; SOUTH AFRICA; /XAM; ANIMALS; BELIEFS; FOLKLORE; LANGUAGES; LINGUISTICS; RESEARCH
p 960.05 AST

0033 Bleek, Dorothea F.
CUSTOMS AND BELIEFS OF THE /XAM BUSHMEN: PART VI: RAIN-MAKING
Bantu Studies, Vol.7, 1933. pp.375–392.
The article records /Xam Bushman beliefs regarding rain-making and is taken from material collected by W.H.I. Bleek and L.C. Lloyd between 1870 and 1880. The information was dictated by Dia!kwain, /Hankasso and //Kabbo. The text is in the /Xam language and names medicine men known to the three informants. Describes the methods by which they were believed to make rain which included catching and killing the rain-bull. Also recounts beliefs regarding solar eclipses and means taken to end them.
CAPE; SOUTH AFRICA; /XAM; BELIEFS; COSMOLOGY; FOLKLORE; LANGUAGES; LINGUISTICS; RESEARCH
p 960.05 AST

0034 Bleek, Dorothea F.
CUSTOMS AND BELIEFS OF THE /XAM BUSHMEN: PART VII: SORCERORS
Bantu Studies, Vol.9, 1935. pp.1–47.
The article records /Xam Bushman beliefs relating to sorcerers and their powers and is taken from material collected by W.H.I. Bleek and L.C. Lloyd between 1870 and 1880. The information was dictated by //Khabbo, /Han/kasso and Dia/kwain and includes explanations of the meanings of rock paintings copied by J.M. Orpen in the Drakensberg and published in the *Cape Monthly Magazine* in July 1884. Describes beliefs which include sorcerers turning themselves into animals and their spirits entering animals after death. Mentions healing methods used by sorcerers including "snoring" or breathing deeply on patients to drive out their illness.
CAPE; DRAKENSBERG; SOUTH AFRICA; /XAM; ANIMALS; ANTHROPOLOGY; BELIEFS; FOLKLORE; HEALING; LANGUAGES; LINGUISTICS; RELIGION; RESEARCH; ROCK ART
p 960.05 AST

0035 Bleek, Dorothea F.
CUSTOMS AND BELIEFS OF THE /XAM BUSHMEN: PART VIII: MORE ABOUT SORCERORS AND CHARMS
Bantu Studies, Vol.10, 1936. pp.163–199.
The article records /Xam Bushman customs and beliefs relating to sorcerers and charms and is taken from material collected by W.H.I. Bleek and L.C. Lloyd between 1870 and 1880. The information was dictated by Dia/kwain, /Kasin, //Khabbo and /Han/kasso. The text is in the /Xam language with an English translation and records uses of herbal medicines, bewitchment and cursing. Dia/kwain tells stories which his father had learnt from the rain-maker who taught him about the "rain's things".
CAPE; SOUTH AFRICA; /XAM; ANTHROPOLOGY; BELIEFS;

FOLKLORE; HEALING; LANGUAGES; LINGUISTICS; RESEARCH
P 960.05 AST

0036 Bleek, Dorothea F.
NOTES ON THE BUSHMAN PHOTOGRAPHS
Bantu Studies, Vol.10, 1936. pp.200–204.
The photographs were taken by Dorothea F. Bleek in 1910 and 1911 in the northern Cape and portray Bushmen wearing European dress in most cases. Gives names and biographical details for each subject portrayed and in some cases, descriptions of customs given by the person in the photograph. One depiction shows a woman using a digging stick.
NORTHERN CAPE; SOUTH AFRICA; CULTURE; LIFE STORIES; PHOTOS
P 960.05 AST

0037 Bleek, Dorothea F.
SPECIAL SPEECH OF ANIMALS AND MOON BY /XAM BUSHMEN
Bantu Studies, Vol.10, 1936. pp.163–199.
The article is based on material collected between 1870 and 1880 by W.H.I. Bleek and L.C. Lloyd from /Xam Bushmen and provides examples of special speech attributed to certain animals and the moon. Points out that this speech attempts to imitate the shape or position of the mouth of the animal concerned. Gives examples of such speech patterns attributed to the blue crane, the ostrich, tortoise, ichneumon, jackal and anteater. Shows how, in each case, a consistent use of particular clicks or a change from a click to a labial characterises the specific "language" of the animal while the anteater and the moon have a peculiar click of their own and the speech of the jackal is characterised by a strange labial click. Includes other brief pieces relating to speech patterns.
CAPE; SOUTH AFRICA; /XAM; BELIEFS; CLICKS; LANGUAGES; LINGUISTICS
P 960.05 AST

0038 Bleek, Dorothea F.
THE //N!KE OR BUSHMEN OF GRIQUALAND WEST: NOTES ON THE //N!KE OR BUSHMEN OF GRIQUALAND WEST.
Khoisan Forum, Working Paper No.15, 2000, ISSN 14331306, Cologne: University of Cologne, 2000. 28pp.
The book contains three sections: The introduction by the editor, and the two papers by Dorothea Bleek. The Introduction concludes that rather than being from a single language, the linguistic data presented by Bleek represents a cluster of related dialects which differ in linguistic detail. Reports that speakers of related languages have recently been identified in the area in which the research was originally conducted. The first Bleek paper describes huts, food, weapons, dress, and a few customs of the //n!ke who lived north of the Orange River and west of the Vaal River. The second paper states that //n!ke is related to //kx'au and /Xam-ka-!ke belonging to the Southern group of Bushman languages. Examines orthography and grammar. Notes that there are five clicks and three tones and that the accent lies mostly on the last syllable of a word.
SOUTH AFRICA; CLICKS; CULTURE; LANGUAGES; LINGUISTICS; MATERIAL CULTURE; N/U; SOCIAL ORGANISATION; SOUTHERN
R/B 496.1 BLE

0039 Bleek, W.H.I.
REYNARD THE FOX IN SOUTH AFRICA IN HOTTENTOT FABLES AND TALES
1864. pp.1–94.
The book contains a collection of Hottentot (Khoekhoe) folktales. In the Introduction the author attempts to establish the philological connections of the Hottentot language. Suggests that the sex-denoting languages of Africa are related. Looks at the probable origin of myths and fables and considers that these are only found among peoples speaking sex-denoting languages, so that there is a connection between grammatical structure and imaginative content.
SOUTH AFRICA; FOLKTALES; KHOEKHOE; KHOEKHOEGOWAB; LANGUAGES; LINGUISTICS; RESEARCH
98/041

0040 Bleek, W.H.I.; Lloyd, L.C.
SPECIMENS OF BUSHMAN FOLKLORE
London: Allen and Unwin. 1911. 468pp.
The collection contains myths, fables, legends and poetry in addition to descriptions of customs and superstitions and autobiographical material from two of the Bushman informants. All texts give both /Xam and English versions. The Preface by L.C. Lloyd explains the orthography used, particularly the symbols for clicks and tones. The Appendix contains letters and papers of W.H.I. Bleek concerning the Bushman language and a Report to the Cape House of Assembly on his research.
CAPE; SOUTH AFRICA; /XAM; CLICKS; CULTURE; FOLKLORE; LANGUAGES; LIFE STORIES; LINGUISTICS; MYTHOLOGY; RESEARCH
R/B 398.20968 BLE

0041 Bleek, W.H.I.; Lloyd, L.C.; Bleek, Dorothea F.
MANTIS AND HIS FRIENDS: BUSHMAN FOLKLORE
68pp.
The book contains a selection of tales collected by W.H.I. Bleek and L.C. Lloyd. Dorothea Bleek edited the volume and shortened some of the tales. The Introduction deals with the lifestyle of the Cape Bushmen at the period before their contact with other races. Explains the effects upon the Bushmen of the misconceptions which outsiders had regarding Bushman use of water-holes and the land itself which led to their eventual disappearance from the Cape as a distinct people.

CAPE; SOUTH AFRICA; /XAM; BELIEFS; FOLKLORE; HISTORY; INTERGROUP RELATIONS
R/B 398.096872 BLE

0042 Blurton-Jones, Nicholas; Hawkes, Kristen; O'Connell, James
THE GLOBAL PROCESS AND LOCAL ECOLOGY: HOW SHOULD WE EXPLAIN DIFFERENCES BETWEEN THE HADZA AND THE !KUNG?
Kent, Susan. *Cultural diversity among twentieth-century foragers: an African perspective.* Cambridge: Cambridge University Press, ill., maps. xiii, 344pp. 1996. pp.159–187. ISBN 0521482372.
The paper discusses explanations for the diversity of behaviour in two forager groups, the Hadza of northern Tanzania and the !Kung of north-western Botswana. Notes the following differences between the two groups: a) Hadza children collect their own food while !Kung children seldom do so; b) Hadza women seem to be less responsive parents than !Kung women; c) Hadza women are more fertile than !Kung women; d) !Kung men trap much small game while Hadza specialise in big game; e) Relationships between the sexes tend be egalitarian among !Kung but segregated or oppositional among Hadza. Discusses these differences using a combination of theoretical methods. Defines and discusses global process theory. Points out the weaknesses in this theory which preclude it from claiming to be a serious scientific theory although it may stimulate re-examination of many issues in anthropology.
BOTSWANA; TANZANIA; !KUNG; ANTHROPOLOGY; FORAGING; HADZA; INTERACTION; SOCIAL ORGANIZATION
306.364 CUL

0043 Boko, Duma Gideon
INTEGRATING THE BASARWA UNDER BOTSWANA'S REMOTE AREA DEVELOPMENT PROGRAMME
Mazonde, Isaac N. *Minorities in the millennium: perspectives from Botswana.* Gaborone: Lightbooks, refs. 2002. vii, 136pp. pp.97–110. ISBN 9991271244.
The paper looks at the legal displacement and marginalization of the Basarwa in the context of how it came about both under the colonial laws regarding tribal land rights and under the constitution of independent Botswana. Examines the philosophy underlying the Remote Area Development Programme which is seen basically as an attempt to integrate Basarwa into the Tswana mainstream while denying the reality of their different cultural norms and their attitude towards the land they traditionally occupied. Considers that the approach of both the colonial government and the government of independent Botswana towards Basarwa was wrong. Examines the situation of Basarwa as an indigenous group in the light of international law. Points out that after 26 years the RADP has not succeeded in empowering the Basarwa but has provided a settlement arrangement by means of which they are engulfed by other ethnic groups who regard them as inferior. While the scheme has provided schools, boreholes and small scale agricultural projects it has neither analysed the real problems of the Basarwa nor provided a workable mechanism for doing so.
BOTSWANA; EMPOWERMENT; LAND RIGHTS; POVERTY; REMOTE AREA DEVELOPMENT; SETTLEMENT POLICY
R/B 968.72 MIN

0044 Bolaane, Maitseo
FEAR OF THE MARGINALISED MINORITIES: THE KHWAI COMMUNITY DETERMINING THEIR BOUNDARY IN THE OKAVANGO, BOTSWANA, THROUGH A DEED OF TRUST
Barnard, Alan; Kenrick, Justin. *Africa's Indigenous Peoples: "First Peoples or Marginalised Minorities"?* Edinburgh: University of Edinburgh, Centre of African Studies, refs., xv, 322pp., 2001. pp.145–171. ISBN 0952791757.
The paper attempts to understand the model of wildlife development chosen by the Khwai community in Ngamiland. Examines how this differs from the standard model developed by the Botswana Government. Discusses the reluctance of the Government to recognise this community, grant it leasehold title and a hunting quota, all of which would enable it to develop a wild-life based community enterprise. Points out that although theoretically communities do have a choice between joint venture agreements and joint venture partnerships, in effect only parts of the first model have been tried and tested. Notes that in preferring a more participative model, the Khwai community are opting for becoming active rather than passive in the management of their resources.
BOTSWANA; KHWAI; NGAMILAND; OKAVANGO DELTA; CONFERENCE PAPERS; DEVELOPMENT POLICY; GOVERNMENT POLICY; NATURAL RESOURCES; NATURE CONSERVATION; RESOURCES MANAGEMENT; SELF-DETERMINATION; WILDLIFE
R/B 305.80968 AFR

0045 Botelle, A.; Rohde, R.
THOSE WHO LIVE ON THE LAND: A SOCIOECONOMIC BASELINE SURVEY FOR LAND USE PLANNING IN THE COMMUNAL AREAS OF OTJOZONDJUPA. LAND USE PLANNING SERIES: REPORT, NO.1,
Ministry of Lands, Resettlement and Rehabilitation, 1995. 208pp.
The report provides a description and analysis of socioeconomic conditions in Eastern Otjozondupa. The report was commissioned by the Ministry of Lands, Resettlement and Rehabilitation and analyses the social and cultural dynamics of the region's population in relation to the appropriate use of the natural resource base. Notes that this socioeconomic re-

port will be combined with an environmental assessment and a water study to form a comprehensive land use plan for the area. Emphasises the need for community participation in the planning process and the strengthening of both leadership structures and community decision-making. Suggests guiding principles for future development.
NAMIBIA; OTJOZONDUPA;!KUNG; DEVELOPMENT PLANNING; ECONOMY; GOVERNMENT POLICY; LAND RIGHTS; LAND USE; LEGAL RIGHTS; NATURAL RESOURCES
R/B 333.1 BOT

0046 Botswana Christian Council, Gaborone
THE TWENTY SEVENTH ANNUAL ASSEMBLY 1992 REPORTS
78pp.
The reports deal with all the work carried out by the Botswana Christian Council in 1991. Notes, under the Report of the Christian Services Committee, fieldwork/outreach to projects in Gantsi, D'Kar, Kang, New Kganagas and Kacgae. Observes the effect of drought upon remote area dwellers and the response of local authorities. Provides details of the operation of Kuru Development Trust and projects it is responsible for. Lists problem issues raised by Basarwa at KDT. Comments on the use of the Small Scale Project Fund to enable churches to use funding for support of programmes/projects which will address root causes of socioeconomic problems. Observes that areas of concern for which the Fund will be used are rural and urban poverty and the plight of the under-privileged (mainly Basarwa).
BOTSWANA; D'KAR; GHANZI; KACGAE; KANG; DEVELOPMENT PLANNING; DROUGHTS; NON-GOVERNMENTAL ORGANISATIONS; POVERTY
98/719

0047 Botswana Christian Council, Gaborone
BOTSWANA CHRISTIAN COUNCIL ASSEMBLY BOOK 1993
104pp.
The report of the Botswana Christian Council's 28th Assembly deals with all the work carried out by the Council in 1992. The General Secretary's Report notes among other priorities, those of enabling the poor to lead a better life, and concern for the marginalised and oppressed. Indicates that the Council is becoming the main facilitator in efforts to secure equal rights for Basarwa in Botswana society. Draws attention to the publication "Who was (t)here first?" in which the human rights situation of Basarwa in selected areas of Gantsi District asassessed. Lists intended follow-ups on the issues raised in the publication. Notes that these will include field trips by BCC staff and Basarwa to allow consultation between different Basarwa groups to be followed by four regional workshops and a national workshop. Notes aims of the "Programme on Basarwa Development" as assistance with housing/shelter by means of:

appropriate technology; community motivation; income generation; food security; nutrition/water; human resources development; and community art. Records projects assisted and amounts of money provided.
BOTSWANA; GHANZI DISTRICT; CHURCH; DEVELOPMENT AID; DROUGHTS; EDUCATION; NON-GOVERNMENTAL ORGANISATIONS; SELF-DEVELOPMENT; WATER
98/1016

0048 Botswana Christian Council, Gaborone
DEMOCRATIZATION AND THE CHURCH
1994, multiple pagings.
Reports deal with all the work done by the Botswana Christian Council in 1993. Notes that efforts with Basarwa continue to grow from strength to strength and have included cooperation with other NGOs. Comments that BCC's advocacy on behalf of Basarwa is often viewed with suspicion by the Botswana authorities. Records staff visits to contact and listen to Basarwa as they highlight issues such as their lack of education, landlessness, lack of self-respect and dislike of the term "Remote area dwellers". Includes financial reports which detail amounts spent on the Basarwa hostel at Motokwe and on the Small Scale Basarwa Project Fund in the programme on Remote Area Dwellers. Notes that the theme of the Assembly was "Democratisation and the Church".
BOTSWANA; D'KAR; MOTOKWE; ADVOCACY; CHURCH; DEVELOPMENT PLANNING; NON-GOVERNMENTAL ORGANISATIONS; WATER
R/B 261.8 DEM

0049 Brearley, J.
NARO FEMALE PUBERTY RITE: AN INTERVIEW WITH MARY OF KURU
Kuru Development Trust, 1997.
The unpublished field-notes describe the puberty rite observed by the author when a fourteen year old girl at Kuru experienced her first menstruation. Describes the dance by the women round the hut in which the girl was secluded and notes that the songs, known as "Eland songs" were similar to those used at healing dances with similar melodic patterns. Includes explanation of the rite by Mary, a San woman who explained that after the girl had finished menstruating she would be taken to the veld for further ceremonies which would ensure that the plants flourished and failure to do this would result in drought.
BOTSWANA; BELIEFS; DANCE; INITIATION; NARO; RITUALS
99/183

0050 Bredekamp, Henry C. Jatti
KHOISAN REVIVALISM AND THE INDIGENOUS PEOPLE'S ISSUE IN POST-APARTHEID SOUTH AFRICA
Barnard, Alan; Kenrick, Justin. Africa's Indigenous Peoples:

"First Peoples or Marginalised Minorities"? Edinburgh: University of Edinburgh, Centre of African Studies, refs., xv, 322pp., 2001. pp.191–209. ISBN 0952791757.
The chapter looks at the topic of the revivalism of Khoisan identity taking place in modern day South Africa. Points out that this topic is linked to the issue of "coloured" identity in post-apartheid South Africa. Refers to W.M. Macmillan's "Cape colour question: a historical survey" which reflects the views of 19th century missionary John Philip regarding the identity and political situation of the Hottentots. Discusses the Griqua revivalism of the first half of the 20th century led by A.A.S. le Fleur. Focuses on the pivotal role of the Griquas in current Khoisan revivalism. Lists a number of contemporary groups and organizations claiming Khoisan identity. Explains the links between Khoisan self-identification in the South African context and that of indigenous peoples in the international context. Looks at ways in which South African policy-makers are dealing with this controversial issue.
EASTERN CAPE; NORTHERN CAPE; SOUTH AFRICA; WESTERN CAPE; ADVOCACY; CONFERENCE PAPERS; GRIQUA; HISTORY; INDIGENOUS PEOPLES; KHOEKHOE; KHOESAN; MISSIONARIES; POLITICAL LEADERSHIP; TERMINOLOGY
R/B 305.80968 AFR

0051 Bregin, Elana
REPRESENTING THE BUSHMEN THROUGH THE COLONIAL LENS
English in Africa, Vol.27 No.1, refs. 2000. pp.37–54.
The paper seeks, by assessing the writings of the 19th and early 20th century on the Bushmen, to establish the extent to which the notions of "otherness" and "difference" were a legitimising factor for the genocidal policies employed against them. Notes that the obsessive fear of "the other" arose from the social conditions pertaining in 19th century Britain where the urban poor were stigmatised as degraded, degenerate and living in squalor and filth, in contrast to the virile and healthy life-style of the "true Briton" from the upper and wealthy classes. Shows how the new scientific theories based on social Darwinism postulated human social evolution, but this included the possibility of racial decline. Points out that most accounts of the Bushmen written during this period describe them as a degenerate and degraded species of humanity doomed to extinction. Provides a detailed account of the various campaigns against the Bushmen suggesting that the above attitudes were used to justify their enslavement and extermination.
SOUTH AFRICA; COLONIALISM; CONFLICT; HISTORY; INTERACTION; LITERATURE
P 820.05 EAF

0052 Brenzinger, Matthias
SAN IN ANGOLA AND ZAMBIA: REGIONAL ASSESSMENT OF THE SAN IN SOUTHERN AFRICA. NO.2
Robins, Steven; Madzudzo, Elias; Brenzinger, Matthias. An assessment of the status of the San in South Africa, Angola, Zambia and Zimbabwe. *Windhoek: Legal Assistance Centre, iii, 105pp.2001. pp.53–75. ISBN 9991676546.*
The chapter looks at the status of the San in Angola and Zambia. Notes that by November 1999 only 1,300 San speaking a Khoisan language could be located in Angola and that this number has probably decreased owing to the fighting between UNITA and the Angolan Army. Reports that three linguistic groups exist: Kwedi; Xu and possibly Khoe. Provides details on the linguistic and geographic distribution of Angolan San. Discusses their living conditions under the following headings: a) security and human rights; b) health and education; c) socio-economic situation. Suggests that the Namibian government should be approached to secure the integrity of its borders with Angola without threatening the lives of civilians. Regarding San in Zambia, reports on the only two San communities living in Zambia in 1999: Kxoe of Simone Plains, and Xhoe in the Mehetta refugee Camp. Makes recommendations regarding the legal status of these people. The appendix includes an overview of recent events in Angola and Zambia relevant to the situation of San in these countries.
ANGOLA; ZAMBIA; !XUN; HISTORY; INTERGROUP RELATIONS; KHWE
R/B 305.80968 ROB

0053 Brenzinger, Matthias
PERSONAL NAMES OF THE KXOE: THE EXAMPLE OF TCOO-NAMES. KHOISAN FORUM WORKING PAPER, NO.10, 1999
Cologne: University of Cologne, 1999. pp.5–18. ISSN 14331306.
The paper on Kxoe personal names highlights their individual nature, the bearer being known as the "true owner" of the name. Notes that whereas many names may be derived from other languages or from the Bible, the majority are taken from ordinary Kxoedam words. Shows that surnames are only used in response to a demand for them from officials, in which case the name of the person's father is provided though never used in everyday life. Points out that such surnames are frequently so misspelled as to render them meaningless. Provides a list of names with the word "t coo" or "supernatural power" as a component. Explains the importance of the concept "t coo" in everyday life: it has both positive and negative aspects and may, for example, both cause and cure illness.
NAMIBIA; BELIEFS; KHWE; KHWEDAM; LANGUAGES; LINGUISTICS
99/930

0054 Brown, David Maughan
THE NOBLE SAVAGE IN ANGLO-SAXON COLONIAL IDEOLOGY, 1950–1980: 'MASAI' AND 'BUSHMEN' IN POPULAR FICTION
refs. 1983. pp.55–77.

The paper looks at images of the San and Masai as depicted in 19th and early and mid-20th century fiction in the context of the "Noble Savage". Considers the development of Social Darwinism, a theory according to which human societies might evolve and equally well, might decline. Shows how living Bushmen exhibited in 19th century Britain were seen not as "Noble Savages" but as degraded examples of humanity. Notes that their supposed degradation was then used to justify policies of genocide by the colonisers. Finds that novels by Laurens van der Post, Wilbur Smith and H. Raubenheimer which deal with terrorist attacks against white settlers, include Bushmen and Masai who are favourably contrasted with black terrorists. Considers that the settlers needed to reassure themselves on the correctness of their own viewpoint, assumed to be a "balanced" view of Africa which permitted the resurrection of the "Noble Savage".
SOUTH AFRICA; ATTITUDES; LITERATURE
P 820.05 EAF

0055 Brown, Duncan
THE SOCIETY OF THE TEXT: THE ORAL LITERATURE OF THE /XAM BUSHMAN
Critical Arts: a Journal of Cultural Studies, Vol.9 No.2, 1995 refs. pp.76–109.
The paper explores ways in which the texts of poetry and narrative by San informants may be seen as both a starting point for and a continuing thread in South African literary history. Suggests therefore that future studies of South African literary history should begin with the creation stories, historical and hunting narratives and personal mood songs which reveal a complexity and rich imaginative detail very unlike the stereotype of their creators as child-like primitives. Notes also that the history of the Bushman as depicted in their oral literature, rock paintings and engravings represent some of the earliest accounts of colonization from the viewpoint of the colonised.
SOUTH AFRICA; /XAM; COLONIALISM; HISTORY; LITERATURE
PH/B 305.80968 CRI

0056 Brörmann, Magdalena
WORKING GROUP OF INDIGENOUS MINORITIES IN SOUTHERN AFRICA (WIMSA)
2002. 6pp.
The article written for a special issue of *Cultural Survival Quarterly* of March 2002 on the history, structure, objectives and activities of the Working Group of Indigenous Minorities in Southern Africa (WIMSA). Notes that the organization was established in 1996 in Windhoek in Namibia and D'Kar in Botswana. Observes that WIMSA offers the San communities support to enable them to gain political recognition, to secure access to natural and financial resources, to raise human rights awareness, and to regain their self-esteem. Sees as its ultimate goal the establishment of a Regional San Council which will be fully representative of the San of southern Africa. Points out that currently most San are illiterate, live in remote areas without access to telecommunications links, and have no familiarity with bureaucratic demands. Highlights major activities of WIMSA since its inception which have included on-the-job training at the Windhoek office, the organization of training workshops, and the setting up of an oral testimony collection project and facilitation of San attendance at conferences and meetings regionally and abroad. Points out that WIMSA does not itself implement projects but only offers advice on them. Outlines the challenges facing WIMSA currently.
BOTSWANA; NAMIBIA; SOUTH AFRICA; EDUCATION; NON-GOVERNMENTAL ORGANISATIONS; REGIONAL COOPERATION; SELF-DEVELOPMENT; TRAINING
PH/B 305.8 WOR

0057 Budack, K.F.R.
THE AONIN OR TOPNAAR OF THE LOWER !KHUISEB VALLEY, AND THE SEA
Traill, A. Khoisan Linguistic Studies 3. 1977. pp.1–42. ISBN 0854944540.
The article describes the traditional economy of the =Aonin or Topnaars of the Lower !Khuiseb Valley in Namibia. Describes in detail the fishing and gathering methods employed by these Nama-speaking people. Shows how they depended heavily on the harvested fruits and seeds of the Nara melon and developed special tools for processing the fruit. Notes that previously the tribe consisted of two sections, Hurinim or Sea People and !Khuiseb who lived up-river and only immigrated seasonally to the coast. Gives vocabulary in the language and examples of praise-songs. Mentions references to the !Khuiseb in the writings of early travellers to the region.
NAMIBIA; CULTURE; FISHING; FOOD; FORAGING; KHOEKHOEGOWAB
496.2709 KHO

0058 Butler, F.G.
NOSE-BLEEDS IN SHAMANS AND ELANDS
Southern African Field Archaeology, Vol.6, 1997. pp.82–87.
The article looks at nose-bleeding in shamans and eland. Proposes, as a result of a re-examination of the ethnographical evidence for nose-bleeding during trance dancing, that it was not an automatic accompaniment of entry into the state of trance (as is widely believed) but that it was induced by the deliberate insertion by the dancer, of powerful snuff into his nostrils. Further suggests that the technique was also employed by shamans/hunters to induce nose-bleeds in the eland, the "totem" animal of the San over much of southern Africa.
SOUTHERN AFRICA; ANIMALS; BELIEFS; DANCE; HEALING;

RELIGION; ROCK ART; SHAMANISM; TRANCE
P 930.105 SAF

0059 Campbell, C.
IMAGES OF WAR: A PROBLEM IN ROCK ART RESEARCH
World Archeology, Vol.18, No2, ill., refs., 1986. pp.255–268.
The article relates to paintings of conflict which are not uncommon in the rock art of southern Africa and are distributed over a wide area. Notes that a variety of weapons and forms of conflict are portrayed. Points out that these paintings can be considered from two viewpoints: either they are realistic depictions of actual events or they are essentially hallucinatory, portraying the non-real world of trance experience. Argues that, although the selected paintings are highly detailed, they contain postures and hallucinatory features which indicate that they are intimately associated with medicine men and trance.
SOUTHERN AFRICA; ZIMBABWE; CONFLICT; DANCE; HISTORY; TRANCE
P 930.105 WAR

0060 Carstens, P.
THE SOCIO-ECONOMIC CONTEXT OF INITIATION CEREMONIES AMONG TWO SOUTH AFRICAN PEOPLES
Canadian Journal of African studies, Vol. 16 No. 3, 1982. pp.505–522.
The paper seeks to establish the socio-economic context of initiation ceremonies among the Nama and Xhosa peoples of southern Africa as well as their responses to social change. Notes that among the Nama, girls' initiation ceremonies were long retained while the Xhosa have kept male initiation as part of their contemporary culture. Examines the role and status of women and men in each of the societies, particularly in the context of work and the rearing of cattle. Describes what is known of the initiation ceremonies of the two peoples and observes that in modern Xhosa society, there is a close relationship between initiation and migrant labour.
SOUTHERN AFRICA; CULTURE; INITIATION; NAMA; XHOSA
98/1159

0061 Cassidy, Lin; Good, Kenneth; Mazonde, Isaac N.; Rivers, Roberta
AN ASSESSMENT OF THE STATUS OF THE SAN IN BOTSWANA: REGIONAL ASSESSMENT OF THE STATUS OF THE SAN IN SOUTHERN AFRICA REPORT, SERIES, NO.3
Windhoek: Legal Assistance Centre, refs. 2001. xiv, 170pp.
The report deals in considerable detail with the current status of San in Botswana. Observes that most San are rural dwellers characterised by extreme poverty, landlessness, lack of access to training or to paid wage labour and stigmatised owing to their low social status. Looks at the Government policies affecting San particularly the Remote Area Development Programme (RADP). Considers that while the RADP has achieved significant success in terms of infrastructural development it has achieved little in terms of capacity-building, income generation or economic empowerment. Highlights the value of advocacy groups and NGOs in the development of the San. Lists main recommendations as follows: a) provision of assistance in the areas of land claims, lobbying, community mobilization, media-relations and fund-raising; b) training in political literacy; c) integration of San languages, history and culture in schools; d) training courses similar to those run in Namibia for traditional leaders and tourism guides; e) appointment of a San "Specially elected" Member of Parliament; f) recognition of San political leaders. Appendices provide socio-economic data on a district-by-district basis and statistical tables give information on every aspect of the status of the San. Chapters on the political status of the San and San perceptions are separately annotated under the names of the authors.
BOTSWANA; CENTRAL DISTRICT; CHOBE DISTRICT; GHANZI DISTRICT; KGALAGADI DISTRICT; KGATLENG DISTRICT; KWENENG DISTRICT; NGAMILAND; SOUTHERN DISTRICT; EDUCATION; GOVERNMENT POLICY; LAND RIGHTS; LITERACY; LOCAL GOVERNMENT; POLITICAL LEADERSHIP; POLITICS; REMOTE AREA DEVELOPMENT; RESOURCES MANAGEMENT; SELF-DETERMINATION; TRAINING; WAGES
R/B 305.8096872 CAS.

0062 Chebanne, Anderson
MINORITY LANGUAGES AND MINORITY PEOPLE: ISSUES ON LINGUISTIC, CULTURAL AND ETHNIC DEATH IN BOTSWANA
Mazonde, Isaac N. Minorities in the millennium: perspectives from Botswana. Gaborone: Lightbooks, vii, 136pp. 2002. pp.47–55. ISBN 9991271244.
The paper focuses on language and cultural preservation which are seen as fundamental human rights. Considers that the exclusion of minority languages of which there are a number in Botswana, has led to the threat of their extermination in the long term. Notes that in the challenge of nation-building faced by the newly independent state, acceptance of only one national language was taken to be one of the building blocks of national unity. Points out that this approach denies important issues in socio-political development and is basically unfair to the communities whose languages are not chosen as "national." Shows that the denial of language rights is linked to the denial of rights to land ownership and culture which are only granted to "majority" tribes. Suggests options which would prevent the disappearance of the minority languages by allowing them into the domains hitherto only occupied by English and Setswana. Looks at possible effects of globalization on language in Botswana and shows that, in spite of threats posed, for example by English as a world language, modern technology could have positive benefits for minority languages. Concludes

that efforts to strengthen and promote minority languages require government support and encouragement.
BOTSWANA; CONSTITUTIONS; HUMAN RIGHTS; LANGUAGES; MINORITY RIGHTS; POLITICS; SETSWANA
R/B 968.72 MIN

0063 Chebanne, Anderson
THE PHONOLOGICAL SYSTEM OF THE CUAA LANGUAGE
Batibo, H.M.; Tsonope, J. The State of Khoesan Languages in Botswana. Mogoditshane: Tasalls, ill., refs.. viii, 169pp, 2000. pp.18–32. ISBN 9991295208.
The paper describes the phonological system of the Cuaa language (Tshwa), a member of the eastern Khoe language family. Notes that Cuaa is spoken around the southern tip of the Sua Pan and further east towards the Shashe River and Mabebesekwa areas, and further eastwards towards Serowe. Comments upon the fundamental dialectical differences occurring in the various geographic locations. Discusses word order, phonology and tone. Remarks that there are currently only two clicks in Cuaa and that this may point towards impending language death. Also notes in this context that while parents may speak their own language, their children frequently only use Setswana or Kalanga. Emphasises the need for additional research into all linguistic aspects of Cuaa. Notes that in view of the sociolinguistic factors assailing the language the quality of data collected may at times be distorted.
BOTSWANA; CLICKS; CONFERENCE PAPERS; KUA; LANGUAGES; LINGUISTICS; PHONOLOGY
R/B 496.1 STA

0064 Chumbo, Sefako; Mmaba, Kotsi
//XOM KYAKYARE KHWE: +AM KURI KX'ÚÎÁ = THE KHWE OF THE OKAVANGO PANHANDLE: THE PAST LIFE: PART 1: ORIGIN, LAND, LEADERS AND TRADITIONS OF BUGAKHWE PEOPLE
Shakawe, Botswana: The Teemacane Trust, 2002. 78pp.
The booklet is the first in a series of Buga and ||Anikwe oral testimonies. Deals with the origin of the Khwe and with their relationship towards the land, their leaders, traditions, the foods eaten, housing, clothing and hunting traditions. The Introduction explains that in 1997 two ||Anikwe men, Michael Biase and Jesi Segole discussed the need for young people as well as outsiders to know how their people had lived previously and collected information from relatives and friends. Sefako Chumba and Kotsi Mmaba also conducted interviews and translated the results into English.
BOTSWANA; OKAVANGO DELTA; //ANIKHWE; BUGAKHWE; CULTURE; FOOD; HUNTING-GATHERING; ORAL HISTORY; SOCIAL ORGANIZATION
R/B 305.8096872 CHU

0065 Coetzee, C.
VISIONS FOR DISORDER AND PROFIT: THE KHOIKHOI AND THE FIRST YEARS OF THE DUTCH EAST INDIA COMPANY AT THE CAPE
Social Dynamics, Vol. 20 No. 2, 1994. pp.35–66.
The paper provides a detailed account of early relations between the Dutch East India Company and the Hottentot inhabitants of the Cape. Quotes extensively from official documents including the journal of Jan van Riebeeck, first governor at the Cape. Notes that, initially, the Company, under instructions from the Heren XVII in Holland, attempted to trade with the Hottentots, who regarded the settlers as temporary sojourners. Shows how an increasingly hostile relationship developed between the two groups. Gives the example of Krotoa/Eva who was taken into van Riebeeck's home, learnt Dutch and acted as interpreter and guide to the Company and married one of the settlers. Although she was baptised, her children were eventually taken from her and she died in exile on Robben Island. The story of Eva is seen to epitomise the relationship between the Hottentots and white settlers at the Cape.
CAPE; SOUTH AFRICA; COLONIALISM; HISTORY; KHOEKHOE; LIFE STORIES
98/1122

0066 Coetzee, J.M.
IDLENESS IN SOUTH AFRICA
Social Dynamics, Vol. 8 No. 1, 1982. pp.1–13.
The paper makes use of contemporary records to show the extent to which the Hottentots in the early period of white settlement at the Cape were censured for their idleness. Finds that this censure arises partly from the prevailing Calvinist work ethic of the writers but also from their frustration when attempting to fit the Hottentot lifestyle into certain preconceived categories. Notes that after 1795 the idleness of frontier farmers was equally heartily condemned by visiting commentators. Points out that no observers see Hottentot idleness in the light of the Eden myth when man lived a life of blissful ease.
CAPE; SOUTH AFRICA; HISTORY; KHOEKHOE; WORK
98/1123

0067 Coetzee, Paulette
BUSHMAN WOMEN IN BESSIE HEAD'S *MARU* AND DAPHNE ROOKE'S *MARGERETHE DE LA PORTE*
Current Writing, Vol.5 No.1, refs., 1993. pp.65–78.
The article examines two books written in the 1970's which feature San women. Introduces the two characters: Margaret in Bessie Head's novel *Maru* and Katjie in Daphne Rooke's novel *Margarethe de la Porte*. Notes that both these women have their origins in the Kalahari and are drawn in ways which

challenge the conventional, essentialist stereotypes while also suggesting aspects of the dominant myths. Notes that in both novels, the San characters do, to a certain extent perpetuate the negative stereotypes yet they also present the characters in an individual light, Margaret, as the artist discovering her own creative powers and Katjie, succeeding in keeping the secret of her deepest thoughts and feelings intact. Concludes that the depiction of San in these novels does not provide a final or completely satisfactory answer to the question of the San in the modern world but they should be seen as part of the ongoing debate.
BOTSWANA; SOUTH AFRICA; GENDER ISSUES; LITERATURE; WOMEN
P 820.05 CWR

0068 Collins, Chris
PLURALITY IN =HOAN. KHOISAN FORUM WORKING PAPER NO.9
Cologne: University of Cologne, 1998. 71pp.
The paper deals with plurality in =Hoan, a Khoisan language classified by Traill as either S7 or N4 which is spoken in south-eastern Botswana. Notes that the most closely related language is Sasi and that the two are mutually intelligible. Finds that in =Hoan both nouns and verbs can be pluralised and share deep and systematic properties. Points out that plurals of inalienable nouns are formed differently than those of alienable nouns. Discusses the use of the grammatical morpheme "ki" with inalienable nouns. Shows that there are basically three classes of inalienable nouns, each defined by independent morphological and notional criteria. Discusses different interpretations of postpositional phrases. Observes that plurals of verbs and adjectives are formed in a similar way to plurals of inalienable nouns and that the plural of a verb is known as a "pluractional" verb. Shows how adjectives and verbs are marked as being plural. Reviews issues related to data in the paper, including noun phrase structure and analysis of pluractional verbs and summarises the implications of this work for Khoisan linguistics.
BOTSWANA; =HUA; GRAMMAR; LANGUAGES; LINGUISTICS; RESEARCH
R/B 496.1 COL

0069 Conference on Human Rights and Democracy
CONFERENCE ON HUMAN RIGHTS AND DEMOCRACY, GABORONE, 17TH – 19TH NOVEMBER, 1998
Gaborone: Ditshawanelo, the Botswana Centre for Human Rights, 1998. 212pp.
The conference focused on the following human rights issues: democracy and human rights; globalization; poverty; education; right to sexual orientation; land and environment; worker's rights and rights of the elderly. Provides both the main papers presented at each major session and a summary of the discussion which followed. Papers dealing specifically with topics relating to the San are separately abstracted under names of the authors but reference is also made to their status and problems in other papers not so abstracted. The Appendix includes the Universal Declaration of Human Rights.
BOTSWANA; CONFERENCE REPORTS; DEVELOPMENT AID; GOVERNMENT POLICY; HUMAN RIGHTS; LAND RIGHTS; NON-GOVERNMENTAL ORGANISATIONS; POVERTY
R/B 321.8096872 DIT

0070 Cooke, C.K.
EVIDENCE OF HUMAN MIGRATIONS FROM THE ROCK ART OF SOUTHERN RHODESIA
Africa: Journal of the International African Institute, Vol.35 No.3, ill., maps, refs., 1965. pp.263–285.
This paper is the result of a study undertaken in 1963 and 1964 of all the known rock painting copies and photographs available from museums and collections in Southern Rhodesia. In the first instance it was done to plot the occurrence of giraffe paintings against those only in silhouette but the list had grown and all animal and human depictions were indexed and plotted on distribution maps and all the information was finally synthesised. Presents an analysis of the human types and domesticated animals recorded on the rock art of Southern Rhodesia. Discusses the significance of the items plotted in the distribution maps. Examines the importance of the Mopani Belt and its significance as a barrier facing sheep herders heading south, as sheep cannot eat mopani. Suggests a possible route from the east of Southern Rhodesia to the Cape of Good Hope which could have been used by sheep herding Hottentots. Notes linguistic evidence to support the Hottentot origin of sheep-herding in the region. Attempts to date the arrival of sheep in Southern Rhodesia as between 1700 and 1400 BP.
ZIMBABWE; HERDERS; PREHISTORY; ROCK ART; SHEEP
P 960.05 AJI

0071 Cooke, C.K.
LATE STYLES IN ROCK ART COMPARED WITH DRAWINGS MADE BY A BUSHMAN ARTIST
South African Archaeological Bulletin, Vol.30, refs., 1975. pp.25–28.
The article shows examples of drawings by a Bushman from the Tsodilo Hills area of Botswana which are compared to those of late cave art from Botswana and Rhodesia with a strong resemblance being noted. Discusses the question of who painted the late series or "Style 5" paintings in Rhodesia but comes to no definite conclusion apart from observing that the

paintings were made after the introduction of sheep and cattle to both Botswana and Rhodesia.
BOTSWANA; TSODILO HILLS; ZIMBABWE; ROCK ART
p 930.105 SAA

0072 Corrington, Matt
ON THE TRAIL OF THE BUSHMEN
Refs., 1999. pp.12–19.
The article outlines the current situation of the Bushman communities in Botswana, Namibia and South Africa. Pays particular attention to the resettlement of the G/wi and G//ana from the Central Kalahari Game Reserve to the village of New Xade. Reports on the situation of Bushmen in West Caprivi, Namibia, many of whom have recently fled to Botswana as refugees following political unrest in their area. Notes the implications for Bushmen in southern Africa of the establishment of the Peace Parks in which two national parks in South Africa and Botswana have been merged, and in which Khomeini Bushmen, who originally lived in the area may be granted land rights. Considers that recognition of the land rights of Bushmen in South Africa could put pressure on Botswana to change its policy on Bushman land rights.
BOTSWANA; CENTRAL KALAHARI GAME RESERVE; NAMIBIA; NEW XADE; XADE; =KHOMANI; !KUNG; CONFLICT; GAME RESERVES; G/UI; G//ANA; KHWE; LAND RIGHTS; POLITICS; RESETTLEMENT
p 910.5 GMA

0073 Coulson, David; Campbell, Alec
AFRICAN ROCK ART: PAINTINGS AND ENGRAVINGS ON STONE
New York: Harry N. Abrams, 2001. 256pp.
The book deals with the rock art, both engraved and painted, of the entire continent. The chapter entitled "Africa: the land and the people" includes a section on the Bushmen of southern Africa, their history, languages and religious beliefs. Points out that only through an understanding of the way in which the Bushman viewed their world can the meaning of their rock art be interpreted. Looks at early attempts to understand its meaning and at modern interpretations. Considers various methods of dating the art, and the various styles found in different parts of Africa. Notes that throughout the continent three main subjects are represented in the drawings or engravings: characterless human beings; animals; and designs or geometric shapes. Points out that the many other objects shown in paintings, such as weapons, digging sticks, carrying bags, and other artefacts used in daily life are mostly depicted as adjuncts to the human or animal figures. Chapter 4 covers the areas in southern Africa where Bushman art is found and the vivid photographs reveal the richness of this heritage. Chapter 9 looks at geometric designs and their possible significance.
ANGOLA; BOTSWANA; NAMIBIA; SOUTH AFRICA; ZAMBIA; ZIMBABWE; BELIEFS; CULTURE; HISTORY; RELIGION; RESEARCH; ROCK ART
R/B 709.0113096 COU

0074 Cowley, Clive
FABLED TRIBE: A JOURNEY TO DISCOVER THE RIVER BUSHMEN OF THE OKAVANGO SWAMPS
Harlow: Longmans, 1969. xix, 232pp.
The expedition described took place in 1966 under the auspices of the University of the Witwatersrand Kalahari Research Committee and aimed to study Bushmen of the northern Kalahari. Records the discovery of a small family group of Tanneke deep in the Okavango swamps. Notes the conclusion reached by the expedition leader, based mainly on linguistic investigations, that these people were of Hottentot rather than Bushman origin but most were the result of intermarriage with peoples of other ethnic origins. Comments on their life style and points out that they did not hunt using bows and arrows but fished and gathered plant products to survive. Admits that a brief visit could provide little useful information about social customs or beliefs.
BOTSWANA; OKAVANGO DELTA; //ANIKHWE; ANTHROPOLOGY; FISHING; FOOD; KHOEKHOE; RIVER BUSHMEN
301.296872 COW

0075 Crawhall, Nigel
WRITTEN IN THE SAND: AUDITING AND MANAGING CULTURAL RESOURCES WITH DISPLACED INDIGENOUS PEOPLES: A SOUTH AFRICAN CASE STUDY
Rondebosch: South African San Institute, UNESCO, ill., refs. 2001. 32pp.
Provides an overview of the issues surrounding language endangerment. Cites research conducted by different linguists and non-linguistic members of minority communities to highlight how languages are lost, from sociological and economic as well as from linguistic perspectives. Associates language death with a larger problem of the destruction of minority peoples' livelihoods across the globe. Expresses concern that languages, especially of societies that were based on hunting and gathering, are at risk of becoming obsolete due to a number of factors mentioned in the document. Notes that instead of protecting the minority groups, governments tend to be interested in protecting tangible heritage such as buildings, monuments and museum contents. Emphasises the need for awareness raising and action to educate governments on what is lost as languages die. Stresses the need for indigenous peoples, governments, and non-governmental organizations (NGOs) to work together to maintain linguistic and cultural diversity. Explains the importance of language maintenance in protecting people's entire cultural heritage, ensuring management of the environment, access to land

and other important natural resources, and redressing issues of marginalization and poverty.
BOTSWANA; KALAHARI; SOUTH AFRICA; =KHOMANI; CULTURE; EMPOWERMENT; GOVERNMENT POLICY; HISTORY; HUNTING-GATHERING; INDIGENOUS PEOPLES; KHOESAN; LANGUAGES; LINGUISTICS; MINORITY RIGHTS; POVERTY
R/B 305.9063 CRA

0076 Cukiri, Tshau Frisca; Kuela, Kiema
NARO LANGUAGE PROJECT OF THE D'KAR REFORMED CHURCH
Oussoren, Otto. Education for remote area dwellers in Botswana. Gaborone: University of Botswana, Research and Development Unit; WIMSA, Regional San Education Project, 2001. 107pp., pp.66–67.
The joint paper introduces the Naro Language Project which operates under the auspices of the Dutch Reformed Church in D'Kar. Each speaker gives a short resume of his work and educational background. Points out the common fallacy among those unfamiliar with San languages that there is one "Sarwa language" which is similar to suggesting that one can speak of "the Bantu language" as if there were only one while in fact there are a number. Explains that the Naro Language Project is developing an orthography for Naro and one in which the click sounds will be accommodated. Notes that most non-San have difficulty in distinguishing click sounds resulting in misunderstandings between people. Shows the value of providing information to public officers who have to write San names so that identity cards are correctly dealt with. Notes that clicks may be written in several ways and that an unstable and unofficial Setswana system has been developed which is often used by teachers in schools. Concludes by pointing out the value of mother tongue education because of the difficulty of grasping concepts in an unknown language.
BOTSWANA; CONFERENCE PAPERS; CLICKS; EDUCATION; LITERACY; NARO; ORTHOGRAPHY
R/B 372.7096872 WIM

0077 Darkwah, R.K.H.; Mgadla, P.T.
PRELIMINARY INVESTIGATION INTO GAPS IN BASARWA HISTORY
Lane, Paul; Hermans, Janet; Molebatsi, Chadzimula. Proceedings from the Basarwa research workshop, Gaborone, 24–25 August, 1995. 106pp. 2001. pp.26–30.
The paper describes the social, political and economic history of Basarwa in Botswana. Notes that in 1985 there were estimated to be around 35,000 Basarwa in Botswana. Notes that elements of change have been observed in the 20th century which are attributed to contact with their non-Basarwa neighbours. Observes that 19th century historiography ignored Basarwa because they did not have an organised state system or any written documents. Claims that their more settled neighbours have exploited Basarwa workers. Concludes that Basarwa have been dispossessed of their land, giving as an example government policy, where large tracts of land formerly accessible to the Basarwa for their traditional economic activities were taken over for environmental and conservation purposes and demarcated as game reserves.
BOTSWANA; ANTHROPOLOGY; CONFERENCE PAPERS; FORAGING; GOVERNMENT POLICY; HUNTING-GATHERING; LAND OWNERSHIP; SOCIAL CHANGE
R/B 305.8096872 PRO

0078 Deacon, Janette
A REVIEW OF 'ROCK ENGRAVINGS OF SOUTHERN AFRICA' BY T.A. DOWSON
South African Archaeological Bulletin, Vol.49 No.159, 1994. 54pp.
The reviewer comments favourably on the excellence of the presentation of rock engravings. Notes that the book is aimed at non-specialists and provides details on the history of rock engraving studies, dating, recording and engraving techniques as well as examining the quality and meaning of the art. Shows that the author deals with interpretation in two ways, by showing that rock engravings were part of a very long enduring religious tradition and that there are similarities between Bushman religious beliefs and practices and what was depicted in their art. Notes the importance of particular sites in the rainmaking rituals and provides photos of the setting of the engravings shown. Points out that the author's discussion with Namibian Bushmen has been helpful in the understanding of the art.
SOUTHERN AFRICA; BELIEFS; BOOK REVIEWS; MYTHOLOGY; RELIGION; RESEARCH; ROCK ART
P 930.105 SAA

0079 Deacon, Janette
PROMOTION OF A NEGLECTED HERITAGE AT STONE AGE SITES IN THE WESTERN CAPE, SOUTH AFRICA
Conservation and management of archaeological sites, Vol. 1 No. 2, James and James Publishers, London, 1995. pp.75–86.
The paper explores efforts to conserve rock art sites in South Africa and to deal with the results of deliberate damage done by visitors. Comments that efforts to minimise damage by limiting access or keeping a low profile has had a negative effect. Notes the limited knowledge of most South Africans about the meaning and value of rock art which is linked to the fact that precolonial history was not in school curricula in the past nor is there much public awareness of either the results of rock art research or of the legislation covering the protection of rock art sites. Provides examples of active intervention at Stone Age living sites in the Cape which provide a dynamic response to

the challenge of conserving rock art.
SOUTH AFRICA; ARCHAEOLOGY; HISTORY; ROCK ART
98/1188

0080 Dedering, T.
THE MURDER OF WILLIAM THRELFALL: THE MISSIONARIES IN SOUTHERN NAMIBIA AND THE CAPE GOVERNMENT IN THE 1820's
South African Historical Journal, Vol. 24 1991, pp.90–111.
The paper deals with the role of missionaries as political agents in Southern Namibia during the early nineteenth century and focuses on two aspects. Firstly it gives the background against which Threlfall's murder took place at a time of crisis between missionaries and the Khoikhoi. Secondly it shows that the murder of the missionary resulted in improvements in relations between the Cape Government and the Khoikhoi and explains how this came about. Points out that before the advent of German colonisers, mission work in Southern Namibia had transformed the social structures of the Khoikhoi.
NAMIBIA; SOUTH AFRICA; CONFLICT; HISTORY; MISSIONARIES; NAMA
98/1167

0081 Deetz, James
'THE ROCK ART OF SOUTHERN AFRICA' BY JAMES DAVID LEWIS-WILLIAMS: A REVIEW
South African Archaeological Bulletin, Vol.39, 1984. pp.146–147.
The reviewer examines the book in detail and commends the new approach to Bushman rock art which it introduces. Considers it intriguing and credible. Shows that the central thesis of the book is the symbolic significance of the paintings. Introduces the three main concepts which support this argument: a) The significance of the superposition of paintings; b) The identification of a powerful motif, the dying eland as a metaphor for the trancing medicine man; c) A different concept of artistic composition and execution. Notes the use of corollary ethnographic information to substantiate the author's claims.
SOUTH AFRICA; ANIMALS; BELIEFS; BOOK REVIEWS; DANCE; RELIGION; RESEARCH; ROCK ART; SHAMANISM; TRANCE
P 930.105 SAA

0082 Denbow, James
INTERFACES: THE STUDY OF THE HISTORICAL CONTEXT OF HUNTER-GATHERERS IN AFRICA
Bernd Heine Sprach und Geschichte in Afrika, Vol.7 No.2. Hamburg: Helmut Buske, 465pp.1986. pp.455–458. ISBN 3871187607.
The paper contains a summary of the ideas and topics presented at the symposium on African hunter-gatherers held at Sankt Augustin, January 3–5,1985. Observes the extent to which knowledge of the more recent past of African hunter-gatherers has grown in the 20 years since the first such symposium held in 1966. Notes that as the knowledge of the history of hunting-gathering societies has increased, so the context of investigations have shifted from a focus on the band as an isolate towards more regional perspectives which examine relations between foragers and their herding and farming neighbours. Notes the organization of the conference around three major themes: linguistic reconstruction and ethnohistory, social structure, territoriality and ecology, symbiosis, assimilation and ethnicity. Reports that the areas in which the studies were carried were east, central and southern Africa.
CENTRAL AFRICA; EAST AFRICA; SOUTHERN AFRICA; ANTHROPOLOGY; ETHNOHISTORY; FORAGING; INTERGROUP RELATIONS; RESEARCH; ROCK ART
95/824

0083 Denbow, James; Campbell, Alec
THE EARLY STAGES OF FOOD PRODUCTION IN SOUTHERN AFRICA AND SOME POTENTIAL LINGUISTIC CORRELATIONS
Bernd Heine Sprache und Geschichte in Afrika, Vol.7 No.1. Hamburg: Helmut Buske, 457pp. 1986. pp.83–104. ISBN 3871187593.
The paper discusses the origins of herding in southern Africa and investigates the archaeological and linguistic evidence of early interaction between Early Iron Age (EIA) and Later Stone Age (LSA) peoples. Queries the usual assumptions that EIA in southern Africa originated from a single source west of Lake Victoria. Instead suggests that EIA communities were spread over a wider area and could have been in contact with Khoisan pastoralists before their southward migration. Notes that the terms for cattle and sheep in Southern Bantu languages are of Khoisan origin. Suggests that it is uncertain whether the spread of herding was due to diffusion or population movements but probably both.
SOUTH AFRICA; ARCHAEOLOGY; LANGUAGES; LINGUISTICS; PASTORALISM; RESEARCH
85/825

0084 Dickens, Patrick; Traill, Anthony
COLLECTIVE AND DISTRIBUTIVE IN !XOO
Traill, Anthony. Khoisan Linguistic Studies 3, 1977. pp.132–144.
The paper examines the notion of "collective versus distributive plural" in !Xoo. Follows closely the analysis made by J.S. Gruber in his paper: "Plural predicates in =Hua" published in *Bushman and Hottentot linguistic studies*, ASI Communications 2 (1975). Finds that there is no evidence of a systematically made collective versus distributive distinction in !Xoc and therefore the structure of !Xoo does not parallel that of =Hua in this regard.

BOTSWANA; !XOO; =HUA; GRAMMAR; LANGUAGES; LINGUISTICS
496.2709 KHO

0085 Dintwa, Bathusi
RESEARCH NEEDS OF THE MINISTRY OF LOCAL GOVENMENT, LANDS AND HOUSING
Lane, Paul; Hermans, Janet; Molebatsi, Chadzimula. Proceedings from the Basarwa Research Workshop, Gaborone, 24–25 August, 1995. 106pp. 2001. pp.100–103.

The paper, presented at the Basarwa Research Workshop held at the University of Botswana on August 24–25, 1995 sets out the requirements of the Ministry of Local Government, Lands and Housing regarding the type of research it would find useful if the Remote Area Development Programme is to be successful. Suggests that the following target areas for research would be of particular interest: a) research which would provide a better understanding of the nature of the Programme's target group who are not homogenous; b) the significance of nomadism, hunting and gathering in the lives of Basarwa; c) the land issues concerning Basarwa vis-à-vis other Batswana and other land uses; d) access to land and its distribution; e) the attitudes of the Basarwa and other Batswana regarding each other; f) affirmative-action development; g) mother tongue education. In addition comments on the urgent need for research on development in order to prevent intensification of poverty and inequality.
BOTSWANA; CONFERENCE PAPERS; DEVELOPMENT PLANNING; GOVERNMENT POLICY; REMOTE AREA DEVELOPMENT; RESEARCH
R/B 305.8096872 PRO

0086 Ditshwanelo: The Botswana Centre for Human Rights
SUMMARY OF THE FACTS RELATING TO THE RELOCATION OF RESIDENTS OF THE CENTRAL KALAHARI GAME RESERVE (CKGR)
n.d., 2pp.

This brief paper sets out the details concerning the relocation of residents of the Central Kalahari Game Reserve (CKGR) by the Botswana Government. Gives the grounds for the resultant court case in the High Court of Botswana held on April 10, 2002. Explains the role of the Negotiating Team in consultation with the Department of Wildlife and National Parks (DWNP) in the development of a draft management plan which would have permitted the residents of the CKGR to use and manage the natural resources in and around their residential areas for income generation.
BOTSWANA; CENTRAL KALAHARI GAME RESERVE; GAME RESERVES; GOVERNMENT POLICY; RESETTLEMENT
PH/B 333.954916 SUM

0087 Doke, Clement M.
AN OUTLINE OF THE PHONETICS OF THE LANGUAGE OF THE CHU BUSHMEN OF NORTH-WEST KALAHARI
Bantu Studies, Vol.2, 1925. pp.129–165.

The paper provides an outline of the phonetics of Ju/'hoan and is based on research carried out in the Grootfontein District of Namibia in 1925. Notes the main features of the language including the fact that it is an isolating language, with mainly monosyllabic words and that musical tone on each syllable replaces stress so that a change of tone may change the meaning of words. Points out that the employment of clicks is a distinguishing feature of all Bushman languages. Includes a short vocabulary and a few words of Nama and Hai//om.
NAMIBIA; HAI//OM; JU/'HOANSI; KHOEKHOEGOWAB; LANGUAGES; LINGUISTICS; NAMA; PHONETICS
P 960.05 AST

0088 Douglas, Stuart
THE HUMAN ISTHMUS: DANGEROUS DILUTED SEWERAGE POISON — RECUPERATING 'BUSHMAN' IN THE 'NEW SOUTH AFRICA'
Critical Arts: A Journal of Cultural Studies, Vol.9 No.2, refs., 1995. pp.65–75. ISSN 02560046.

The article, with a title taken from the warning on the sewerage tankers at Schmidtsdrift, is strongly critical of the attempt to present Bushmen as a bridge between past and present in the new South Africa. Recounts the attempt by the right wing Afrikaner Freedom Front Party to recruit Schmidtsdrift Bushmen to their party. Also notes the effort of the Freedom Front to present Afrikaners as "First People", even to sending a delegation to the UN Working Group for Indigenous People in Geneva in 1994. Finds that political elements from Left and Right in South Africa tend to see "Bushmanness" as "Otherness" of a primordial and quintessential nature and this does not augur well for reconciliation in South Africa. Considers that this approach may contribute to the re-establishing of competing nationalisms rather than contributing to the creation of a new, unified South Africa.
SCHMIDTSDRIFT; SOUTH AFRICA; CULTURE; INDIGENOUS PEOPLES; POLITICS
PH/B 305.80968 CRI

0089 Dowson, Thomas A.
ROCK ART RESEARCH'S UMBILICAL CORD: A REVIEW OF *AFRICA PRAEHISTORICA*, VOL. 1
Cimbebasia, Dec 1990, Vol. 12. pp.172–176.

The review of Harald Pager's *Rock Paintings of the Upper Brandberg, Amis Gorge* (the first in the Cologne-based Heinrich-Barth Institut's *Africa Praehistorica* series), while appreciative of the excellent reproductions in the book, criticises its methodological approach. Points out that apart from

the reproductions of the paintings, there is a detailed catalogue which defines each depiction or scene. Takes issue with this empirical approach to the interpretation of rock art which ignores its diversity and precludes a more penetrating interpretive discussion. Calls for rock art scholars to "cut the methodologically flawed umbilical cord" leading back to now discredited interpretations and rather to adopt methods that will allow rock art research to develop and ask new and more interesting questions.
NAMIBIA; BOOK REVIEWS; RESEARCH; ROCK ART
99/740

0090 Dowson, Thomas A.; Holliday, Anne L.
ZIGZAGS AND ELAND: AN INTERPRETATION OF AN IDIOSYNCRETIC COMBINATION
South African Archaeological Bulletin, Vol.44, No.149. 1993. pp.46–48.
The article explains the probable significance of rock paintings of eland and rain-animals with associated zigzags surrounding and issuing from their bodies. Refers to the neuropsychological research on altered states of consciousness which has indicated that rock art often depicts hallucinations experienced by shaman artists. Considers that the zigzags represent the potency associated with the eland and the rain-animals. Uses information from 19th century and modern ethnological sources to confirm these insights.
FREE STATE; SOUTH AFRICA; ANIMALS; ANTHROPOLOGY; DANCE; RELIGION; ROCK ART; SHAMANISM; TRANCE
P 930.105 SAA

0091 Draper, Patricia
THE LEARNING ENVIRONMENT FOR AGGRESSION AND ANTI-SOCIAL BEHAVIOR AMONG THE !KUNG
Montagu, Ashley. Learning non-aggression: the experience of non-literate societies. London: Oxford University Press. n.d., refs. pp.31–53. ISBN 0195023439.
Discusses case study of !Kung on whether they are harmless or murderous. Addresses the interpersonal conflict and aggression among !Kung. Emphasises the learning environment of children and how it relates to the learning of aggressive behaviour. Notes parental attitudes towards children's behaviour and techniques for dealing with conflict. Describes dimensions of social organization relevant to the ability of !Kung to discourage interpersonal aggression and to encourage group cooperation. Concludes that the !Kung are successful in discouraging harmful and malicious behaviour in young people.
BOTSWANA; NAMIBIA; !KUNG; ANTHROPOLOGY; CULTURAL CHANGE; ENVIRONMENT; FORAGING; INTERACTION
PH/B 301.427 DRA

0092 Draper, Patricia
!KUNG WOMEN: CONTRASTS IN SEXUAL EGALITARIANISM IN FORAGING AND SEDENTARY CONTEXTS
Reiter, Rayna R. (ed.). Towards an anthropology of women. New York: Monthly Review Press, 416pp.1975. pp.77–109. ISBN 0853453721.
The paper describes male/female relations in two !Kung communities one of which is sedentary and the other traditional hunting-gathering. Emphasises the extent to which, in the traditional life-style women have considerable autonomy and influence which tends to diminish with sedentism. Comments that in the hunting-gathering context, women are not subordinate to men. Shows the ways in which sex roles of both adults and children tend to be more rigidly defined in sedentary villages. Finds that while men interact with outsiders and travel more frequently in the village context, women are more home-bound and involved in a multiplicity of tasks not required in the foraging way of life.
BOTSWANA; !KUNG; ANTHROPOLOGY; FARMING; GENDER ISSUES; HUNTING-GATHERING; SEDENTISM; WOMEN
301.412 REI

0093 Draper, Patricia
IF YOU HAVE A CHILD, YOU HAVE LIFE: DEMOGRAPHIC AND CULTURAL PERSPECTIVES ON FATHERING IN OLD AGE IN !KUNG SOCIETY
Refs., 1992. pp.131–152.
The chapter is based on data collected from !Kung of Western Botswana, collected in 1987–1988 by means of interviews. Provides demographic information on various aspects of ageing and survival into old age, particularly as relating to males. Focuses on the ties between older parents (particularly fathers) and their adult children. Notes that parent-child relationships continue to be important throughout life and, because of the limited technological sources available to the society, physically infirm old people are dependent on younger people (hence the title of the chapter). Points out that the low fertility rate of the !Kung and high childhood and adult mortality means that many people reaching old age may have no surviving children. Notes that the incursion of non-!Kung into the area has had a negative effect on gender relations between !Kung as many !Kung women now bear children to fathers who are outsiders while some !Kung men do not have any children. Points out that all informants claimed that the two vital factors relating to successful aging were having children to support one, and one's own bodily strength. Notes that this was demographically supported in the case of women but not in that of men.
BOTSWANA; !KUNG; AGED; DEMOGRAPHY; GENDER ISSUES
PH/B 305.8096872 DRA

0094 Duggan-Cronin, Alfred Martin,
THE BUSHMAN TRIBES OF SOUTHERN AFRICA
Kimberley: Alexander McGregor Memorial Museum, 1942, various pagings.
The book contains a large number of photographs with accompanying text describing where the photograph was taken and giving details about the subject and in most cases indicating the "tribe" to which the subject belongs. Includes pictures of the now extinct /Xam. Many of the photographs are portraits of individuals but some show daily activities such as processing skins, collecting water or dancing.
BOTSWANA; GHANZI DISTRICT; NAMIBIA; SOUTH AFRICA/XAM; /'AUNI; =KHOMANI; CULTURE; MATERIAL CULTURE; PHOTOS
301.2968 DUG

0095 Eastwood, Edward B.
CAPTURING THE SPOOR: TOWARDS EXPLAINING KUDU IN SAN ROCK ART OF THE LIMPOPO-SHASHI CONFLUENCE AREA
South African Archaeological Bulletin, Vol.54 No.170, 1999. pp.107–119.
The paper examines the selection of kudu rather than eland by the San of the Limpopo-Shashi confluence area (LSCA) with reference to the distribution of the kudu, its biological and behavioural characteristics and its significance in San thought. Comments that images of kudu predominate in San rock art north of northern South Africa. Notes that two bodies of evidence contribute to an understanding of the significance of the kudu in the rock art of the LCSA; firstly there are the ethnographic sources and secondly there are the context and associations of the kudu in the art itself that provide primary and secondary evidence for the social, ritual and metaphoric importance for San hunter-gatherers who once occupied the area.
SOUTH AFRICA; ZIMBABWE; ANIMALS; BELIEFS; RELIGION; ROCK ART
P 930.105 SAA

0096 Ebert, James I.; Thoma, Axel; Oabile, Malebogo; Ebert, Melinda; Hitchcock, Robert K.
REPORT AND RECOMMENDATIONS FOR LAND ALLOCATION AND BASARWA DEVELOPMENT IN THE SANDVELD REGION OF THE CENTRAL DISTRICT, BOTSWANA
1976, various pagings.
The report reflects the results of a year's fieldwork by the authors and provides a number of recommendations regarding future possibilities for the area and economic development of the Basarwa living there. Some key recommendations include suggestions that the location of boreholes be mapped to assist in the later allocation of land and that Basarwa handicrafts be developed and arrangements be made for marketing of handicrafts. Further suggests the following as strategies to improve income of Basarwa: a) payments of wages to all employed Basarwa; b) involvement of Basarwa in tourist industry; c) training and employment of Basarwa in mechanics and borehole maintenance. Recommends incentive and experimentation with larger-scale Basarwa "commercial" enterprises in their own communal areas. Suggests ways of improving educational opportunities for Basarwa children. Remaining recommendations refer to suggestions on the types of land use planning needed and improvement in the alignment of the main road.
BOTSWANA; DEVELOPMENT PLANNING; EDUCATION; FARMING; HANDICRAFTS; LAND USE
PH/B 305.8 REP

0097 Ehret, Christopher
PROPOSALS ON KHOISAN RECONSTRUCTION
Bernd Heine Sprache und Geschichte in Afrika, Vol.7 No.2. Hamburg: Helmut Buske, 465pp. 1986. pp.105–130. ISBN 3871187607.
The paper investigates the evidence to suggest the existence of a wider Khoisan language family comprising the southern African languages and, from East Africa, Sandawe and Hadza which are more distant from each other and from the southern African branch. Notes differences between the phonological systems of the Southern and East African groups of languages, but observes that the major systemic differences in phonology are all potentially explainable, and in the case of Sandawe and Hadza, partly by borrowings from Cushitic and Bantu languages. Presents comparative data on sound shifts and the evolution of click sounds from earlier non-click consonants.
SOUTHERN AFRICA; TANZANIA; CLICKS; HADZA; KHOESAN; LANGUAGES; LINGUISTICS; SANDAWE
95/824

0098 Eistein, A.
AN OBSERVATIONAL BIOLOGY: AFRICA: SAN BUSHMEN
Wisdom of the elders: sacred native stories of nature. Bantam Books, 1993. pp.79–85.
The chapter, based largely on the findings of Richard Lee and Hans-Joachim Heinz, provides details of the ethnobiology and ethnobotany of the Bushmen. Shows that the knowledge of animal and bird behaviour is extensive, extremely detailed and exceeds the knowledge required merely for hunting purposes. Sees the Bushman as "the original scientist" with a knowledge of animal physiology based upon acute observation. Considers that the relationship with nature is linked to religious beliefs: the experiences of those in the trance state is believed to provide them with a unique perspective on the natural world.
BOTSWANA; !KUNG; !XOO; DANCE; ETHNOBIOLOGY; ETHNOBOTANY; HEALING; TRANCE
99/187

0099 Elbourne, Elizabeth
EARLY KHOISAN USES OF MISSION CHRISTIANITY
Bredekamp, Henry; Ross, Robert. Missions and Christianity in South African history. 1995. pp.65–95.
The paper examines the religious, political and economic ways in which descendants of the Cape Khoisan communities used Christian missions in the 17th century. Shows how Khoisan, a traumatised and dispossessed group of mixed ethnic origin, accepted Christian teaching more readily than did other indigenous peoples. Explains that they found in Christianity new explanations for their condition and were able to combine it with aspects of their own religious beliefs. Notes the hostility towards the missions shown by farmers who opposed the baptism of "heathen" and who attempted to block efforts of their Khoisan labourers to resettle at the mission station of Bethelsdorp (Genadendal). Shows that the farmer's opposition was largely economic as they feared the loss of Khoisan labour which was seen as bonded to particular places or persons and denied free movement by the pass system. Comments on the political involvement of Bethelsdorp missionaries on behalf of Khoisan.
CAPE; SOUTH AFRICA; CONFLICT; HISTORY; INTERGROUP RELATIONS; KHOEKHOE; KHOESAN; MISSIONARIES; POLITICS; RELIGION
209.68 MIS

0100 Elderkin, E.D.
DIACHRONIC INFERENCES FROM BASIC SENTENCE AND NOUN STRUCTURE IN CENTRAL KHOISAN AND SANDAWE
Bernd Heine Sprache und Geschichte in Afrika, Vol.7 No.2. Hamburg: Helmut Buske, 465pp. 1986. pp.131–156. ISBN 3871187607.
The article presents the hypothesis that there is an affinity between the Central Khoisan languages and Sandawe. Examines this hypothesis looking at the syntactical structure and simple nominals in Sandawe, Nama, and Kxoe. The multiple functions of the series of suffixes designated as (p)erson (g)ender (n)umber series form the main focus of this study. Employs the classification proposed by Köhler in which Sandawe and Central Khoisan form one unit.
NAMIBIA; TANZANIA; CLICKS; LANGUAGES; LINGUISTICS; KHOE; KHWEDAM; NAMA; RESEARCH; SANDAWE
95/824

0101 Ellis, William
BUSHMAN IDENTITY, LAND CLAIMS AND THE THREE AGENDAS
Barnard, Alan; Kenrick, Justin. Africa's Indigenous Peoples: "First Peoples or Marginalised Minorities"? Edinburgh: University of Edinburgh, Centre of African Studies, refs., xv, 322pp., 2001. pp.255–272. ISBN 0952791757.
The paper addresses what are referred to as the "three agendas" articulated by the =Khomani living on the farms they won as a result of their successful land claim in the vicinity of the Kalahari Gemsbok National Park. Notes that in spite of their expressed nostalgia for life in the park, most of the =Khomani are several generations from the hunting and gathering life style, do not know how to hunt with bows and arrows and do not speak a San language. Shows that they expect to survive by producing artefacts for sale to tourists and by game farming and ethnotourism activities. Describes the tensions that exist between those wishing to live a perceived "traditional" life style and "westernised Bushmen" who are stock owners and wealthier but form a minority within the group. Concludes that the commonly expressed third agenda is that of the dire poverty in which most are living and that this is what needs to be addressed by the people themselves who need to learn to live as a group with common goals.
KALAHARI GEMSBOK NATIONAL PARK; NORTHERN CAPE; SOUTH AFRICA; =KHOMANI; CONFERENCE PAPERS; FARMING; HUNTING-GATHERING; INTERGROUP RELATIONS; LAND RIGHTS; LIVESTOCK; POVERTY; TOURISM
R/B 305.80968 AFR

0102 Elphick, Richard
THE CAPE KHOI AND THE FIRST PHASE OF SOUTH AFRICAN RACE RELATIONS
Thesis (Ph.D.), University of Yale, Department of History, xii, 314pp. refs., 1972.
Deals with the Cape Khoi (i.e. those Khoi living in modern times South of the Orange river) before white intrusion. Notes that the Khoi expanded southwards towards the Orange river valley. Explains the Khoi split into the Cape Khoi and the Namaqua. Discusses Khoi-White contact from 1652–1700. Notes two Khoi-Dutch wars and Khoi economic decline. Comments on the rapid assimilation of Khoi into the colony's labouring class and subordination of Khoi chiefs to the authority of the Cape government. Observes that by late 17th century, white racial attitudes towards the Khoi resembled South African white racial attitudes towards Blacks. Notes that the smallpox epidemic of 1713 killed the majority of Khoi in the Western Cape, though the disintegration of traditional Khoi society was advanced by 1713.
CAPE; SOUTH AFRICA; HISTORY; INTERGROUP RELATIONS; KHOEKHOE; LANGUAGES; LINGUISTICS; NAMAQUA
TH 968.1 ELP

0103 Elphick, Richard
KRAAL AND CASTLE: KHOIKHOI AND THE FOUNDING OF WHITE SOUTH AFRICA
New Haven: Yale University Press, xxii, 266pp. 1977.
The book is a history of the Khoikhoi from before the arrival

of whites at the Cape until the collapse of Khoikhoi society towards the end of the 17th century. Contains four parts: 1. The Cape Khoikhoi before the arrival of whites. 2. Europeans and the western Cape Khoikhoi,1488–1701. 3. Processes of decline among the western Cape Khoikhoi,1652–1701. 4. Denouement and retrospect. Examines in some detail the relationships between Khoikhoi and hunters (San). Shows, using evidence from linguistics, cultural anthropology and physical anthropology, that Khoikhoi originated in southern Africa and were initially hunters probably with a "Bush" culture. Indicates that they later interacted with San at many stages of their history. Uses historical written records to describe each of the Khoikhoi groups in turn, giving a history of their interaction with white invaders. Seeks to establish reasons for the decline of Khoikhoi society. Shows the conditions needed for the Khoikhoi to have survived as an independent people and shows that these were not fulfilled in the period under review.
CAPE; SOUTH AFRICA; ANTHROPOLOGY; COLONIALISM; CULTURAL CHANGE; HERDING; HISTORY; INDIGENOUS PEOPLES; INTERGROUP RELATIONS; KHOEKHOE; KHOESAN; LIVESTOCK; PHYSICAL ANTHROPOLOGY; SOCIAL ORGANISATION
968 ELP

0104 Elphick, Richard; Malherbe, C.
THE KHOISAN TO 1828
Elphick, Richard; Giliomee, Herman. The shaping of South African society. Cape Town: Maskew Miller Longman, xix, 624pp.1989. pp.3–65. ISBN 0636010767.
The chapter records the history of the Khoisan from the onset of white settlement at the Cape under the Verenigde Oostindische Compagnie up till 1828 when the Cape was under British rule. Provides reasons for the collapse of Western Cape Khoikhoi society by 1720. Shows that loss of sheep and cattle and the land needed to graze the animals were among the factors responsible for Khoikhoi decline and their subsequent dependence upon the settlers for the necessities of life. Refers to the resistance of the Bushmen to white domination and to absorption of dispossessed Khoikhoi into Bushman bands. Notes the development of a racial order based on white domination. Considers that this provided the model which was carried by white colonists to new regions and peoples as they moved away from the Cape.
CAPE; SOUTH AFRICA; COLONIALISM; CONFLICT; HERDING; INDIGENOUS PEOPLES; INTERGROUP RELATIONS; KHOEKHOE; KHOESAN; LAND USE
968.03 SHA

0105 Endicott, Karen L.
GENDER RELATIONS IN HUNTER-GATHERER SOCIETY
Lee, Richard; Daly, Richard. The Cambridge encyclopedia of hunters and gatherers. Cambridge, Cambridge University Press, 1999. xx, 511pp., ill, maps. pp.411–418. ISBN 052157109X.
The chapter looks at gender relations in a number of hunter-gatherer societies world wide. Explores interpretative differences and examines some common misconceptions about hunter-gatherer relationships. Traces changes in interpretation of gender relations by anthropologists which have resulted from the feminist movement and the work of female anthropologists. Deals with various questions relating to meat-sharing and power relations, the effect of incorporation into nation-states upon gender relations, and whether men control women in foraging societies. Refers to the !Kung particularly with regard to meat-sharing and the fact that the owner of the arrow which killed the prey is responsible for sharing out the meat and can be female. Describes the mechanism whereby !Kung hunters are prevented from turning the meat-sharing network into a power-base.
BOTSWANA; !KUNG; ANTHROPOLOGY; CULTURE; EGALITARIANISM; GENDER ISSUES; SOCIAL ORGANIZATION
R 306.36403 CAM

0106 England, Nicholas M.
MUSIC AMONG THE ZU'/'WA-SI OF NAMIBIA AND BOTSWANA
Harvard dissertations in folklore and oral tradition. New York: Garland, ill., music., refs., 1995. xvii, 417pp.
The book deals in considerable detail with the instrumental and vocal music of Zu/asi and related peoples. Includes details concerning their ethnic and linguistic background, social organization and the known history of the Nyae Nyae area of Namibia. Part I covers instrumental music, describing the manufacture of the instruments and analysing their music. Provides illustrations of the various instruments and examples in staff notation of the music they produce. Part II covers vocal music and the instruments which accompany it. Describes the curing ritual carried out by medicine men during the healing dance and the associated beliefs. Covers vocal music of women and girls and the dances and songs connected with girls' menarchal ceremony. Appendices include transcriptions in staff notation of Bushman songs recorded by the author.
ANGOLA; BOTSWANA; NAMIBIA; NYAE NYAE; BELIEFS; DANCE; HEALING; JU/'HOANSI; MUSIC; RELIGION; RESEARCH; RITUALS; SHAMANISM; TRANCE
R/B 780 ENG

0107 English, Mark
"WE, THE PEOPLE OF THE SHORT BLANKET": DEVELOPMENT PROPOSALS BASED ON THE NEEDS AND ASPIRATIONS OF THE CENTRAL KALAHARI GAME RESERVE POPULATION
Gaborone, 1980, 67 leaves.

The report was written as a planning document to be used as a basis for implementing assistance for residents of the Central Kalahari Game Reserve (CKGR). Provides a brief history of the three groups inhabiting the area: G/ui, G//ana and Bakalagadi. Notes that all these groups have resided in this part of Botswana for many generations. Explains the two types of mobility pattern as either movement within the Game Reserve or out migration to the villages and settlements. Notes that the latter type of movement takes place regularly but increases considerably during periods of drought when neither food nor water are obtainable. Describes the subsistence methods which in addition to hunting and gathering include stock rearing and small-scale arable farming as well wage labour outside the reserve. Notes that the CKGR residents either have no cash income at all or one that is extremely small and irregular. Mentions how income is used and comments that wealthier families tend to invest in domestic stock especially horses. Looks at the effects of the 1979/80 drought and the lack of drought relief support from the Botswana authorities which is largely as a result of bureaucratic delays associated with logistical problems. Examines negative and positive effects of the settlement of many Bushmen at Xade. Makes recommendations regarding future development, both short and long term, and warns that resettlement of the CKGR communities out of the Reserve could lead to their destruction.
BOTSWANA; CENTRAL KALAHARI GAME RESERVE; BAKGALAGADI; FORAGING; G/UI; G//ANA; GOVERNMENT POLICY; INTERACTION; POVERTY; REMOTE AREA DEVELOPMENT; SETTLEMENT POLICY
R/B 307.72096872 WET

0108 Erni, C.
RESETTLEMENT OF KHWE COMMUNITIES CONTINUES
Indigenous Affairs, No. 3/4, July 1997, pp.8–11.
The paper examines the policy of the Botswana Government regarding the resettling of Central Kalahari Game Reserve residents. Describes living conditions at New Xade, the settlement to which 500 former residents of !Xade were relocated in May 1997. Notes that promises made to them regarding compensation, provision of an adequate water supply and building materials for their new homes have not been fulfilled. Comments that prospects for improved economic opportunities in this area remain bleak and lack of land rights continues to be a serious problem. Suggests reasons for the intransigence of the Botswana government in pursuing its resettlement policy in the face of both local and international protest.
BOTSWANA; CENTRAL KALAHARI GAME RESERVE; NEW XADE; XADE; GAME RESERVES; GOVERNMENT POLICY; LAND RIGHTS; RESETTLEMENT; WATER
98/1137

0109 Fagan, Brian M.
THE KHOIKHOI OF THE CAPE OF GOOD HOPE
Fagan, Brian M. Clash of cultures (2nd edn.). Walnut Creek: Altamira Press, 1998. pp.35–56.
The chapter traces the history of the interaction between the Khoikhoi and the white settlers at the Cape, emphasising the negative reaction of the latter towards the original inhabitants. Shows how the Khoikhoi were dispossessed of land and cattle and finally disappeared as a separate people. Reveals the duality in the approach of Europeans towards the non-Western world. This included both dreams of an earthly paradise inhabited by noble savages and the exploitation and degradation of the races they actually encountered in their conquests.
CAPE; SOUTH AFRICA; COLONIALISM; HISTORY; INTERACTION; KHOEKHOE
PH/B 302 FAG

0110 Felton, Silke
A GENDER PERSPECTIVE ON THE STATUS OF THE SAN IN SOUTHERN AFRICA
Regional assessment of the status of the San in Southern Africa report series, No.5, xiv, 105pp., Windhoek: Legal Assistance Centre, 2001.
The assessment looks closely at the situation of San women in southern Africa. Comments that although all San in the region continue to be extremely marginalised, the position of San women is worse than that of men. Shows that they are discriminated against as San, as women, and as San women both within their own communities and in the wider society in which they live. Notes that these forms of discrimination are mutually reinforcing. Looks at the gender situation in the various conditions under which San are living today, namely: on farms, in settlements, and, in the case of Schmidtsdrift San, in military camps. Notes the effects of sedentarization upon gender relations. Devotes a chapter to each of the following topics: work and division of labour; education; health; gender; violence and abuse; policy frameworks to address San gender concerns; leadership; non-governmental organizations; and gender concerns. Challenges governments, San support organizations, San community-based and non-governmental organizations to develop strategies to address the many facets of gendered discrimination.
BOTSWANA; NAMIBIA; SOUTH AFRICA; ADVOCACY; BOOK REVIEWS; GENDER ISSUES; NON-GOVERNMENTAL ORGANISATIONS; REGIONAL COOPERATION; WOMEN
R/B 305.48068 FEL

0111 Fewster, Kathryn Jane
PETSO'S FIELD: ETHNOARCHAEOLOGY AND AGENCY
K. J. Fewster; M. Zvelebil. Ethnoarchaeology and hunter-gatherers: pictures at an exhibition. London: Archaeo Press, 2001.

pp.81–89. ISBN 1841712469.
The paper addresses the study of interaction between contemporary hunter-gatherers and farmers, and the implications of this for the origins and spread of agriculture in Europe at the mesolithic–neolithic transition. Reports that ethnoarchaeological research was carried out in Botswana among groups of Bamangwato agro-pastoralists and Basarwa (San) hunter-gatherers. Makes analogies from this research to prehistoric south-east Spain in order to demonstrate that there are various levels at which ethnographic analogy can be applied to archaeological data. Argues that many ethnoarchaeological enquiries incorporate the use of generalizations which serve ultimately to reduce the privilege of ethnoarchaeology: the opportunity to observe living human beings and their relationships to material culture. Notes that this is important because at the time of the fieldwork the Basarwa as a community had not adopted agro-pastoralism, with the exception of a man called Petso. Concludes that his action serves as a model for the Giddensian concept of agency and for those interested in using such a concept in their understanding of prehistory, there is a need to develop epistemology that critically examines the use of generalization in ethnoarchaeology.
BOTSWANA; MARULAMANTSE; SEROWE; AGRICULTURE; BANGWATO; ETHNOARCHAEOLOGY; FARMING; INTERACTION; PREHISTORY
PH/B 930.1 FEW

0112 Fischer, Jean
THE BUSHMAN'S BATTLE FOR SURVIVAL
Growth, October, 1982. pp.6–7.
The article describes the problems facing !Kung in the eastern area of Namibia in the 1980s. At this time the government was threatening to reduce the land area of Bushmanland by a quarter in order to set up a nature reserve in the traditional hunting grounds of the !Kung, a move opposed by local inhabitants and those concerned with their wellbeing. John Marshall's report to the Council of Ministers mentions an exceedingly high death rate probably caused by poor diet, lack of hygiene, alienation, lack of employment, drunkenness, and apathy, conditions which, if allowed to continue, could only result in the continuing population decline. Refers to the Cattle Fund, set up in order to initiate animal husbandry and promote self-sufficiency. Notes the effects on the community of the recruitment of many men into the South African Defence Force and the accompanying introduction of a cash economy. Considers that only the development of a new economy will enable the !Kung to survive and that animal husbandry will be the answer for them.
NAMIBIA; !KUNG; ARMY; CATTLE; FARMING; SELF-DETERMINATION
98/940

0113 Frolov, B.A.
ON SOUTHERN SAN ROCK ART
Current Anthropology, Vol.24, 1983, refs., pp.237–238.
The paper forms part of the comments on Lewis-Williams' article entitled "The economic and social context of southern San rock art" *Current Anthropology* Vol. 23 No. 4, 1982 p. 429–438. Compares themes identified in the art of north-western Asia with those identified in Bushman art by Lewis-Williams. Points out that this finding confirms the conclusion that economic and social factors were determinants of artistic creativity in entirely different geographic and ethnic contexts.
SOUTHERN AFRICA; CULTURE; ECONOMY; RESEARCH; ROCK ART
P 301.05 CAN

0114 Gall, Sandy
THE BUSHMEN OF SOUTHERN AFRICA: SLAUGHTER OF THE INNOCENT
London: Chatto and Windus, ill., refs, 2001. xxxix, 264pp.
The book champions the cause of Bushmen in southern Africa, recounting both their tragic history and the current situation in Botswana and Namibia. Uses dialogue and photos to document encounters with Bushmen leaders and groups in the two countries. Provides information from various books on the Bushmen but does not include page references. Includes a foreword by Prince Charles and a Preface by George Silberbauer who originally recommended the establishment of the Central Kalahari Game Reserve and who calls for respect without which the "dispossessed" will never be seen to be deserving of the right to choose their own way of life.
BOTSWANA; CENTRAL KALAHARI GAME RESERVE; KALAHARI GEMSBOK NATIONAL PARK; KAGGA KAMMA; NAMIBIA; NEW XADE; SOUTH AFRICA; !KUNG; =KHOMANI; ADVOCACY; EXPLOITATION; GAME RESERVES; HISTORY; INTERACTION; KHOEKHOE; NON-GOVERNMENTAL ORGANISATIONS; SELF-DETERMINATION; SERFDOM
R/B 301.296872 GAL

0115 Garlake, Peter S.
THEMES IN THE PREHISTORIC ART OF ZIMBABWE
World Archaeology, Vol.19 No.2, 1987. ill., maps, refs, pp.178–193.
The article provides an impressionistic survey of the rock art of Zimbabwe and is set within a framework of San belief about dance, trance, trancers and their potency. Notes that the interpretation follows on the work of J.D. Lewis Williams in South Africa and seeks to extend his approach, using Zimbabwean rock art. Considers that Zimbabwean rock art is within the same tradition as that of South Africa, with many basic similarities in materials, techniques, subject matter and representational conventions. Observes the differences that can be

noticed, with the inclusion of more trees and plants depicted in the Zimbabwean tradition, a different emphasis given to certain animals and in larger complex abstract paintings from the north. Finds no depictions of historical subjects and suggests that the paintings were produced at an earlier period than those on the Drakensberg and ceased when pastoralists settled in the area.
ZIMBABWE; DANCE; HISTORY; PASTORALISM; RESEARCH; SHAMANISM; TRANCE
P 930.105 WAR

0116 Garlake, Peter S.
SYMBOLS OF POTENCY IN THE PAINTINGS OF ZIMBABWE
South African Archaeological Bulletin, Vol.45 No.151, pp.17–27. 1993.
The paper examines the forms, contexts and associations of a particular motif, the dot, in the San paintings of Zimbabwe. Shows how different forms connotated different aspects of potency. Concludes that this motif, particularly when incorporated in compositions based on a particular form of oval shape, was an element in a powerful graphic system of symbols which, of their nature, should not be restricted to any precise single set of meanings. Suggests that this is characteristic of San art as a whole in Zimbabwe and that this has important implications for the interpretation of the art.
ZIMBABWE; ANIMALS; BELIEFS; RELIGION; RESEARCH; ROCK ART
P 930.105 SAA

0117 Garlake, Peter S.
THE HUNTER'S VISION: THE PREHISTORIC ART OF ZIMBABWE
London: British Museum Press, c1995. 24pp. of plates: ill. (some col.), refs. 176pp.
The book examines the rock art of Zimbabwe in great detail, providing numerous black-and-white tracings and coloured photographs of both the actual paintings and their physical setting. Compares Zimbabwe rock art with that of South Africa and finds many dissimilarities. Notes that the Zimbabwe rock art dates back many millennia while that of at least the Drakensberg is far less ancient. Considers that although there is evidence that the San of Zimbabwe shared religious beliefs with those of the rest of southern Africa, their art is not essentially shamanistic in emphasis. Notes the importance of potency or spiritual power depicted by means of animals, humans and partially human figures which may represent spirits. Finds that the elephant replaces the eland as the major source of this power in Zimbabwean rock art. Concludes that this art was connected with the daily life of San society not as a record of how it was lived but as celebration of its values, economic, moral and spiritual worth.
ZIMBABWE; ANIMALS; BELIEFS; DANCE; RELIGION; RESEARCH; ROCK ART; TRANCE
R/B 759.0113096891 GAR

0118 Gaski, Harald
RESEARCH ON AND BY INDIGENOUS PEOPLES
Lane, Paul; Hermans, Janet; Molebatsi, Chadzimula. Proceedings from the Basarwa research workshop, Gaborone, 24–25 August, 1995. 106pp. 2001. pp.55–57.
This is a contribution from a member of one of the indigenous peoples at the Basarwa Research Workshop held at the University of Botswana from 24–25 August, 1995. Raises concern that research conducted by academics on indigenous peoples differs from research master-minded by indigenous peoples on their own matters. Makes comparisons from situations of the different indigenous groups like Basarwa and the Sami of Norway. Explains that, because these groups are in the minority, they are usually assimilated by the major groups and regarded as inferior. They are often not given a chance to manage their own affairs as they are considered not capable. Explains the task of the Sami political awakening in ensuring their right to recognition of their own language and cultural activities.
BOTSWANA; NORWAY; CONFERENCE PAPERS; HUMAN RIGHTS; INDIGENOUS PEOPLES; RESEARCH
R/B 305.8096872 PRO

0119 Geingos, Victoria; Brörmann, Magdalena
SAN, LAND RIGHTS AND DEVELOPMENT: CAN SAN SURVIVE WITHOUT LAND?
Indigenous Rights in Commonwealth Africa Meeting. Cape Town, South Africa. 16–18 October, refs, 2002, 8pp.
The paper deals extensively with the problem of San communities' lack of legal access to land, their dispossession from the land they had traditionally used for generations and their resultant marginalization, economic dependency and lack of political influence. Observes that out of six Namibian San Traditional Authorities, only two have been officially recognised. Points out that this effectively denies them access to the Land Boards which allocate land in communal areas and denies them of any possibility of negotiating with government or of having any possibility of political representation or negotiation with government. Concludes that without legal access to land, San cannot survive.
NAMIBIA; OMAHEKE SOUTH; WEST CAPRIVI; !KUNG; !XOO; JU/'HOAN; LAND RIGHTS; MARGINALIZATION; POLITICS; POVERTY
PH/B 333.72096872 TAY

0120 George, Kipi
NAMIBIAN GOVERNMENT DEPRIVES KXOE COMMUNITY OF RIGHTS TO ANCESTRAL LAND

Fifth session of the Working Group on Indigenous Populations, Land and Environment in Relation to Indigenous People, 1997, 2pp.

This report by the elected chief of the Kxoe community of West Caprivi in Namibia describes the current situation of his community of 6,000 people. Shows how, under the South African government, this community was deprived of its traditional right to hunt. Points out that since the independence of Namibia, this right was not restored and the Kxoe have become impoverished and marginalised. Emphasises the problem of land rights which has been exacerbated by the fact that land upon which the community hoped to establish a tourist camp has been taken by the government for an extension to a prison rehabilitation centre and the Kxoe told to leave the area. Along with this is the problem that though the Namibian government previously recognised Kipi George as the legitimate chief of his people they are now supporting the claims of the Mbukushu chief who disputes this and wishes to be seen as the paramount chief of the area. Calls upon the other indigenous people and the international community to support the Kxoe in their struggle for land and political rights.
NAMIBIA; WEST CAPRIVI; GAME RESERVES; LAND RIGHTS; NATURAL RESOURCES; GOVERNMENT POLICY; KHWE
PH/B 301.305 GEO

0121 Glasser, Sylvia
APPROPRIATION AND APPRECIATION
Texts and images of people, politics and power: representing the Bushman people of southern Africa. Johannesburg. 4th–7th September, 1994, 13pp.

The paper by a South African choreographer with a degree in social anthropology, looks at questions relating to the relationship between indigenous South African culture and the dominant western culture. Explains the background from which these considerations arose. Describes receiving a request from a ballet examining body wanting to include a "Bushman deer dance" among its primitive dance section and requiring information on such dances. Examines issues of cultural appropriation which may mean taking something from another culture with appreciation and understanding or appropriating it without any such considerations. Looks at cultural appropriation in the context of cultural fusion in which forms of cultural expression from different traditions may be combined or integrated. Finally describes the choreography of a 30 minute dance entitled "tranceformation" which encapsulated aspects of trance dancing and the belief system it represents.
SOUTH AFRICA; CULTURE; DANCE; RELIGION; SHAMANISM; TRANCE
PH/B 792.80968 GLA

0122 Godwin, Peter
BUSHMEN: SOUTHERN AFRICA'S HUNTER-GATHERERS SEEK A FOOTHOLD
National Geographic, Vol.199 No.2, 2001, pp.90–117.

The article provides a brief outline of the current situation of the Bushman communities of Namibia, Botswana and South Africa. Comments that one of the few remaining communities of Bushmen living a more-or-less traditional life-style are Ju/'hoansi in the Nyae Nyae District of north-eastern Namibia. Comments on changes in life-style observed at Molopo, a settlement in the Central Kalahari Game Reserve in Botswana where hunting on horseback, using dogs has superseded bow and arrow hunting and where donkeys and goats are kept. Describes the advocacy efforts of the First People of the Kalahari (FPK) and the Working Group of Indigenous Minorities in Southern Africa (WIMSA). Comments on conditions at Schmidtsdrift in South Africa, home to Angolan Bushmen relocated by the South African Defence Force. Reports on discussions with leaders of the !Xu and Kwe communities living there. Concludes that little of Bushman culture is likely to survive.
BOTSWANA; CENTRAL KALAHARI GAME RESERVE; NAMIBIA; NYAE NYAE; SCHMIDTSDRIFT; SOUTH AFRICA; !XUN; ADVOCACY; GAME RESERVES; JU/'HOANSI; KHWE; NON-GOVERNMENTAL ORGANISATIONS
P 910.5 NGE

0123 Good, Kenneth
INEQUALITIES AND THE SAN IN BOTSWANA TODAY
Texts and images of people, politics and power: representing the Bushman people of Southern Africa. Johannesburg. 4th–7th Aug, 1994. Johannesburg: University of Witwatersrand, 1994. 13pp.

The paper points out that Government opposition to San political organization is a key issue when solutions to their problems are sought. Notes the following areas as crucial for San development: land rights, cattle ownership, lack of adequate economic opportunities, the wage structure, and the domination of local organizations in settlements by office-bearers of political parties.
GHANZI DISTRICT; CENTRAL KALAHARI GAME RESERVE; POLITICAL LEADERSHIP; RESETTLEMENT; LAND RIGHTS; FARMING
PH/B 320.96872 GOO

0124 Good, Kenneth
THE STATE AND EXTREME POVERTY IN BOTSWANA: THE SAN AND DESTITUTES
The Journal of Modern African Studies, Vol.37 No.2, 1999. refs. pp.185–205.

The paper considers how the rise of wealth and power within

the cattle-owning economy of Botswana has been accompanied by the creation of poverty and weakness. Observes that the impoverishment of the San and "destitutes" was a structured, comprehensive, and long-term process caused less by phenomena such as periodic drought than by members of an elite possessing economic and political power and the exploitation which they practised. Notes that the growth economy of recent decades has not ameliorated the situation but has strengthened the wealthy while neglecting or worsening the plight of the San. Concludes that the state possesses the financial resources and developmental capacity to alleviate poverty but its controllers continue to prioritise other matters.
BOTSWANA; CATTLE; GOVERNMENT POLICY; POVERTY; REMOTE AREA DEVELOPMENT
PH/B 320.9096872 GOO

0125 Gordon, Robert J.
SAVING THE LAST SOUTH AFRICAN BUSHMEN: A SPECTACULAR FAILURE
Critical Arts: a Journal of Cultural Studies, Vol.9 No.2, 1995, pp.28–48. ISSN 02560046.
The paper recounts the story of a failed attempt in the 1930s, to have an area set aside in South Africa where the "last South African Bushmen" would be able to continue their hunting and gathering tradition undisturbed. Describes the work in this regard by Donald Bain with support from parliamentarians and newspapers plus the formation of a committee to further the cause. Notes that it failed due to opposition from the National Parks Board and local farmers. Concludes that the failure of the scheme, launched at the time of the Empire Exhibition in 1936, when Donald Bain brought a group of Bushmen to the Exhibition to display aspects of their life-style, was also due to the general indifference of the public.
SOUTH AFRICA; ADVOCACY; ATTITUDES; HISTORY
PH/B 305.80968 CRI

0126 Gordon, Robert J.; Sholto-Douglas, Stuart
THE BUSHMAN MYTH: THE MAKING OF A NAMIBIAN UNDERCLASS
Conflict and social change series, 2nd ed. Boulder: Westview Press, 2000. xviii,: ill., maps, refs. 342pp.
The second edition is a revised and enlarged version of the 1992 publication which brings the situation of Namibian Bushmen up to date for the period since independence. Looks at the studies which have appeared during the period noting those dealing with hitherto neglected farm Bushmen who form the majority of Bushmen in the country. Examines the increasing self-awareness of Bushmen and changes in the approach of those studying them as newer methods of interpretive anthropology are adopted.
NAMIBIA; ANTHROPOLOGY; COMMUNICATION; CONFLICT; FARM WORKERS; JU/'HOANSI; HAI//OM; HISTORY; INTERACTION; LAND USE
306.096881 GOR

0127 Greenberg, Joseph H.
THE CLICK LANGUAGES
Greenberg, Joseph H. Studies in African linguistic classification. New Haven: Compass Publishing, 1955. 120pp. pp.80–94.
The chapter examines the classification of click or Khoisan languages of Africa. Considers that the three branches of click languages are Khoisan, Sandawe and Hatsa. Discusses in detail earlier claims that Hottentot is a Hamitic language and dismisses these showing that certain linguistic developments in Hottentot cannot be traced to a Hamitic influence. Examines morphology and phonology of Hottentot, comparing it to other Khoisan/Bushman languages. Examines the two East African click languages, Sandawe and Hatsa and concludes that while Sandawe is clearly related to the other Khoisan languages, the relationship of Hatsa to both Sandawe and Khoisan is fairly remote.
SOUTH AFRICA; TANZANIA; CLICKS; HADZA; KHOEKHOEGOWAB; KHOESAN; LANGUAGES; LINGUISTICS; SANDAWE
496 GRE

0128 Guelke, Leonard; Shell, Robert
LANDSCAPES OF CONQUEST
Journal of Southern African Studies, Vol.18 No.4, 1992, refs., pp.803–824.
The paper shows how the Khoikhoi and San were gradually squeezed out of lands they formerly occupied as the Europeans took over the springs and watercourses. Notes that, in the 17th and 18th centuries, European settlers used a strategic combination of technology and bureaucracy to oust the Khoikhoi from the land they had previously inhabited. Comments that it was the use of firearms and horses (a new fighting technology) which enabled settlers to hold and defend lands taken from the Khoikhoi. This was combined with the legitimization by the Dutch East India Company of land seizure when settlers were granted freehold rights on lands so acquired. Notes that, eventually, the surviving Khoikhoi became clients of the European settlers and applied their skills in animal husbandry to the livestock of the invaders rather than to their own.
CAPE; SOUTH AFRICA; CONFLICT; COLONIALISM; HISTORY; INTERGROUP RELATIONS; KHOEKHOE; LIVESTOCK; PASTORALISM
P 968.05 JSA

0129 Guenther, Mathias
KALAHARI BUSHMEN IN TRANSITION
Rotunda, Summer 1971. ill., pp.8–15.

The article describes a collection of Nharo cultural articles deposited in the Royal Ontario Museum in the 1970s. Shows that the items displayed demonstrate the cultural conflict and social regimentation of the Nharo of the Ghanzi District. Describes the hierarchy existing in the district by means of which the Nharo are permitted entrance into the economic sphere as labourers but are excluded from other areas of community life. Finds that the exclusion of the Bushmen from the belief system of the white farmers allows them to retain their own values, norms and beliefs which are also reflected in the material culture. Shows how the acquisition of such useless items as dead batteries, broken watches and lamps represent prestige markers and indicate the attraction of a way of life from which the Nharo are excluded.
BOTSWANA; GHANZI DISTRICT; CULTURE; INTERACTION; MATERIAL CULTURE; NARO
PH/B 303.4 GUE

0130 Guenther, Mathias
"THE PATTERN IS THE THING": DIVERSITY AND CONFORMITY AMONG THE KHOISAN. HUNTERS AND HERDERS OF SOUTHERN AFRICA BY ALAN BARNARD
Current Anthropology, Vol.33 No.4, 1992, pp.478–481.
The review of *Hunters and herders of southern Africa* commends the book as a worthy successor to Isaac Schapera's *The Khoisan peoples of South Africa. Bushmen and Hottentots* (1930), pointing out that it has as one of its stated aims the updating of Schapera's work. Shows that an important premise requiring revision is that the hunter-gatherer San and the herder Khoikhoi were two distinct peoples whereas Barnard considers their sociological and historical similarity to be a central feature. Notes that the title of the review is a quotation from Bateson and reflects the methodology employed in a book which seeks to understand "Khoisan regional structure" by providing a thorough study of the historical, linguistic and societal-structural relationships amongst the herding and foraging peoples. Explains the arrangement of the book and observes that the author dissociates himself from the current postmodernist-revisionist trend in Khoisan studies.
SOUTHERN AFRICA; ANTHROPOLOGY; BOOK REVIEWS; KHOEKHOE; KHOESAN; RESEARCH; REVISIONISM
P 301.05 CAN

0131 Guenther, Mathias
DIVERSITY AND FLEXIBILITY: THE CASE OF THE BUSHMEN OF SOUTHERN AFRICA
Kent, Susan. *Cultural diversity among twentieth-century foragers: an African perspective*. Cambridge: Cambridge University Press, 1996. xiii, 344pp., ill., maps pp.65–86. ISBN 0521482372.
The paper focuses on the cultural diversity that existed historically and still exists in Bushman culture. Examines the following cultural aspects which manifest diversity: subsistence technologies; trade patterns; spatial organization and political leadership. Shows that the social structure of all Bushman groups has the band as its main feature but even this manifests wide regional diversity. Contends that similarly, a "Khoisan religious system" exists but shows great variation regarding beliefs. Notes the Bushman propensity to "forage" for ideas which has allowed them to adapt to new influences and which is an important element in their cultural survival. Considers, with regard to the "Kalahari debate" that there is evidence to support both "traditionalist" and "revisionist/integrationist" positions so that the new research strategy should be one of synthesis.
BOTSWANA; NAMIBIA; !KUNG; /XAM; ANTHROPOLOGY; BANDS; BELIEFS; CULTURE; HAI//OM; NAMA; POLITICAL LEADERSHIP; RELIGION; RESEARCH; REVISIONISM; SOCIAL STRUCTURE
306.364 CUL

0132 Guenther, Mathias
TRICKSTERS AND TRANCERS: BUSHMAN RELIGION AND SOCIETY
Bloomington: Indiana University Press, ix, 288pp., map., refs., 1999.
The book presents an extremely detailed analysis of the essential elements of Bushman religion. Shows how the lack of structure of both Bushman religion and the society in which it functions have presented major problems to researchers seeking to unravel their complexity and ambiguity. Reveals that attempts to impose a structure upon this unstructured religion has led to distortion and misunderstanding of its basic characteristics. In fact some researchers have concluded that Bushmen neither live in societies nor practice any form of religion. Chapters cover the following topics: Bushman society; values and individuals; religious beliefs and cosmology; the trickster; the trance curing dance; stories and story telling; myth and gender; initiation rites; missionaries and Bushmen; Bushman religion and the tolerance for ambiguity. Notes that at present aspects of Christian belief are being incorporated into the Bushman religious system.
BOTSWANA; BELIEFS; COSMOLOGY; DANCE; FOLKLORE; HEALING; INITIATION; MISSIONARIES; MYTHOLOGY; SHAMANISM; SOCIAL ORGANIZATION; TRANCE
R/B 299.681 GUE

0133 Guenther, Mathias
FROM TOTEMISM TO SHAMANISM: HUNTER-GATHERER CONTRIBUTIONS TO WORLD MYTHOLOGY AND SPIRITUALITY
Lee, Richard and Daly, Richard. *The Cambridge encyclopedia of hunters and gatherers*. Cambridge, Cambridge University Press, 1999. xx, 511pp., ill., maps. pp.426–433. ISBN

052157109X.
The chapter deals with the two complexes of ritual and belief, namely totemism and shamanism, which are typically associated with hunter-gatherer societies. Notes that in spite of the differences between hunter-gatherer societies it is yet possible to trace a sub-strata of ritual, cosmological and symbolic commonality. Comments that this commonality is essentially shamanistic and that shamanism is a religious phenomenon which can be differentiated from other religions. Outlines the key elements of hunter-gatherer religion which are closely linked to the natural world. Shows that shamanism is a method and a thought system for entering this universe and by relating to its beings and forces, transforming and channelling them for the benefit of humans. Sees ecstasy and the transformation into spirit-beings as the key elements of shamanistic ritual. Notes the trickster as a central protagonist of hunter-gatherer mythology. Refers to !Kung, Nharo and other San groups and their beliefs and practices.
BOTSWANA; !KUNG; BELIEFS; COSMOLOGY; NARO; RELIGION; RITUALS; SHAMANISM; TRANCE
R 306.36403 CAM

0134 Haacke, W.H.G.
THE SO-CALLED "PERSONAL PRONOUN" IN NAMA
Traill, A. Khoisan Linguistic Studies 3. pp.43–62, 1977, ISBN 0854944540.
The paper looks at the way in which Nama grammar and in particular the pronoun has traditionally been dealt with by linguists. Suggests a new approach to the so-called "pronoun" and introduces the term "minimal designant" to replace "suffix". Emphasises the need for a revision of outdated concepts of Nama grammar based on a traditional "school grammar" suitable for Latin or German and originally established by Vedder at the beginning of the 20th century.
NAMIBIA; GRAMMAR; LANGUAGES; LINGUISTICS; KHOEKHOEGOWAB
496.2709 KHO

0135 Hammond-Tooke, W.D.
SYMBOL OR ICON? A BREAKTHROUGH IN THE STUDY OF SOUTHERN AFRICAN ROCK ART: A REVIEW
South African Archaeological Bulletin, Vol.37, 1982, refs., pp.72–74.
This is a review of the book "Believing and seeing: symbolic meanings in southern San rock paintings" by J.D. Lewis-Williams. Regards Lewis-Williams' explication of the meaning of San rock art as a major advance. Considers that the importance of the book lies in the attempt to ascertain the meaning of the art. Notes that the author rejects the approach which sees paintings as merely "icons" or scale model depictions of San social life or produced for aesthetic reasons only. Shows instead that the paintings are depictions of the two dominant symbols in San life: the eland and the trance experience which in effect are symbols of each other. Recounts the author's use of the Bleek/Lloyd materials in the University of Cape Town Library and the collection of texts made in 1873 by J.M. Orpen. Notes that both these sources relate to now extinct San groups. Shows how use of modern ethnography among contemporary !Kung bridges the gap between the /Xam and living San leading to the discovery of a broadly similar worldview common to the two groups.
BOTSWANA; CAPE; NAMIBIA; SOUTH AFRICA; /XAM; !KUNG; ANIMALS; ANTHROPOLOGY; BELIEFS; BOOK REVIEWS; RELIGION; RESEARCH; ROCK ART; SHAMANISM; TRANCE
P 930.105 SAA

0136 Hammond-Tooke, W.D.
DIVINATORY ANIMALS: FURTHER EVIDENCE OF SAN/NGUNI BORROWING
South African Archaeological Bulletin, Vol.54 No.170, 1999. refs., pp.128–132.
The paper seeks to extend the debate as to the nature of possible San influence on the mediumistic divinatory practice of Nguni and thus contribute to the understanding of forager/farmer contacts as well as casting a cautionary light on the selective way in which cultural borrowing occurred in the past. Suggests that, in addition to the trance dance, the Cape Nguni also adopted, in the (modified) form of divinatory animals, San cosmological ideas of the power of animals in the healing process. Discusses the nature of this adoption and the highly selective way in which it occurred.
CAPE; KWAZULU-NATAL; ANIMALS; BELIEFS; COSMOLOGY; DANCE; HEALING; INTERGROUP RELATIONS; MYTHOLOGY; RELIGION
P 930.105 SAA

0137 Hardbattle, John
THE "SHOW THE LAND" PILOT PROJECT
Lane, Paul; Hermans, Janet; Molebatsi, Chadzimula. Proceedings from the Basarwa Research Workshop, Gaborone, 24–25 August, 1995. 106pp., pp.31–32. 2001.
The short paper reports on the work and aims of First People of the Kalahari (Kgeikani Kweni) and describes in particular the nature of the "Show the Land" project being carried out in the part of the Central Kalahari Game Reserve occupied by the Molapo community. Explains the objectives of the mapping project as follows: a) to identify areas for potential agricultural activities and development of water resources; b) to identify veld production areas; c) To collate cultural and historical data for preservation. Explains the type of data to be collected and the methods to be used for the mapping which include experimenting with geographic information systems (GIS) and

global positioning systems (GPS) technology, use of satellite imagery and observation made by walking and driving through the areas concerned. Notes that local historical, cultural and local knowledge will be collected from the communities using group discussions and interviews.
BOTSWANA; CENTRAL KALAHARI GAME RESERVE; ECOBOTANY; ORAL HISTORY; RESEARCH
R/B 305.8096872 PRO

0138 Hargrove, Thomas Henry
FOOD PRODUCTION AND CULTURE CHANGE AMONG HUNTER-GATHERERS OF SOUTHERN AFRICA
Dissertation (M.A.), University of New Mexico. 1980, 120 pages.
The study explains the causes and consequences of food production technologies in sub-Saharan Africa. Explains the late arrival of food production in southern Africa around 2,000 years ago and a sudden massive migration of Iron Age Bantu herders and farmers into the south from Central Africa. Notes that as a result of this pushing, the Khoisan-speaking hunters and gatherers of southern Africa moved into the deserts. Places emphasis on the development of long-term adaptations to a wide range of environments with unpredictable resources. Describes the initial appearance of immigrant Bantu food producers to give a clear picture of the ultimate origins of southern African food producing technologies and how it impacted on the hunter-gatherers of southern Africa. Explains that archaeological, linguistic, and historical evidence show that the spread of food production which followed these earliest appearances was a slow and fragmented movement along several paths of development that included Khoisan as well as Bantu cultures.
BOTSWANA; !KUNG; AGRICULTURE; CULTURAL CHANGE; ENVIRONMENT; FARMING; FOOD PRODUCTION; FORAGING; HUNTING-GATHERING; KHOESAN; KINSHIP; LIVESTOCK; PREHISTORY
TH 305.80968 HAR

0139 Hasselbring, Sue
REFLECTIONS ON MTE: LINGUISTIC RESEARCH AND TEACHING EXPERIENCES
Oussoren, Otto Education for remote area dwellers in Botswana. Gaborone: University of Botswana, Research and Development Unit; WIMSA, Regional San Education Project, 2001. 107pp., pp. 73–76.
The paper provides research findings on literacy and education and gives personal experiences of teaching literacy at a cattle post. Reveals that the students in Botswana who are educated through the medium of their mother tongue, Tswana, show a far lower drop-out rate as compared to students whose mother tongue is a non-Tswana Bantu language or a San language. Points out that San languages are least like Tswana from a grammatical point of view and it is San-speaking students who drop out of school in the largest numbers. Likewise shows that the literacy rate of Remote Area Dwellers, the majority of whom are San is lower than that for the rest of the population. Notes that San people do continue to use their own languages in addition to frequently knowing another language such as Tswana or Kgalagadi. Relates methods used to teach Tsoa speakers at cattle posts west of Mosolotsane to read and write Tswana. Finds that pupils are happy with a mixed age group of learners, learn better if the use of Tsoa is integrated in the learning process and that pupils are prepared to help each other. Suggests reasons for school drop out among San children and possible solutions.
BOTSWANA; !XOO; BUGAKHWE; EDUCATION; G//ANA; G/UI; JU/'HOANSI; LITERACY; NARO; TSHWA
R/B 372.7096872 WIM

0140 Hasselbring, Sue; Segatlhe, Thabiso
LANGUAGE CHOICE IN TEN DOMAINS AMONG KHOESAN SPEAKERS IN BOTSWANA
Batibo, H.M.; Tsonope, J. The state of Khoesan languages in Botswana. Mogoditshane: Tasalls, 2000. viii, 169pp., ill.. pp. 76–99, ISBN 9991295208.
The chapter presents data provided by Botswana citizens regarding the languages they use in nine different domains or spheres. Reports that the survey was undertaken by the Botswana Language Use Project. Provides information statistically and then discusses the data. Covers the following categories: number and age ranges of the respondents from each language group; educational level attained; languages spoken by respondents to a variety of people in a number of different contexts. Also reports on languages used when singing; praying; talking to people at church, and which languages respondents can read. Tabulates and discusses domains of language use by district. Notes the names of two languages not hitherto mentioned in the literature on the Khoesan languages of Botswana, namely /Ibe and !Goro which are spoken in the southern part of the Boteti subdistrict. Comments on endangered languages and foresees that the following may die out within a generation: /Xaisa, Danisi, Nama, Teti and Tshwa while so few speakers of =hua, //Ani and =Aba were found that they are also probably endangered. Calls for research and documentation of these endangered languages and encouragement to their speakers to continue using and developing the languages.
BOTSWANA; DANISI; KHOEKHOEGOWAB; KUA; LANGUAGES; LINGUISTICS; NARO; TETI; TSUA; TSHWA
R/B 496.1 STA

0141 Hays, Jennifer
EDUCATION AND THE SAN OF SOUTHERN AFRICA: THE SEARCH FOR ALTERNATIVES

Mazonde, Isaac N. *Minorities in the millennium: perspectives from Botswana*. Gaborone: Lightbooks, 2002. refs., vii, 136pp. pp.73–87, ISBN 9991271244.

The article reports on the education of San children in southern Africa, showing that there are similarities in the education of the indigenous world-wide. Lists major characteristics by which indigenous peoples may be identified: a) pre-existence; b) non-dominance; c) they make different uses of land and natural resources; d) self-definition. Points out however that all indigenous peoples face a major problem of loss of land rights and rights to natural resources. Both San and other indigenous children face similar educational problems which frequently result in their dropping out of school. These include: a) being taught foreign systems of knowledge in languages different from their own; b) being taught in a foreign language by teachers unfamiliar with their culture and using disciplinary and instructional methods unlike those used in the home environment. Finds that as a result San children may end up alienated from their own culture and lacking in self-esteem with a negative attitude to life. Suggests positive alternatives and provides several examples of successful attempts to address the problems of San children in the formal school system in Botswana.

BOTSWANA; ACCESS TO EDUCATION; ATTITUDES; EDUCATION; SCHOOL DROP OUTS

R/B 968.72 MIN

0142 Headland, D.T.; Reid, L.
HUNTER-GATHERERS AND THEIR NEIGHBOURS FROM PREHISTORY TO THE PRESENT
Current Anthropology, Vol.30, 1989, pp.43–66.

The paper presents arguments which refute the widely assumed notion that modern hunter-gatherer societies lived until very recently in isolation from food-producing societies and states, and practised neither cultivation, pastoralism nor trade. Presents data suggesting a very different model of middle to late Holocene hunter-gatherer economies. Argues that such groups were in fact heavily dependent upon both trade with food-producing populations and part-time cultivation or pastoralism. Refers to recent publications on a number of hunter-gatherer societies, including the !Kung San, which establish that the symbiosis and desultory food production observed among them to-day, are neither recent nor anomalous, but represent an economy practised by most hunter-gatherers for hundreds if not thousands of years. Discusses psychological and political reasons for Westerners' attachment to the myth of the "savage other". Includes responses by other researchers on the paper which in the main agree with the hypothesis presented.

BOTSWANA; ANTHROPOLOGY; !KUNG; HUNTING-GATHERING; RESEARCH

P 301.05 CAN

0143 Heine, Bernd
ON SPATIAL ORIENTATION IN KXOE: SOME PRELIMINARY OBSERVATIONS. KHOISAN FORUM WORKING PAPER, NO. 6
Cologne: University of Cologne, 1997. 28pp.

The paper seeks to determine how spatial reference is conceptualised and expressed in Kxoe. Distinguishes three kinds of orientation system: a) deictic, used when items are visible to the speaker. This system is associated with such concepts as "up", "down", "back", "front", "left" and "right"; b) landmark orientation is used with regard to such physical features as mountains, rivers etc. known and in reach of the speaker; c) cardinal orientation is defined in terms of fixed reference points which exist independently of the speaker such as "north", "south" etc. Seeks to establish a correlation between choice of orientation markers and relative distance of the located items. Concludes that for micro-space, deictic markers are employed; for middle-range space, landmarks are commonly used while use of cardinal markers which denote macro-space depend on the mobility of the speaker and his/her educational level. Finds landmark orientation to be the most dynamic marker and notes that it is susceptible to new political and environmental changes.

NAMIBIA; KHWEDAM; LANGUAGES; LINGUISTICS

PH/B 496.1 HEI

0144 Heinz, H-J.
THE SICK BUSHMAN
South African Practitioner's Digest of Treatment, October, 1962. pp.9–15.

Focuses on the Bushmen's knowledge and uses of medicine. Clearly describes different ailments and viruses that usually affect Bushmen and the ways in which they treat them. Describes their ways of life, initiation of boys and girls, different types of dances and their significance. Explains their beliefs, their sex roles and their foods.

BOTSWANA; BELIEFS; CARE-GIVING; CULTURE; HEALING; HEALTH; INITIATION; SEX ROLES

PH/B 362.1042 HEI

0145 Heinz, H-J.
TERRITORIALITY AND THE BASARWA
Lane, Paul; Hermans, Janet; Molebatsi, Chadzimula. Proceedings from the Basarwa Research Workshop, Gaborone, 24–25 August, 1995. 106pp., 2001. pp.98–99.

Paper presented at the Basarwa Research Workshop, held on 24–25 August, 1995 at the University of Botswana focuses on the idea of territoriality among Basarwa and other indigenous groups. Starts by explaining what is meant by territoriality. Explains that some indigenous groups from around the world attach land claims to certain pieces of land which belonged to their ancestors, most of which they cannot now access. Ob-

serves that, however, territoriality with Basarwa is associated with their social organization based on three different things a) family; b) extended family; and c) the band. Explains the importance of the band in Basarwa territoriality as it possesses land and all its natural resources. Therefore, observes that Basarwa cannot be regarded as nomadic because they move within their defined territory looking for animals and gathering plant foods.
BOTSWANA; CONFERENCE PAPERS; INDIGENOUS PEOPLES; LAND RIGHTS; TERRITORIALITY
R/B 305.8096872 PRO

0146 Hermans, Janet; Cassidy, Lin; Bowie, Hamish
"SOFTWARE" FOR RAD HOSTELS: A MANAGEMENT PLAN FOR PRIMARY SCHOOL HOSTELS IN REMOTE AREAS
Gaborone, 1999, iii, 40pp.
The report seeks to develop a management framework for all primary school hostels located in the remote areas which serve some of the most disadvantaged children in the country. Explains that the report arises from realization that in addition to attending to the physical infrastructure of the hostels, the need for attention to the social aspects of the hostel environment was recognised. Weaknesses in the existing hostel situation include lack of standards and guidelines, inadequate facilities, infrastructure, staffing and poor relations with both the school and the local community.
BOTSWANA; CHILDREN; HOSTELS; PRIMARY EDUCATION; REMOTE AREA DEVELOPMENT
R/B 327.7096872 HER

0147 Hitchcock, Robert K.
HUNTING IS OUR HERITAGE: THE STRUGGLE FOR HUNTING AND GATHERING RIGHTS AMONG THE SAN OF SOUTHERN AFRICA
Senri Ethnological Studies, No.59. Eighth International Conference on Hunting and Gathering Societies (CHAGS 8). Osaka. October, 1998. Anderson David G.; Ikeya Kazunobu. Parks, poverty, and power: managing hunting practice and identity within state policy regimes. refs. pp.139–156.
The paper narrates fears of the San and other indigenous peoples of Africa about whether they will be permitted to continue hunting in spite of major changes in land and natural resource conservation legislation, and when development projects favouring other activities are given priority. Mentions a few countries in Africa where indigenous peoples are still allowed to do subsistence hunting while in the rest of Africa they do it at a risk of arrest and imprisonment. Notes that the main concern here is that conservation laws restrict the rights of local people to hunt. In the case of Botswana, gives history of hunting and gathering being permitted but which later changed because of what is regarded as Government bias on issuing Special Game Licences to San. Having experienced all these problems and difficulties, the San and other African minority groups have set up their own non-government organizations and advocacy groups, and approached international fora such as the Human Rights Commission of the United Nations to present their case. Concludes that the future of the San depends on their ability to convince governments and other stakeholders of the importance of economic rights which are a matter of both cultural and physical survival.
BOTSWANA; GHANZI DISTRICT; KALAHARI DESERT; NAMIBIA; SOUTH AFRICA; TANZANIA; CONFERENCE PAPERS; GOVERNMENT POLICY; HUNTING; HUNTING-GATHERING; INDIGENOUS PEOPLES; LEGAL RIGHTS; NON-GOVERNMENTAL ORGANISATIONS; SELF-DEVELOPMENT; SERFDOM; TOURISM
R/B 363.68 PAR

0148 Hitchcock, Robert K.
LAND REFORM, ETHNICITY AND COMPENSATION IN BOTSWANA
Cultural Survival Quarterly, Vol.14 No.4, 1990, refs., pp.52–55.
The paper looks at land reform policy in Botswana, especially the Tribal Grazing Land Policy (TGLP), its effect upon Basarwa, and whether they received compensation when forced to move from lands which were to become commercial ranches. Reports that though commercial services centres were set up in some districts, this did not solve the problems of security of land tenure for Basarwa, and, because of population density, they quickly became subject to resource depletion and overgrazing. Notes that though according to Tswana customary law and the revised TGLP guidelines, individuals and communities should not have their rights removed without compensation, in effect, compensation was only granted to those regarded as "tribespeople". In cases where land boards granted compensation to Basarwa, the payments made to them were considerably lower than those made to members of other groups. Concludes that Botswana is lauded as a country committed to social justice, sustained development and its multi-racial stance, and therefore special attention should have been paid to the equitable distribution of compensation benefits.
BOTSWANA; GOVERNMENT POLICY; LAND REFORMS; LAND RIGHTS
PH/B 301.305 HIT

0149 Hitchcock, Robert K.
HUMAN RIGHTS, LOCAL INSTITUTIONS AND SUSTAINABLE DEVELOPMENT AMONG KALAHARI SAN
90th annual meeting of the American Anthropological Association on human rights and indigenous people. Chicago. November 20–24, 1991, refs., 14pp.
This paper analyses strategies employed by a number of San communities geared towards bringing about sustainable development. Explains that the San of the Kalahari Desert region

of southern Africa have begun to form such local institutions in an effort to promote their socioeconomic, political and civil rights. Notes that these associations have been formed as a partial response to the serious problems of poverty, dispossession and environmental degradation which they face and are aimed at increasing self-sufficiency and enhancing conservation.
BOTSWANA; CONSERVATION; NON-GOVERNMENTAL ORGANISATIONS; POVERTY; SELF-DEVELOPMENT
PH/B 338.8096872 HIT

0150 Hitchcock, Robert K.
GAME PARK VS. THE SAN: CONSERVATION AND SUSTAINABLE DEVELOPMENT IN THE KALAHARI
International Work Group for Indigenous Affairs Newsletter, No.1, July/August, 1991, pp.7–12.
The paper traces the history of changes in government policy regarding the Central Kalahari Game Reserve and its human inhabitants up till the early 1990s. Notes that by this time the decision that the inhabitants be relocated outside the reserve had already been taken, but as yet no-one had been forcibly removed and food was still being supplied. Shows the various factors which led to this outcome and the probable reasons behind the decision of the Botswana Government. Comments on the effect of resettling a large group of people to the area around Xade which resulted in degradation of the surrounding area and changes in foraging and hunting techniques and dependence on food supplied from outside. Looks briefly at the work of the Remote Area Development Programme over more than a decade. Commends the formation of grassroots development organizations among San and other rural people. Considers that resettlement away from their traditional living area should only be done with care and sensitivity if Botswana's aims of self-reliance and unity are to be achieved.
BOTSWANA; CENTRAL KALAHARI GAME RESERVE; GAME RESERVES; GOVERNMENT POLICY; RESETTLEMENT
PH/B 338.96872 HIT

0151 Hitchcock, Robert K.
AFRICAN WILDLIFE: CONSERVATION AND CONFLICT
Johnson, Barbara Rose. Life and death matters: human rights and the environment at the end of the millennium. Walnut Creek: Altamira Press, refs., 1997. pp.81–95.
The paper looks at conservation and development projects and their effect on local communities continent-wide. Lists a number of conservation efforts in Africa which have had negative impacts on the wellbeing of local populations including those in Botswana, Namibia and South Africa. Examines the following aspects: a) hostility between wildlife officers and local communities; b) depletion of wildlife numbers owing to military activity; c) resettlement of local communities to make way for wildlife reserves; d) efforts by local people in the setting up of social and environmental organizations to ensure a better balance between conservation and development. Points out the need for direct links to be made between human rights, the environment and democratic government with local participation to ensure the safeguarding of human rights.
BOTSWANA; CENTRAL KALAHARI GAME RESERVE; CONSERVATION; GAME RESERVES; GOVERNMENT POLICY; HUNTING; RESETTLEMENT; WILDLIFE
PH/B 333.91 HIT

0152 Hitchcock, Robert K.
INTRODUCTION: AFRICA
Lee, Richard; Daly, Richard. The Cambridge encyclopedia of hunters and gatherers. Cambridge, Cambridge University Press, 1999. xx, 511pp., ill., maps., pp.175–184. ISBN 052157109X.
This introduction to the encyclopedia covers all the hunter-gatherer groups on the continent of Africa. Tables provide details of population sizes of indigenous African peoples who are or were formerly hunter-gatherers. Looks at the San of southern Africa in their historical context and in relation to their interaction with other races, and summarises the main problems facing them currently. Finds common characteristics to be a pattern of flexible and fairly egalitarian band organization with less rigid and hierarchical sociopolitical arrangements than their pastoralist neighbours. Points out how recent land reforms in many parts of Africa have led to the dispossession of foragers. Comments on the self-help and advocacy groups which currently support African hunters and gatherers.
SOUTHERN AFRICA; ADVOCACY; GOVERNMENT POLICY; HISTORY; HUNTING-GATHERING; INTERGROUP RELATIONS; LAND USE; NON-GOVERNMENTAL ORGANISATIONS; SELF-DEVELOPMENT
R 306.36403 CAM

0153 Hitchcock, Robert K.
TYUA
Lee, Richard; Daly, Richard. The Cambridge encyclopedia of hunters and gatherers. Cambridge, Cambridge University Press, 1999. xx, 511pp., ill., maps., pp.225–230. ISBN 052157109X.
The article deals with the Tyua, Tshwa, Shua or River Bushmen of Botswana and Zimbabwe. Notes that Tyua have interacted with non-Khoesan populations for up to 2000 years in a variety of patron-client systems. Provides information on the following topics: history, environment, economy, settlement patterns, mobility and land tenure, domestic and political organization, religion and spirituality. Outlines the challenges faced by modern day Tyua in both Zimbabwe and Botswana,

where they have lost their land to cattle ranches and game reserves.
BOTSWANA; ZIMBABWE; ECOLOGY; ECONOMY; ENVIRONMENT; LAND USE; RIVER BUSHMEN; SOCIAL CHANGE; SOCIAL ORGANIZATION; TYUA
R 306.36403 CAM

0154 Hitchcock, Robert K.
'WE ARE THE FIRST PEOPLE': LAND, NATURAL RESOURCES AND IDENTITY IN THE CENTRAL KALAHARI, BOTSWANA
Journal of Southern African Studies, Vol.28 No.4, 2002, refs., pp.797–823. ISSN 03057070.
The article focuses on the ways in which the San and another minority group known as Bakgalagadi, have been treated over time in Botswana. Particularly emphasises treatment of the people residing in the Central Kgalagadi Game Reserve, the largest protected area in the country. Deals specifically with the roles of various institutions and individuals, including the Botswana government, advocacy groups, donors, community-based organizations and, importantly, the San and Bakgalagadi themselves, in promoting minority rights, especially those relating to land, natural resources and identity. Notes that some San organizations, such as First People of the Kalahari, attempted to use the contentious issue of being "indigenous" as a means of arguing for rights to land and resources. In the end efforts to promote indigenous rights and the filing of a legal land claim in the High Court were unsuccessful in preventing the removals of people from their ancestral territories in the Central Kalahari. Points out that there are lessons here for indigenous peoples and minority human rights movements in Africa, including the importance of building inter-group coalitions, the need to use diversified strategies to achieve goals, the significance of striking a balance between outside assistance and working with local groups, and the value of mobilising people at the grassroots over the long term.
BOTSWANA; CENTRAL KALAHARI GAME RESERVE; BAKGALAGADI; INDIGENOUS PEOPLES; LAND RIGHTS; MINORITY RIGHTS; NATURAL RESOURCES; NON-GOVERNMENTAL ORGANISATIONS
P 968.05 JSA

0155 Hitchcock, Robert K.
CONTROLLING THEIR DESTINY: THE JU/HOANSI OF NYAE NYAE
Cultural Survival Quarterly, Vol.26 No.1, 2002, map, pp.13–15.
The Ju/'hoansi of Nyae Nyae, also known as the !Kung, were made famous in the annals of anthropology through the films of John Marshall and the writings of Lorna Marshall and Elizabeth Marshall Thomas. Notes that the turbulent history of the Ju/'hoansi since their resettlement at Tshumkwe by the South African colonial power is less well-known. Points out that the enforced acculturation of the Ju/'hoansi and their severe cultural losses were made worse when they were caught in the cross-fire between the South West African People's Organization (SWAPO) and the South African Defence Force. Concludes that the Ju/'hoansi have survived all this and fought successfully to preserve their land base and cultural identity but still face problems.
NAMIBIA; NYAE NYAE; TSHUMKWE; ADVOCACY; CULTURE; JU/'HOANSI; NON-GOVERNMENTAL ORGANISATIONS; SELF-DEVELOPMENT
R/B 305.8096872 CUL

0156 Hitchcock, Robert K.; Bartram, Laurence E., Jr.
SOCIAL BOUNDARIES, TECHNICAL SYSTEMS AND THE USE OF SPACE AND TECHNOLOGY IN THE KALAHARI
Stark, Miriam T. The archaeology of social boundaries. Washington, D.C.: Smithsonian Institution Press, 1998, pp.12–49.
The paper provides ethnoarchaeological data from agropastoralists, foragers, part-time foragers and wage earners in the central and eastern Kalahari. Uses the information to establish how social space is constructed and how the social boundaries and zones of interaction between ethnically and linguistically distinct groups are established and maintained. Notes a number of factors governing variability in technical systems and points out that it is the material conditions which reflect people's thoughts rather than technical systems. Suggests that the purpose of anthropology is to explore the nature of past and present human systems. Points out that this can only be done by isolating the material conditions under which evolutionary change takes place.
BOTSWANA; CENTRAL KALAHARI GAME RESERVE; KALAHARI DESERT; ANTHROPOLOGY; ARCHAEOLOGY; BANGWATO; EGGSHELLS; FOOD; FORAGING; G/UI; G//ANA; HERERO; HUNTING; KUA; LAND RIGHTS; LAND USE; TERRITORIALITY
PH/B 930.0096872 HIT

0157 Hitchcock, Robert K.; Yellen, John E.
SUBSISTENCE HUNTING AND RESOURCE MANAGEMENT AMONG THE JU/'HOANSI OF NORTHWESTERN BOTSWANA
African Study Monographs, Vol.17 No.4, 1996. pp.153–219.
This assessment of subsistence hunting and natural resource management was carried out among Ju/'hoansi Bushmen (San) over a period of 30 years from the 1960s to 1995 as part of anthropological investigations of remote foraging and food-producing populations in the north-western Kalahari Desert region of Botswana and Namibia. Notes that the Ju/'hoansi pursue a diversified set of resource management and utilization strategies, exploiting over 50 species of mammals, birds, and other fauna using a variety of tools and techniques. Reports that wildlife offtake rates in the 1960s were well below replacement rates. Finds that although changes have occurred over time in technology and in the use of dogs, donkeys and

horses in hunting, the numbers of animals taken by subsistence hunters were still below sustainable yields in 1995, and wildlife products continue to play a significant role in the socioeconomic and ideological systems of Ju/'hoansi. Concludes that these findings underscore the importance of ensuring a continuation of the right to hunt legally and to engage in local community-based natural resource management projects.
BOTSWANA; NAMIBIA; NGAMILAND; /XAI/XAI; CONSERVATION; GOVERNMENT POLICY; G/UI; HUNTING; JU/'HOANSI; RESOURCES MANAGEMENT; WILDLIFE
PH/B 305.8096872 SUB

0158 Hoehn, G.C.
MENTAL IMAGERY AND VISUAL MEMORY
South African Archaeological Bulletin, Vol.45 No.151, 1990, refs., p.61.
This article investigates the human mental imagery and power of visualising. Indicates that visualising is a natural gift and the tendency to inheritance is strong. Provides evidence for the visualising memories of two hunter-gatherer peoples, Eskimoes of the Hudson Bay area and the San of southern Africa. Also comments on copies in London of San rock paintings made in the last century. Discusses a case study of a young San drawing varieties of animals on paper and slate. Comments on the accuracy of the drawing and describes the method used to produce the drawings using a series of isolated dots. Notes that the artist indicated that this was the plan used by his kindred in making their pictures. Concludes that it is likely that these visual powers were inherited by many successive generations of prehistoric painters and engravers.
NAMIBIA; SOUTHERN AFRICA; BOOK REVIEWS; CASE STUDIES; HUNTING-GATHERING; PREHISTORY; ROCK ART; VISUAL PERCEPTION
P 930.105 SAA

0159 Hoff, Ansie
THE WATER SNAKE OF THE KHOEKHOEN AND /XAM
South African Archaeological Bulletin, Vol.52 No.165, 1997, refs, pp36–37.
The article reports on research conducted among the Khoekhoen and descendants of the /Xam San (previously believed by many to have died out) with the purpose of contributing to ethnographic data on the water snake, one of the large snakes depicted in rock art. Finds that a substantial amount of information is still obtainable from the Khoekhoen and /Xam and that distinct /Xam cognitive orientation still exists. Notes that evidence indicates that the water snake was regarded as a symbol for water and therefore as a particularly potent phenomenon. Comments that a dualistic nature was attributed to it, which is presently more pronounced among the /Xam than among the Khoekhoen, the latter tending to emphasise its negative qualities.
NAMIBIA; SOUTH AFRICA; /XAM; BELIEFS; KHOEKHOE; MYTHOLOGY; RELIGION; RESEARCH; ROCK ART
P 930.105 SAA

0160 Hollmann, Jeremy
PRELIMINARY REPORT ON THE KOEBEE ROCK PAINTINGS: WESTERN CAPE PROVINCE, SOUTH AFRICA
South African Archaeological Bulletin, Vol.48 No.157, 1993, pp.16–25.
The article presents data derived from 50 sites in the Koebee area of the western Cape where hitherto little systematic recording of rock art had been undertaken. Notes that humans are portrayed in restricted contexts and outnumber animals in the paintings. Points out that paintings of animals depict a restricted range of species, of which the majority are antelopes. Finds that symbols, metaphors and postures associated with San rituals also occur. Notes also that there are depictions of healing dances, fat-tailed sheep and a complex "fight" scene.
CAPE; SOUTH AFRICA; ANIMALS; CONFLICT; DANCE; RESEARCH; ROCK ART; SHAMANISM; TRANCE
P 930.105 SAA

0161 Honken, Henry
SUBMERGED FEATURES AND PROTO-KHOISAN
Traill, A. Khoisan Linguistic Studies 3, 1977. pp.145–169. ISBN 0854944540.
The paper examines the submerged features detectable in click languages. Defines submerged features as "grammatical features that are both striking and arbitrary and unlikely to be the result of borrowing". Notes that this definition was suggested by Sapir in a paper entitled "The Hokan affinity of Subtiaba of Nicaragua". Bases the investigation of submerged features in click languages on data from Sandawe, =Hoa, Zu/'hoasi, Nama, Xukxoe, !Xo, //egwi and Hadza. Shows that the pronominal, demonstrative and interrogative sub-systems of the click languages are composed each of a number of elements which are widely distributed among the various click languages. Finds that these display structural and phonetic similarities which make it unlikely that they are due to diffusion or chance.
BOTSWANA; NAMIBIA; SOUTH AFRICA; TANZANIA; !XUN; !XOO; =HUA; CLICKS; GRAMMAR; HADZA; JU/'HOANSI; LANGUAGES; LINGUISTICS; NAMA; SANDAWE
496.2709 KHO

0162 Honken, Henry
WORD GROUPS IN THE CLICK LANGUAGES
Khoisan Special Interest Group Newsletter 2, 1984, refs, pp.5–8.
The paper re-examines the evidence for lexical complexities

in the click languages. Discusses two theories mentioned in D.M. Beach's book entitled "The phonetics of the Hottentot language" which favours the "decomposition theory" over "composition theory" with regard to morpheme structure. Provides examples of sets of lexemes with a common phonetic peculiarity. Uses examples from Nama, =hoa, Xam, zu/'hoasi and !xo to display correspondences and makes clear that Beach's rejection of composition theory is not acceptable.
/XAM; !XOO; =HUA; JU/'HOANSI; LANGUAGES; LINGUISTICS; NAMA
PH/B 496.1 KHO

0163 Hovelmann, Wendy
AFRICAN LANGUAGES AND THEIR PLACE IN EDUCATION IN SOUTHERN AFRICA WITH SPECIFIC REFERENCE TO KHOESAN LANGUAGES
Batibo, H.M.; Tsonope, J. The state of Khoesan languages in Botswana. Mogoditshane: Tasalls, 2000. viii, 169pp., ill., refs. pp.100–124. ISBN 9991295208.
The paper aims to provide information on the status of African languages in Namibian basic education and to encourage cooperation on future Khoesan language development. Points out that the Namibia Early Literacy and Language Project (NELLP) working with the South African Molteno Project have already developed teaching and learning materials in eight indigenous Namibian languages. Notes that the only Khoesan language so far included is Khoekhoegowab and that considerable development has taken place with regards to teacher training and the provision of teaching materials and syllabi in this language. Comments that Ju/'hoan will soon be developed in the same manner. Reports on the first of several proposed workshops held in December 1998 on Ju/'hoan research and development. Considers questions of motivation for the promotion of literacy and on the value of standardising cross-border languages. Emphasises the economic advantages for collaboration between countries in the SADC region in the provision of school textbooks. Concludes with a call for communication, consultation, co-ordination and co-operation within the region.
NAMIBIA; CURRICULUM; EDUCATION; JU/'HOANSI; LANGUAGES; LINGUISTICS; LITERACY; ORTHOGRAPHY; REGIONAL COOPERATION
R/B 496.1 STA

0164 Hudson, Derek J.; Isaksen, Jan.
SELECTED BIBLIOGRAPHY ON THE QUALITY OF LIFE IN BOTSWANA
Botswana Society bibliography of Botswana, Part 4: An annotated bibliography on income distribution, social indicators, social welfare and natural resources, Gaborone: The Botswana Society, 1998. iii, 243pp.
The annotated bibliography contains useful references to Basarwa and entries include keywords. The Introduction contains valuable information on the topics covered by the bibliography and additional comments on the Basarwa.
BOTSWANA; BIBLIOGRAPHIES; ECONOMY; NATURAL RESOURCES
R/B 307.72096872 HUD

0165 Humphreys, A.J.B.
BURCHELL'S SHELTER: THE HISTORY AND ARCHAEOLOGY OF A NORTHERN CAPE ROCK SHELTER
South African Archaeological Bulletin, Vol.30, pp.3–18.
The paper examines the history of the terminal occupation by a hunter-gatherer group of a rock shelter in the Kaap escarpment near Campbell in the northern Cape. Quotes from the account of the visit by William Burchell to this shelter which appears in his book *Travels in the interior of South Africa* (1822). This includes the encounter with the inhabitants of the shelter, their appearance, dress, food and the playing of a musical instrument (the gora). Comments that by 1813, when John Campbell visited the site, its Bushman inhabitants had apparently become integrated into the community which developed under the auspices of the London Missionary Society. Provides details of the archaeological remains discovered and concludes that radio-carbon dating suggests an association between the people seen by Burchell and some of the archaeological remains. Notes the value of combining historical and archaeological information to provide a more complete picture.
NORTHERN CAPE; SOUTH AFRICA; ARCHAEOLOGY; FOOD; FORAGING; HISTORY; INTERACTION
P 930.105 SAA

0166 Humphreys, A.J.B.
A REVIEW OF 'PASTORALISM IN AFRICA' BY A.B. SMITH
South African Archaeological Bulletin, Vol.49, No.159, 1994. pp.55–56.
The reviewer considers the book to be a valuable source on pastoralism in Africa. Gives an outline of its arrangement and the major topics it covers. Notes that the coverage is continent-wide and that the book is aimed not merely at an academic readership but is intended to assist governments and development agencies to formulate strategies relevant to specific areas and peoples. Criticises examples of oversimplification and even misrepresentation of some issues and also poor editorship of the text.
SOUTHERN AFRICA; BOOK REVIEWS; PASTORALISM
P 930.105 SAA

0167 Ikeya, Kazonubu
SOME CHANGES AMONG THE SAN UNDER THE INFLUENCE OF RELOCATION PLAN IN BOTSWANA

Senri ethnological Studies, No.59. Eighth International Conference on Hunting and Gathering Societies (CHAGS 8). Osaka. October, 1998. In Anderson, David and Ikeya, Kazunobu Parks. Property and power: managing hunting practice and identity within state policy regimes. refs., pp.183–198. ISSN 03876004.

The paper sets out the situation of the San in the Central Kalahari Game Reserve and in the new settlements of Kaudwane and New Xade up to 1998. Aims to clarify the reasons why San either agreed to leave the Game Reserve in conformity with Government resettlement plans or refused to do so. Documents changes in San lifestyle resulting from their resettlement in New Xade or Kaudwane. Relates the course of negotiations between government and the inhabitants of the Central Kalahari Game Reserve from 1986 to 1997 and the details of the resettlement process from 1996–1998. Also relates the emergence and activities of the advocacy organization First People of the Kalahari and meetings of the negotiating team representing CKGR residents and the Botswana authorities. The paper is based on research carried out in seven areas of the Ghanzi District in 1997 and 1998 and is enhanced by detailed sketch maps indicating the location of the new settlements and which groups moved to each settlement.
BOTSWANA; CENTRAL KALAHARI GAME RESERVE; KAUDWANE; NEW XADE; GOVERNMENT POLICY; G/UI; G//ANA; LIVING CONDITIONS; NON-GOVERNMENTAL ORGANISATIONS; RESETTLEMENT
R/B 363.68 PAR

0168 Imamura-Hayaki, K.
GATHERING ACTIVITY AMONG THE CENTRAL KGALAGADI SAN
African Study Monographs, Supplement 22, Dec. 1996, pp.47–66.
The article aims to analytically describe the present San gathering activities as they change their traditional subsistence and way of life under the influence of the sedentarization programme of the Botswana Government. Notes that firewood and building materials are needed more than before. Reports that San gathering activities have changed remarkably in quantity but not in quality and though the frequency, time length and harvest amount have lessened their favourite plant species, methods and group formation in gathering have not changed. Finds that gathering is more frequently done in groups than individually for greater efficiency and that the size of a group depends on the seasonal and spatial change in plant distribution and the distance to the collecting site. Emphasises the significance of social interaction such as cooperation and information exchange in group gathering. Lists the plants eaten by the Kgalagadi San and the part of the plant utilised.
BOTSWANA; KALAHARI DESERT; ETHNOBOTANY; FORAGING; G//ANA; G/UI; GOVERNMENT POLICY; SEDENTISM
99/809

0169 Imamura-Hayaki, K.
TECHNICAL ASPECTS OF GATHERING AMONG THE CENTRAL KGALAGADI SAN
Vol. 34 No. 1. pp.173–186. Institute of Industrial Sciences, Nagoya Gakuin University, July 1997.
The paper presents the ways in which the /Gui and //Gana of the Central Kalahari gather and cook food and use digging sticks. The data was gathered from July 1991 to February 1991 in the Central Kalahari Game Reserve. Notes the following effects of sedentarization on gathering habits of the San: a) the ratio of gathered plant foods to the total food consumed has dropped because of the availability of water from wells and of food rations provided by the Government; b) the result of a large settled population has caused the depletion of vegetable resources. Notes that San women collect both edible plants and firewood, building materials and grass for thatching. Lists a number of frequently gathered plants with their San and botanical names and describes the cooking method for each plant, also mentions edible caterpillars which are collected and roasted. Mentions a number of methods of using digging sticks including their use as a weapon or hunting tool.
BOTSWANA; CENTRAL KALAHARI GAME RESERVE; FOOD; FORAGING; G/UI; G//ANA; SEDENTISM
99/768

0170 Isaacson, Rupert
THE HEALING LAND: A KALAHARI JOURNEY
maps. xii, 272pp. London: Fourth Estate, 2001.
The autobiographical account of the author's encounters with Bushmen in Botswana, Namibia and South Africa focuses on their struggle for land in the Kalahari region of southern Africa. Looks particularly at that of the =Khomani people of the Northern Cape in the vicinity of the Kalahari Gemsbok National Park. Describes the Kalahari environment, the current situation of Bushmen and the social disintegration common in all the communities visited. Emphasises the importance of the healing dance in the revitalization of Bushman culture.
BOTSWANA; KALAHARI DESERT; KALAHARI GEMSBOK NATIONAL PARK; NAMIBIA; SOUTH AFRICA; =KHOMANI; GENDER ISSUES; HEALING; LAND RIGHTS; RITUALS; SHAMANISM; TRANCE; WOMEN'S ROLE
R/B 305.80968 ISA

0171 James, Alan
THE FIRST BUSHMAN'S PATH: STORIES, SONGS AND TESTIMONIES OF THE /XAM OF THE NORTHERN CAPE
maps, refs, Pietermaritzburg: University of Natal Press, 2001. 269pp.
The book presents poems based on the translations of /Xam folklore collected by W.H.I. Bleek and Lucy Lloyd in the late 19th Century and three future poems from the notebooks of

Dorothea F. Bleek in the 20th century. Each rendering is provided with notes explaining its meaning and giving the name of the original /Xam informant. The Introduction gives background on the status of the /Xam at the time the translations were made, biographical details on the informants and justifications for the work of rearranging and simplifying the earlier texts in order to bring them to the attention of the general reader in a comprehensible way. Sets out the tasks undertaken in order to arrive at literary solutions which would faithfully reflect the nature of the /Xam texts.
CAPE; SOUTH AFRICA; /XAM; FOLKLORE; LITERATURE; ORAL HISTORY
398.089961 JAM

0172 Jean Milmine, M.S.
ECOLOGICAL PROBLEMS AND POSSIBILITIES FOR NGAMILAND BUSHMEN
Research Office for Bushman Development, Ngamiland, 1976. 10pp.
The paper written in collaboration with Megan Biesele, research liaison officer for Bushman development, looks at the situation of the Bushmen in Ngamiland during the 1970s. Identifies three lifestyles prevalent among Bushmen in the area: a) traditional hunting and gathering but combined with occasional labour on cattleposts and involving new hunting methods; b) semi-traditional hunting and gathering combined with stock keeping and carried out in association with cattleposts and villages; c) total dependence on the cattle industry with food obtained through hunting or gathering providing only a very occasional nutritional supplement to the diet. Suggests changes likely to occur as increasingly large numbers of cattle enter the area and explains why this has become possible. Suggests areas for future research.
BOTSWANA; NGAMILAND; CATTLE; CULTURAL CHANGE; HUNTING-GATHERING; LAND RIGHTS
98/770

0173 Jeffreys, M.D.W.
THE MANTIS MYTH
South African Archaeological Bulletin, Vol.26 No.197, p.127.
The letter refers to an earlier letter by the same author in which the confusion between the possible meanings of a Bushman word which could mean either the mantis insect or the name of God according to the tone employed. Refers to a corroborative example in the Hottentot language as shown in the book by Theophilus Hahn, *Tsuni-Goam the supreme being of the Khoi-Khoi* published in 1881 which shows that the same word may mean either God or the mantis according to the tone employed.
BELIEFS; LANGUAGES; LINGUISTICS; RELIGION
P 930.05 SAA

0174 Jeursen, Belinda
ROCK ART AS A BRIDGE BETWEEN PAST AND FUTURE: A COMMON CULTURAL HERITAGE FOR THE NEW SOUTH AFRICA
Critical Arts: a Journal of Cultural Studies, Vol.9 No.2, 1995 refs., pp.119–130. ISSN 02560046.
The paper attempts to explore the implications and motivations for the appropriation of the Bushman image through their art. Lists the books published between 1979 and 1994 which reflect changes in approach in rock art research, but does not attempt to spell these out in detail. Considers that each of the books presents a distinct political message. Points out that rock art is both a recurrent symbol and a motif which may be seen as an original, unique and powerful South African archetype. Concludes, however, that the recuperated vision of the San first emerging in G.W. Stow's "The native races of South Africa" (1905) and more fully developed in the writings of Laurens van der Post, though potentially valuable as a link between past and future must be acknowledged without mystification. Shows that the image of a harmless, hunting and gathering community living in harmony with nature has little relevance for living Bushmen and their current existence. Notes that they do not benefit from further stereotyping provided by both films and advertisements.
SOUTH AFRICA; FILMS; RESEARCH; ROCK ART
PH/B 305.80968 CRI

0175 Jolly, Pieter
MELIKANE AND UPPER MANGOLONG REVISITED: THE POSSIBLE EFFECTS ON SAN ART OF SYMBOLIC CONTACT BETWEEN SOUTH-EASTERN SAN AND SOUTHERN SOTHO AND NGUNI COMMUNITIES
South African Archaeological Bulletin, Vol.50, 1995. pp.68–80.
The paper investigates the possible expression of Nguni and southern Sotho religious concepts and ritual practices in the rock art of south-eastern Africa. Pays special attention to the testimony of the 19th century San informant, Qing, concerning paintings from the caves at Melikane and upper Mangolong, Lesotho. Suggests that the assumption of structural continuities in San religious ideology and ritual practices takes insufficient account of symbiotic interaction between south-eastern San and black farming communities, and changes in the ideological and other systems of the San resulting from such contact. Explores some implications of such changes for the current paradigm of rock art studies and the use of ethnographic analogy in rock art studies.
LESOTHO; BASOTHO; BELIEFS; INTERACTION; RELIGION; RESEARCH; ROCK ART
98/412

0176 Jones, Neville
THE STONE AGE IN RHODESIA
ill., refs. New York: Negro Universities Press, 1969. xiv, 120pp.

The book originally published in 1926 deals with the Stone Age archaeology of Rhodesia (Zimbabwe). Four chapters deal with the rock art and associated stone tools of the Bushmen. Attempts to establish the motives behind the production of the paintings. Considers that the earliest paintings reflect a belief in "imitative magic" by means of which portrayal of an animal was believed to lead to its being successfully hunted. Notes also the existence of paintings of snakes with such features as horns, wings and animal shaped heads which are believed to be related to Bushman mythology. Comments that the significance of circles, crosses and wavy lines is as yet unknown. Records details of an interview with the last Bushman in the Matopos, a middle-aged woman living among the Matabele and whose parents were probably enslaved by them.
MATOPOS; ZIMBABWE; ARCHAEOLOGY; BELIEFS; MYTHOLOGY; PREHISTORY; STONE AGE
968.91 JON

0177 Judson, W.A.
PORANE 'N MASARWA KUNSTENAAR
Bantu, 1966. pp.351–353.
The article (in Afrikaans) discusses drawings done by a "Masarwa" artist from the north-eastern Kalahari north-west of Molepolole. Comments on the possible origin of the word "Masarwa", noted by both S.S. Dornan and I. Schapera and apparently taken over from Tswana and Kgalagadi-speakers by the people so described. Displays examples of the artist's drawings of both animals and abstract designs. Considers some designs to be symbolic while others were apparently produced for purely aesthetic purposes. Notes that Porane, the artist, was in the habit of decorating wooden household objects and ostrich egg-shell water containers but had never previously handled a felt pen of the type used for the drawings.
BOTSWANA; ART; EGGSHELLS
PH/B 305.8096872 JUD

0178 Khoisan Identities and Cultural Heritage Conference
The Digging Stick, Vol.14 No.2, 1997. pp.8–10.
Reviews the Proceedings of the Khoisan conference that was held in Cape Town between 12 and 16 July, 1997. The conference provided unique access to a wealth of up-to-date and previously unpublished information on Khoisan identities and cultural heritage in the mid to late 1990s. According to the review, the proceedings attempt to bridge the divide between scholars of the Khoisan and the Khoisan communities themselves, offering extensive access to the voices of contemporary Khoisan interest groups from South Africa, Namibia and Botswana as well as the most recent scholarly debates around issues of Khoisan culture, history and identity. One contributor who represented the indigenous peoples, Mr Mathambo Ngakaeja from Botswana raised concern that they are deprived of a lot of useful things like land rights, employment, schools and clinics because researchers have described them as nomadic.
BOTSWANA; NAMIBIA; SOUTH AFRICA; CULTURE; INDIGENOUS PEOPLES; KHOESAN; LAND RIGHTS
P 930.105 DST

0179 Kaashe, Tseeku
TEACHING IN THE GHANZI PRIMARY SCHOOL
Oussoren, Otto Education for remote area dwellers in Botswana. Gaborone: University of Botswana, Research and Development Unit; WIMSA, Regional San Education Project, 2001. 107pp., p.53.
The paper provides a brief resume of the problems facing San children in Ghanzi District primary schools. Explains that there are only three San teachers in the district, one of whom is the author of the paper. Notes the following causes of drop-out of San children: Unfamiliarity with the language used in the classroom so that children may take up to four years to become fully conversant with Setswana; corporal punishment; abusive language towards San pupils from children of other language groups.
BOTSWANA; GHANZI DISTRICT; CONFERENCE PAPERS; EDUCATION; PRIMARY EDUCATION; SCHOOL DROP OUTS; SCHOOLS
R/B 372.7096872 WIM

0180 Kagaya, Ryohei
A CLASSIFIED VOCABULARY OF THE SANDAWE LANGUAGE
Asian & African Lexicon, 26, ill.,Tokyo: ILCAA, 1993. x, 144pp.
The book contains three sections: a classified vocabulary of Sandawe; a Sandawe-English Index (dictionary) and an English-Sandawe Index (dictionary). The Introduction describes the phonology, tones and grammar of Sandawe and lists the abbreviations and symbols employed in the text.
TANZANIA; DICTIONARIES; GRAMMAR; LANGUAGES; LINGUISTICS; PHONOLOGY; SANDAWE
496.1 KAG

0181 Kazombungo, Jerson
GHANZI DISTRICT FARM WORKER'S PROJECT
Oussoren, Otto. Education for remote area dwellers in Botswana. Gaborone: University of Botswana, Research and Development Unit; WIMSA, Regional San Education Project, 2001. 107pp., pp.35–36.
The paper outlines the activities of the Ghanzi District Council Farm Worker's Project initiated by the Ghanzi District Council in collaboration with the Dutch Development Organisation (SNV). Lists aims as the ameliorization of the living and working conditions of farm workers through the improvement of

communication between workers and employers; health situation of workers; education of their children; physical infrastructure such as housing and sanitation. Explains structure of the Project and membership of the Steering Committee. Comments on the establishment of two pre-schools on farms and the commissioning of a demographic survey to determine the number of school-age children not attending school. Notes as a constraint the fact that the committee has no authority to effect changes as it can only make recommendations to Council management and has no access to education committees which have political power.
BOTSWANA; GHANZI DISTRICT; ACCESS TO EDUCATION; CONFERENCE PAPERS; FARM WORKERS; LABOUR; LABOUR RELATIONS; PRE-SCHOOL EDUCATION; SCHOOL ENROLMENT; SCHOOL DROP OUTS
R/B 372.7096872 WIM

0182 Keineetse, Keitseope; Beurden Van, J.
BASARWA IN TRANSITION
Gaborone: SNV, Jun 1989. 57pp.
The report compiled for use by the Netherlands Development Organisation (SNV) staff was produced by two journalists, a Motswana and a Dutchman. Provides historical background on the Ghanzi District and the position of Basarwa on the Ghanzi farms; the effects of the cattle economy; government programmes and policies regarding wildlife. Reports on visits to the following settlements: Xade, East Hanahai, D'Kar and Kacgae. Highlights problems of land use conflicts particularly in Kacgae where cattle overrun the settlement in search of water. Recommendations for the Netherlands Development Organisation include support for a seminar of NGOs, government workers and Basarwa to plan a suitable development strategy. Also suggests encouragement of economic activities and help with legal aid.
BOTSWANA; D'KAR; EAST HANAHAI; KACGAE; CATTLE; DEVELOPMENT AID; DIET; EDUCATION; FARMING; GAME RESERVES; HISTORY; NON-GOVERNMENTAL ORGANISATIONS
97/119

0183 Kelly, R.L.
HUNTER-GATHERER MOBILITY STRATEGIES
Journal of Anthropological Research, Vol. 39, 1983. pp.277–307.
The paper aims to initiate development of a theory of hunter-gatherer mobility strategy. Defines this as the nature of the seasonal movement of hunter-gatherers across landscape. Notes that this in turn forms one facet of the way these communities cope with the problem of acquiring resources. Defines several mobility variables which measure resource accessibility, monitoring costs. Uses ethnographic data to show patterning between the nature of mobility strategies and the resource structures of the environment. In the context of the Kalahari, contrasts the availability of water as a determinant of mobility in the case of the G/wi and !Kung with the latter moving more often because of lack of surface water and therefore being dependent on plants for their fluid needs.
BOTSWANA; !KUNG; ANTHROPOLOGY; FORAGING; G/UI; RESEARCH; SOCIAL ORGANIZATION
98/1190

0184 Kent, Susan
AND JUSTICE FOR ALL: THE DEVELOPMENT OF POLITICAL CENTRALIZATION AMONG NEWLY SEDENTARY FORAGERS
American Anthropological Association, 1989, refs. pp.704–712.
The article points out that there are differences in community political centralization, presence of violence and institutionalised mechanisms for the mediation of disputes among established sedentary, newly sedentary and nomadic Basarwa. Attributes the differences to different mobility patterns. Also notes that the shift from nomadism to sedentism led to an increase in political centralization in the form of a community-sanctioned arbitrator and explains what happens if one is not available. Concludes that endemic violence which is common to newly sedentary Basarwa, only superficially resembles violence common to other societies with long histories of sedentism.
BOTSWANA; KUTSE; NATA; !KUNG; CULTURE; EGALITARIANISM; FORAGING; POLITICS; SEDENTISM
PH/B 305.8096872 KEN

0185 Kent, Susan
THE CURRENT FORAGER CONTROVERSY: REAL VERSUS IDEAL VIEWS OF HUNTER-GATHERERS
Man, Vol.27, 1992. pp.45–70.
The paper discusses the validity of previous portrayals of the Basarwa (Bushmen or San) and of foragers in general. Notes that some anthropologists claim that the Basarwa can be viewed as foragers with an autonomous culture distinct from that of their agropastoralist neighbours. Others claim that the Basarwa are the same as other rural poor who make up an underclass within the larger agropastoralist society. Research and literature reviews among recently sedentary Basarwa indicate that there is much more variability among the Kalahari foraging groups than previously recognised. Concludes that although there are Basarwa groups who are little different from their agropastoralist neighbours, other groups pursue a primarily, though by no means exclusively, foraging way of life.
BOTSWANA; KUTSE; NGAMILAND; ZUTSHWA; FORAGING; CULTURE; HUNTING-GATHERING; LANGUAGES; LINGUISTICS; POVERTY; SOCIAL CHANGE
P 301.205 MAN

0186 Kent, Susan
CULTURAL DIVERSITY AMONG TWENTIETH-CENTURY FORAGERS: AN AFRICAN PERSPECTIVE
Cambridge: Cambridge University Press, 1996. ill., refs., xiv, 344pp.
The book was compiled in order to counter the tendency among anthropologists to focus on similarities in hunter-gatherer societies while not recognising their diversity. Comments on what brought this focus into being, namely such seminal studies as Lee and deVore's *Man the hunter* (1965) and Dahlberg's *Woman the gatherer* (1981). Notes that these and later books tended to stress the "commonality among hunter-gatherers" to an extent that the diversity of such groups was overlooked. Suggests three possible reasons why hunter-gatherers have been seen as homogenous: a) lack of knowledge among researchers about the variability which can occur within particular hunter-gatherer societies such as Pygmies or Bushmen, groups of whom differ quite substantially from each other so that no one language group should be seen as representative of the rest; b) because of very rapid culture changes occurring among modern hunter-gatherers, earlier studies of each group can be seen as inaccurate and this may result in lack of recognition of their diversity; c) conclusions may be based only on particular theoretical approaches such as subsistence strategies, while ignoring other aspects of culture. Notes that the book is a textbook on methodological approaches and thought in anthropology.
BOTSWANA; ANTHROPOLOGY; G/UI; G//ANA; HUNTING-GATHERING; KUA; NARO; RESEARCH
306.364 CUL

0187 Kinahan, John
PASTORAL NOMADS OF THE CENTRAL NAMIB DESERT: THE PEOPLE HISTORY FORGOT
Windhoek: Namibia Archaeological Trust, 1991. ill., refs. 167pp.
The study presents a new and challenging approach to the precolonial history of Namibia. Uses primarily archaeological methods to uncover a wealth of evidence for the development of an indigenous pastoral society during the last two millennia. Presents the detailed picture of the pastoral economy in Namibia which emerges from the remains of seasonal encampments and an integrated system of management encompassing all but the most remote and waterless parts of the desert. Examines the collapse of nomadic pastoralism in the light of both archaeological and archival evidence, establishing a continuity of events which radically extends the time depth of precolonial history.
NAMIBIA; NAMIB DESERT; ARCHAEOLOGY; HISTORY; HUNTING-GATHERING; PASTORALISM; PREHISTORY
968.81 KIN

0188 Kinahan, John
THE ARCHAEOLOGY OF SOCIAL RANK AMONG EIGHTEENTH CENTURY NOMADIC PASTORALISTS IN SOUTHERN AFRICA
African Archaeological Review, Vol.13 No.4, 1994. pp.225–245.
The paper shows that investigations of a complex stone-walled encampment at //Khauxa!nas in Namibia, provide new insights into the social consequences of European contact with the pastoral Khoi in the past. Points out that the Namibian evidence contradicts the general view that the eighteenth century Khoi were little more than a colonial underclass. Notes that details of layout and construction of dwellings at //Khauxa!nas point to the rise of a hierarchical organization uniting autonomous households within the pastoral alliance. Concludes that this development reflects the social evolutionary potential of Khoi society at a crucial moment in its history, immediately prior to the rise of armed resistance against colonial rule.
NAMIBIA; ARCHAEOLOGY; KHOEKHOE; PASTORALISM; RESEARCH
98/1164

0189 Kirby, Percival R.
THE GORA AND ITS BANTU SUCCESSORS
Bantu Studies, Vol.5, 1931. refs. pp.89–109.
The article is based on material collected for "A survey of music and musical practices of the native peoples of southern Africa". Provides a very detailed study of the gora, a musical instrument which probably originated amongst the Korana along the Orange River and spread west, east and south. Considers that it was adopted by the Hottentots and Bushmen and from them passed to other ethnic groups such as the Zulu, Xhosa, Basotho and Tswana with various adaptations and names. Analyses a number of early references to the gora. Reports in detail upon the manufacture and methods of performance of the instrument. Provides several examples of tunes in staff notation recorded by various observers. Provides technical notes on the harmonics employed by players of the gora and considers that both the unique method of sound production and the use for melodic purposes of the upper portals of the harmonic scale make this instrument of great importance.
!ORA; KHOESAN; KHOEKHOE; MUSIC; RESEARCH
p 960.5 AST

0190 Kirby, Percival R.
A STUDY OF BUSHMAN MUSIC
Bantu Studies, Vol.10 No.2, 1936. pp.205–252.
The article is in two parts: firstly it deals with historical, mainly 19th century references to Bushman music with examples of Bushman songs accompanied by staff notation; secondly it provides the contents of two music manuscript books recorded by Lucy Lloyd and containing both the words of songs and the

music accompanying them. Concludes that Bushman music was strongly influenced by both European and Hottentot music. Notes the close connection between Bushman speech and song, melody being largely determined by speech-tone and rhythm by verbal emphasis. Provides details of the forms, measures and scales of Bushman music and notes its close association with dance.
SOUTHERN AFRICA; DANCE; LANGUAGES; LINGUISTICS; MUSIC; RESEARCH
P 960.05 AST

0191 Köhler, Oswin von
ALLGEMEINE UND SPRACHLICHE BEMERKUNGEN ZUM FELDBAU NACH ORALTEXTEN DER KXOE-BUSCHLEUTE
Bernd Heine. Sprache und Geschichte in Afrika, Vol.7 No.1. Hamburg: Helmut Buske, 1986. 457pp., pp.205–272.
The paper deals with the origins of agriculture as a supplementary economy among the Kxoe Bushmen on the Lunyama River of Angola. Shows that the assumption by F. Seiner (1909) that the Kxoe only became familiar with the cultivation of food plants after the arrival of Mbukushu farmer/herdsmen after 1750, could not be confirmed by investigating names of cultivated plants or analysing agricultural vocabulary. Notes that apart from Mbukushu loanwords in Kxoe relating to cereal production, there are a number which appear to be of Khoi origin. Observes that the study of the names of the cultivated plants and of cultivation vocabulary indicates complex cultural-historical processes in the history of the region while the dating of sorghum, millet and cowpea seeds from at least 1000 BP, found at an archaeological site on the edge of the Okavango Delta near Maun suggest a new perspective on the origin of agriculture among hunter-gatherers.
ANGOLA; AGRICULTURE; ARCHAEOLOGY; KHWE; LANGUAGES; LINGUISTICS
95/825

0192 Koketso, Gaewetse
THE REMOTE AREA DEVELOPMENT PROGRAMME OF THE MINISTRY OF LOCAL GOVERNMENT
Oussoren, Otto. Education for remote area dwellers in Botswana. Gaborone: University of Botswana, Research and Development Unit; WIMSA, Regional San Education Project, 2001. 107pp., pp.48–50.
The paper gives the history of the Remote Area Development Programme, defines its target group and sets out its objectives. Shows how the programme is implemented at national and local level and in collaboration with district-based departments of the Ministries of Agriculture, Education and Commerce and Industry. Sets out the following problems facing remote area dwellers (RADs) in Botswana and requiring attention: poverty, low literacy levels, inadequate education and training, weak institutions and leadership, and lack of awareness about their land rights. Notes the main issues concerning the education of RAD's children and the solutions attempted by the programme in addressing them. Considers that the programme has had success in some areas, notably in the provision of social services and that its objectives remain relevant. Promises that the programme will continue to confront the remaining problems in collaboration with appropriate stakeholders.
BOTSWANA; CONFERENCE PAPERS; EDUCATION; GOVERNMENT POLICY; LAND RIGHTS; LOCAL GOVERNMENT; REMOTE AREA DEVELOPMENT; RURAL DEVELOPMENT; TRAINING
R/B 372.7096872 WIM

0193 Kuru Development Trust
KURU DEVELOPMENT TRUST ACTIVITY REPORT FOR 1997 AND ANNUAL PLAN FOR 1998
1997. 49pp.
The introduction to the report provides the background to the programme. Outlines the situation currently facing the San of southern Africa with particular emphasis on Botswana. Notes economic problems faced by communities in settlements who have become dependent upon aid from government and donors. Comments on reasons for San children dropping out of school and thus remaining illiterate. Notes changes in organizational structure which will allow Kuru to assist local groups with the organization of their own community structures and income-generating projects. Provides reports from the following departments: Extension, Education and culture, Business and Dquae Qare Game Farm Project, with each department including its main objectives and achievements for the year and plans for the following year.
BOTSWANA; D'KAR; GHANZI DISTRICT; ADVOCACY; COMMUNITY DEVELOPMENT; ECONOMIC DEVELOPMENT; EMPOWERMENT; NON-GOVERNMENTAL ORGANISATIONS; RURAL DEVELOPMENT; SELF-DETERMINATION; TRAINING
PH/B 338.96872 KUR

0194 Kuru Development Trust
KURU DEVELOPMENT TRUST ACTIVITY REPORT FOR THE YEAR 1998 AND PLANS FOR 1999
1998, 47pp.
The report contains an introductory chapter outlining the structure and programmes of Kuru Development Trust. Provides detailed reports from the following departments: extension; education and culture; business and the Game Farm Project. Individual reports indicate the activities undertaken in 1998, constraints faced, and plans for 1999. Notes that the departments are attempting to fulfil the primary objective of Kuru "to assist marginalised communities in Botswana with the establishment and development of self-sustainable community

self-help organizations, which will increase the capacity of these communities to gain control over their social and economic lives and which will be able to define, direct and implement the communities' own development."
BOTSWANA; D'KAR; GHANZI DISTRICT; COMMUNITY DEVELOPMENT; EMPOWERMENT; NON-GOVERNMENTAL ORGANISATIONS; SELF-DETERMINATION; TRAINING
PH/B 338.96872 KUR

0195 Kuru Development Trust. Bokamoso Preschool Programme
THE CHALLENGES OF CHANGE: A SURVEY ON THE EFFECTS OF PRESCHOOL ON BASARWA PRIMARY SCHOOL CHILDREN IN THE GHANZI DISTRICT OF BOTSWANA
Ghanzi: Kuru Development Trust, 1995, ill., iii, 64pp.
Report of a survey undertaken in Ghanzi District primary schools between 1993 and 1995 to ascertain the progress of Basarwa children who had completed preschool. Gives the history and aims of the Bokamoso Preschool Programme operating in several settlements in the district. Provides information on the cross-cultural difficulties experienced by children, teachers and parents of primary school children. Looks at reasons for children dropping out of school and finds them complex. Concludes that a wide gap in understanding exists between teachers and parents owing to lack of cultural knowledge of the other party. Suggests areas requiring further investigation.
BOTSWANA; BERE; D'KAR; GHANZI DISTRICT; HANAHAI; EDUCATION; INTERACTION; NARO; NON-GOVERNMENTAL ORGANISATIONS; PRE-SCHOOL EDUCATION
305.233 CHA

0196 König, Christa; Heine, Bernd
THE !XUN OF EKOKA: A DEMOGRAPHIC AND LINGUISTIC REPORT. KHOISAN FORUM WORKING PAPER, NO.17, 2001
refs., 192pp. ISSN 14331306.
The paper deals mainly with the !Xun language but contains a brief section containing demographic information. The Introduction places the !Kun language within its linguistic setting among the other related "lects" which are spoken in southern Angola, northern and north-eastern Namibia and north-western Botswana. Prefers the term "lect" to the more commonly used term "dialect" to refer to a particular variety of !Kun which differs in some linguistically definable way from other varieties of the language. Explains that these linguistically related speech forms are otherwise entitled "Northern Khoisan". Provides a detailed grammatical sketch of the language, a fairly extensive !Xun-English and English-!Xun vocabulary and three folktales in !Kun with English translations and a short description of hunting.
NAMIBIA; !XUN; DICTIONARIES; GRAMMAR; LANGUAGES; LINGUISTICS; PHONOLOGY; SOCIAL ORGANISATION
R/B 496.1 KON

0197 Lane, P.; Reid, A.; Segobye, A.
DITSWAMMUNG: THE ARCHAEOLOGY OF BOTSWANA
Gaborone: Pula Press, 1998. ill., maps, refs. 263pp.
The book, the first to deal in any detail with the archaeology of Botswana, is based upon the papers read at a conference on the above topic, which was held in October 1996. Notes that the book reflects cooperation between the authors of the papers and three discussants invited to participate in the programme, namely Professors Alison Brooks, Jim Denbow and Tom Huffman. Chapters cover the following topics: the origins and growth of archaeology in Botswana; the late Stone Age; herding traditions; early farming communities; the late Iron Age; ethnoarchaeological research; Botswana's prehistoric rock art; the organization of archaeology; archaeology and museums; and the present state of archaeology in Botswana. Shows the need for future research and participation of locally trained researchers.
BOTSWANA; ARCHAEOLOGY; HERDERS; PASTORALISM; PREHISTORY; RESEARCH; ROCK ART
R/B 968.72 DIT

0198 Lanham, L.W.; Hallowes, D.P.
LINGUISTIC RELATIONSHIPS AND CONTACTS EXPRESSED IN THE VOCABULARY OF EASTERN BUSHMAN
Foundations in southern African linguistics. Johannesburg: Witwatersrand University Press, 1993. xv, 293pp., ill. pp.253–256. ISBN 1868142337.
The chapter deals with linguistic relationships of the Eastern Bushman language spoken by a small group of twenty to thirty Bushmen in the Lake Chrissie area of the eastern Transvaal. The study is based on research conducted from March 1954 to September 1955. Finds that the language has close links with the =Khomani language spoken in the southern Kalahari. Notes the presence of words borrowed from Siswati, English and Afrikaans which are all currently spoken in the area while words taken from Sotho and Tswana suggest contact with speakers of these languages in the past.
SOUTH AFRICA; 'AUO; //XEGWI; LANGUAGES; LINGUISTICS; N/U; SOUTHERN
PH/B 496.1 FOU

0199 Le Roux, Braam; Thoma, Axel
PROJECT PROPOSAL FOR THE ESTABLISHMENT OF THE WORKING GROUP OF INDIGENOUS MINORITIES IN SOUTHERN AFRICA: A REGIONAL NETWORK – ANGOLA, BOTSWANA, NAMIBIA, SOUTH AFRICA, ZAMBIA, ZIMBABWE
Lane Paul; Hermans, Janet; Molebatsi, Chadzimula. Proceedings from the Basarwa Research Workshop, Gaborone, 24–25

August, 1995. 106pp. pp.52–54. 2001.
The article indicates that one of the resolutions reached at the regional conference on development programmes for Africa's San population held in Windhoek, Namibia in 1992 was that regional networking should be established to represent San people. Further notes that in order to facilitate networking and development, the following should be taken into consideration: a) all the present resources at the San's disposal should be accommodated and united; b) the San should run their organization; c) people should be organised at grass-roots level; d) networking would have to integrate a development support programme that coordinates all efforts and facilitates the design of new strategies. Also suggests that: a) regional networking organization which could be called Working Group of Indigenous Minorities in Southern Africa (WIMSA) be formed; b) all indigenous people's Community Based Organization (CBO's) should be supported; c) first people of the Kalahari (FPK) will be supported; d) more emphasis should be put on community work. Concludes that WIMSA will have to play a functional role by facilitating the formulation of future development strategies in the different countries.
BOTSWANA; NAMIBIA; CONFERENCE PAPERS; NON-GOVERNMENTAL ORGANISATIONS; SELF-DEVELOPMENT
R/B 305.8096872 PRO

0200 Le Roux, Willemien
A VISIT TO SCHMIDTSDRIFT: THE LARGEST SAN "SETTLEMENT" IN THE WORLD?
Kalahari Support Group Newsletter, refs., 1995. pp.7–8.
The article describes conditions at the Schmidtsdrift camp where 4,000 !Xu (Northern !Kung) and Khwe (Kxoe language group) were resettled when the South African Defence Force (SADF) withdrew from Namibia. Although the SADF and Khwe and !Xu Trust are attempting to introduce income-generating projects, the members of the community have difficulty in overcoming dependency upon the Army and in coming to terms with capitalism. Outlines the aims of the !Ku and Khwe Trust which was formed in 1994 as a resource and advocacy body.
SCHMIDTSDRIFT; SOUTH AFRICA; !XUN; ADVOCACY; KHWE; RESETTLEMENT; SELF-DETERMINATION
99/184

0201 Le Roux, Willemien
SHADOW BIRD
1st ed. Cape Town: Kwela Books, 2000. 192pp.
The setting for this book of sketches is the village of D'kar in western Botswana where the author and her husband worked with the Naro people for many years. Movingly written, it presents the personal stories of a variety of San characters, their struggles and triumphs, their pain and laughter and their interaction with the white and black neighbours who share their lives at different levels. Paints a graphic picture also of the physical background against which the characters live out their lives in a harsh climate, amid heat, dust and the sudden transformation brought about by rain.
BOTSWANA; D'KAR; INTERACTION; LITERATURE; NARO; POVERTY
823.94 LER

0202 Lebotse, Kabelo Kenneth
SELF-DETERMINATION AND MINORITIES IN BOTSWANA: THE CASE OF THE SAN PEOPLE
Mazonde, Isaac N. Minorities in the millennium: perspectives from Botswana. Gaborone: Lightbooks, 2002. refs., vii, 136pp. pp.111–115. ISBN 9991271244.
The paper considers what is meant by self-determination and to what degree it has been extended to the San in Botswana. Notes that in spite of divergent views as to the meaning of the term "self-determination", it has been affirmed as a right in the United Nations Charter of Human Rights. Refers to the well-known but unacceptable ruling by the Attorney General's Chambers in Botswana that because they were "true nomads" Basarwa had no rights except that of being allowed to hunt. Notes that although the Botswana Government denies that its policies towards the San are in accordance with this ruling they appear to be consistent with it. Examines the role and performance of the Remote Area Development Programme (RADP) and observes that it was set up to provide: a) social services; b) economic opportunities; c) political/legal rights for remote area dwellers. Considers that the resettlement of San in Tswana type villages away from their traditional areas has led to the disruption of their cultural life. Suggests that the RADP should be revised to allow San inclusion in the management and conservation of natural resources in their traditional areas. They should also be allowed to benefit from tourism instead of being moved to make way for tourism. Emphasises the need for government to recognise the land rights of the San.
BOTSWANA; CONFERENCE PAPERS; GOVERNMENT POLICY; HUMAN RIGHTS; LAND RIGHTS; REMOTE AREA DEVELOPMENT; SELF-DETERMINATION; SETTLEMENT POLICY; TOURISM
R/B 968.72 MIN

0203 Lee, Richard B.
EATING CHRISTMAS IN THE KALAHARI
Natural History, December, 1969, pp.14–22, 60–63.
The articles relates an incident experienced by the author which illuminated aspects of Bushman culture. Describes his intention of purchasing an ox which would be served at Christmas to the !Kung community whose members had provided him with information during his stay in the Kalahari. However, to his surprise, the very large ox purchased was heavily criticised

as "thin", a "bag of bones" etc and he was solemnly assured that it would not feed the community adequately and fights might break out when its meat was shared out. However, when slaughtered its meat lasted two days and nights. Eventually the author realised that he had been given the type of treatment which would be meted out to any Bushman who was considered to be in danger of becoming arrogant and self-important. As he had power to provide such sought after goods as tobacco, or to withhold them, he could be considered both arrogant and mean and was treated appropriately.
BOTSWANA; DOBE; !KUNG; CULTURE
PH/B 305.8096872 LEE

0204 Lee, Richard B.
POLITICS, SEXUAL AND NON-SEXUAL, IN AN EGALITARIAN SOCIETY
Leacock, E. Politics and history in band societies. Cambridge University Press, 1982. pp.37–59,
The paper deals with egalitarianism and leadership in !Kung society. Finds that men and women play complementary roles with relative equality between the sexes and rape being extremely rare. Notes that two types of leadership are found in the society. Within the band the acknowledged leader may be a senior member of a large family, the "owner" of a N/ore (band territory) or married to a woman so acknowledged and possessing certain characteristics admired by the society. Observes that those representing the !Kung with the outside world tend to be more aggressive and articulate, but arrogance and meanness are the personality traits most disapproved of.
BOTSWANA; !KUNG; CULTURE; EGALITARIANISM; GENDER ISSUES; INTERGROUP RELATIONS; LEADERSHIP; SOCIAL ORGANISATION
95/1041

0205 Lee, Richard B.
THE DOBE JU/'HOANSI
Case studies in cultural anthropology. Fort Worth: Harcourt Brace College, c1993. ill., maps, refs. xv, 207pp.
The second edition of the case-study originally entitled "The Dobe !Kung" is an update of the original material. Describes the environment and settlement patterns, kinship and social organization, marriage and sexuality, subsistence methods, conflict, politics, religion and relations with neighbouring non-Ju/'hoansi. Contains two new chapters: Chapter 11 details events of the last decade and their effect upon the Ju/'hoansi and Chapter 12 looks at changes in anthropological theory and practice partly brought about by the changes in the conditions under which the subjects of their research now live.
BOTSWANA; DOBE; NAMIBIA; ALCOHOL; BELIEFS; CULTURE; JU/'HOANSI; RELIGION; RESEARCH; SETTLEMENTS; SEX ROLES; SOCIAL CHANGE
306.089961 LEE

0206 Lee, Richard B.
PROGRESS OR POVERTY? THE DOBE JU/'HOANSI
Cultural Survival Quarterly, Vol.26 No.1, 2002, pp.16–17.
The report on the present situation of the Ju/'hoansi of the Dobe area notes that this was the site of a series of anthropological studies in the 1970s on the hunting and gathering life-style. Shows the problems faced by Ju/'hoansi over four decades since these studies were made and the people became settled in one area. Comments on the social problems caused by alcohol abuse, difficulties in obtaining ploughs and agricultural equipment, difficulty in building up adequate cattle herds, and the loss of all cattle due to their being slaughtered in 1995 because of cattle disease. Reports on positive developments like drilling of boreholes and establishment on a conservancy at /Xai/Xai which promises improved economic security.
BOTSWANA; DOBE; CATTLE; DEVELOPMENT PLANNING; JU/'HOANSI; RESOURCES UTILIZATION; SELF-DEVELOPMENT
R/B 305.8096872 CUL

0207 Lee, Richard B.; Rosenberg, H.G.
AGE, GENDER AND AUTONOMOUS SPACES
18pp.
The article aims to show how the Bushman method of handling conflict constitutes a comprehensive and effective dispute resolution system which has lessons for those in the field of conflict resolution. Looks at functions performed in a successful conflict management system and finds that they are: the prevention of disputes before they arise; resolving the disputes by healing the emotional wounds; reconciling divergent interests; determining rights and testing if necessary the relative power of the parties, and finally containing any unresolved disputes threatening to escalate into violence and channelling them back into the system for resolution. Explores each function in turn to establish how it is utilised to deal with conflict: emotions; interests; rights and power are each dealt with within the community; which can be seen as an effective "third force" working to prevent; resolve and contain disputes. Comments that this is done without a formal legal or governmental system in spite of the existence of potentially lethal weapons (poisoned arrows). Concludes that much can be learnt from this apparently simple but in many ways more socially advanced society.
BOTSWANA; CONFLICT; CULTURE; SOCIAL ORGANISATION; VIOLENCE
98/1178

0208 Lee, Richard B.; Daly, Richard Heywood
THE CAMBRIDGE ENCYCLOPEDIA OF HUNTERS AND GATHERERS

New York: Cambridge University Press, 1999. ill., maps, refs., xx, 511pp.
The encyclopaedia is divided into two parts: Part 1 contains over 50 case studies of hunting and gathering peoples worldwide with a general introduction for each region as well as an archaeological overview. Part 2 consists of essays on prehistory, social life, gender, music and art, health, religion and indigenous knowledge. The final section looks at hunter-gatherers in a global world and surveys both the encounters of hunter-gatherers with colonialism and their current struggle for survival in modern nation-states. Lists indigenous peoples' organizations and advocacy groups. The general introduction to the encyclopaedia includes the history of hunter gatherer studies including the conferences on hunting and gathering societies (CHAGS) and notes the major trends appearing in late 20th century hunter-gatherer studies. Chapters dealing with specific San groups are separately abstracted under authors in this bibliography but they are also referred to in both case studies and special essays.
ADVOCACY; BELIEFS; ECOLOGY; POLITICS; RELIGION; SELF-DETERMINATION; SOCIAL ORGANIZATION
R 306.36403 CAM

0209 Legassick, Martin
THE NORTHERN FRONTIER TO C.1840: THE RISE AND DECLINE OF THE GRIQUA PEOPLE
Elphick, Richard; Giliomee, Herman. The shaping of South African society, 1652–1840. Cape Town: Maskew Miller Longman, 1989. xix, 624pp., pp.358–420. ISBN 0363010767.
The chapter records the history of the peoples inhabiting Namaqualand, Bushmanland and central Transorangia in the 18th and early 19th century. Describes the emergence of the Griqua, a people with a distinct life-style differing from either that of the Cape settlers or the earlier peoples of the region. Explores the role of missionaries in their development and relationships with the Cape government. Notes economic and political changes from 1840 and their negative effects upon the Griqua. Concludes that the early nineteenth century was the last period in South African history during which "brown" people were able to play a relatively independent role before expansion of the frontier and the white conquest of the area.
CAPE; SOUTH AFRICA; AFRIKANERS; GRIQUA; HISTORY; INTERGROUP RELATIONS; MISSIONARIES
968.03 SHA

0210 Lewis-Williams, James David
SYNTAX AND FUNCTION OF THE GIANT'S CASTLE ROCK PAINTINGS
South African Archaeological Bulletin, Vol.27 1972, pp.49–65.
The paper attempts to find more meaningful ways of discussing the parietal art of the Bushman than that hitherto considered. Suggests that while the "classic" theories have not been supported by the facts and lead to a cul-de-sac, a study of the function of the art, illuminated by an analysis of the mythology, will provide a more promising approach. Notes that a better understanding of the form of the art does not reveal its meaning, which will only be revealed by studying the mythology of the Bushmen.
DRAKENSBERG; KWAZULU-NATAL; SOUTH AFRICA; BELIEFS; MYTHOLOGY; RELIGION; ROCK ART
P 930.105 SAA

0211 Lewis-Williams, James David
SUPERPOSITIONING IN A SAMPLE ROCK PAINTING FROM THE BARKLY-EAST DISTRICT
South African Archaeological Bulletin, Vol.29. 1974. pp.93–103.
The paper reveals that quantitative evidence from three areas bordering the Drakensberg shows that superpositioning is not random but intentional. Contends that this conclusion has far-reaching implications regarding the purpose and significance of the paintings. Notes that certain categories were favoured as the initial elements upon which new paintings would be imposed and the lower painting would exercise a limiting influence on the range of subjects from which the second could be selected. Concludes that the rock paintings investigated are largely concerned with social relationships and together constitute a complex signifying system.
SOUTHERN AFRICA; CULTURE; RESEARCH; ROCK ART; SOCIAL ORGANIZATION
P 930.105 SAA

0212 Lewis-Williams, James David
EZELJAGDSPOORT REVISITED: NEW LIGHT ON AN ENIGMATIC ROCK PAINTING
South African Archaeological Bulletin, Vol.32, 1977, refs., pp.165–169.
The paper discusses possible interpretations of a painting at a site located at Ezeljagdspoort near Oudtshoorn. Explains that the painting was first copied and recopied in the 1870s and was of interest because it apparently depicted what Western observers interpreted as mermaids. Presents comments by Han=kasso, one of Bleek's San informants which suggest that the painting can be explained in terms of rituals used to control the angry being !Khwa (the rain's navel). Warns against Eurocentric interpretations of rock art which should rather be interpreted in terms of San beliefs and customs.
SOUTH AFRICA; BELIEFS; RELIGION; RITUALS; ROCK ART
P 930.105 SAA

0213 Lewis-Williams, James David
FELSBILDER IN SUDAFRIKA: TEIL 1: DIE GRAVIERUNGEN AUF KLIPFONTEIN, KAP-PROVINZ

African Studies, Vol.39 No.2, 1979. pp.79–80.
The review of C.J. Fock's book on the rock engravings from the farm Klipfontein near Kimberley, South Africa, describes it as "a handsome contribution to the upgrading of rock art studies". Commends the large number of engravings reproduced but poses the question as to how the quantitative data provided can be utilised and to what extent the items which have been counted are actually those which were of importance to the engravers. Compares rock engravings with rock paintings and observes that both art forms include peculiar subjects such as eared snakes and animal-headed figures. In addition, the Klipfontein engravings include depictions of domestic animals and some "scenes".
SOUTH AFRICA; BOOK REVIEWS; RESEARCH; ROCK ART
99/765

0214 Lewis-Williams, James David
ETHNOGRAPHY AND ICONOGRAPHY: ASPECTS OF SOUTHERN SAN THOUGHT AND ART
Man, Vol.15, 1980, pp.467–482.
The article considers the unique and detailed explanations given by two nineteenth century San informants regarding four sets of paintings. The interpretations of the paintings appear in J.M. Orpen's article in the *Cape Monthly Magazine (NS)* Vol. 9 of 1874 entitled, "The mythology of the Maluti Bushmen". When shown copies of the paintings, Orpen's informant in the Maluti and Bleek's in Cape Town provided explanations using unfamiliar metaphors which, when interpreted, show that much of the rock art relates to trance performance and to possible hallucinations experienced during the trance experience.
CAPE; LESOTHO; SOUTH AFRICA; ANTHROPOLOGY; BELIEFS; DANCE; MYTHOLOGY; RESEARCH; ROCK ART; SHAMANISM; TRANCE
97/093

0215 Lewis-Williams, James David
BELIEVING AND SEEING: SYMBOLIC MEANINGS IN SOUTHERN SAN ROCK PAINTINGS
Studies in anthropology, London: Academic Press, 1981 ill., refs, xiii, 151pp.
The book provides a detailed analysis of the symbolic meaning of rock paintings. Bases the model employed partly on that suggested by Charles Sanders Pearce and Charles Morris by means of which paintings may be taken as signs which require a certain response from the observer. Discusses the previous interpretations of rock art and the whole theory of signs. Explains the methodology adopted in order to arrive at the conclusions presented. Notes that, whereas previous studies have been selective and have looked at only a random selection of widely scattered paintings, this book deals with only two sites, Barkley East and Giants Castle in the Drakensberg where over 3,600 paintings were recorded and statistically analysed. Uses the ethnography to elucidate the underlying symbolism of the paintings. Relies heavily upon the work of Bleek and Lloyd and the article by J.M. Orpen in the Cape Monthly Magazine of 1874 on the mythology of the Maluti Bushmen, as well as considering the discoveries of anthropologists in the Kalahari and his own brief period of fieldwork among Kalahari Bushmen in 1974. Considers that the eland is the central symbol in Bushman thought, tying all social, spiritual and metaphysical concerns into a consistent whole and playing a part in such significant rituals as female initiation, the young hunter's first kill and marriage. Finds that the eland, an embodiment of the divinity /Kaggen, is associated with rain-making and the trance dance as well as playing a mediating role within basic societal divisions: male/female, child/adult, life/death, man/divinity and that aspects of all these meanings can be seen in the paintings.
DRAKENSBERG; SOUTH AFRICA; DANCE; HEALING; RELIGION; RESEARCH; ROCK ART; SHAMANISM; TRANCE
759.0113 LEW

0216 Lewis-Williams, James David
THE ROCK ART OF SOUTHERN AFRICA
Cambridge: Cambridge University Press, 1983. ill. (some col.) refs., 68pp., [63]pp. of plates:.
The book surveys the rock art, both paintings and engravings, of southern Africa. Recounts the development of rock art research and the various techniques employed in the attempt to unravel the meaning of the art. Shows the weaknesses of the various theories put forward previously to "explain" the purpose of rock art. Concludes that it can only be understood by combining the results of modern ethnological studies of living Bushmen, particularly their folklore and religious beliefs and examining the comments of Bushman informants of the late 19th century and the folklore they related to W.H.I. Bleek and L.C. Lloyd. Shows the complex metaphorical nature of many rock paintings, especially those depicting dying eland and notes that myth, ritual, and art are linked by metaphor. Summarises the final stages in the history of the Bushman artists of South Africa and their eventual demise in the face of encroachment by land-hungry white farmers into the areas they had inhabited for many centuries.
SOUTH AFRICA; ANTHROPOLOGY; BELIEFS; DANCE; HISTORY; MYTHOLOGY; RELIGION; ROCK ART; SHAMANISM; TRANCE
759.0113 LEW

0217 Lewis-Williams, James David
THE ROCK ART WORKSHOP: NARRATIVE OR METAPHOR?
Hall, M. Frontiers: Southern African Archaeology Today: BAR International Series, No. 207, 1984. pp.323–327.

The report on a rock art symposium held in 1984 deals with considerations of the relative importance of the two opposing interpretations of southern African rock art. Shows that the one regards rock art as mainly depictions of daily life or historical events while the other considers it to be mainly symbolic. Examination of examples of reproductions of rock art from different regions led to a consensus that while many were indeed symbolic there were still a number remaining which could not be so interpreted. An exposition of the metaphorical view of the art was provided by J.D. Lewis-Williams who showed that even paintings which appeared to be simply records of actual events also contained symbolic elements as do paintings of animals previously interpreted as merely aesthetic depictions. Questions on regional differentiation led to the comment that there probably existed a pan-San cognitive system.
SOUTHERN AFRICA; ANIMALS; ANTHROPOLOGY; ARCHAEOLOGY; BELIEFS; DANCE; RELIGION; RESEARCH; ROCK ART; SHAMANISM; TRANCE
99/742

0218 Lewis-Williams, James David
DECEPTIVE APPEARANCES: A CRITIQUE OF SOUTHERN AFRICAN ROCK ART STUDIES
Advances in World Archaeology, Vol. 5, 1986. pp.253–289.
The paper seeks to show the ineffectuality of the empirical method employed by earlier rock art researchers in their attempts to understand the meaning of the art. Shows that the collection of large amounts of data did not logically result in any theory which could explain its meaning. Proposes a model employing both ethnography and mythology to throw light upon the art itself. Contends that this leads to the hypothesis that San rock art is essentially shamanistic in nature and often employs complex metaphors which depict the experiences of shamans in the trance state. Evaluates this hypothesis using criteria which demonstrate its superiority over rival hypotheses.
SOUTHERN AFRICA; ANTHROPOLOGY; BELIEFS; DANCE; MYTHOLOGY; RELIGION; RESEARCH; ROCK ART; SHAMANISM; TRANCE
99/748

0219 Lewis-Williams, James David
THROUGH THE VEIL: SAN ROCK PAINTING AND THE ROCK FACE
refs., 1990. pp.5–16.
The article deals with the use made of the actual rock face by the artists who created rock paintings. Notes that in numerous San rock paintings people or animals apparently enter or leave the rock face. Shows that neuropsychological and ethnographic evidence suggests that San shamans were believed to visit the spirit world via a tunnel, which in some instances, started at the walls of rock shelters. Shaman-artists depicted some of the visions they brought back from the spirit world as if they were emerging from the rock face. Considers that this conclusion implies that the rock face was as meaningful as a ritual element as the paint, anything painted on the walls of a rock shelter was thus placed in a shamanistic context.
BOTSWANA; LESOTHO; SOUTH AFRICA; BELIEFS; DANCE; RELIGION; RESEARCH; ROCK ART; SHAMANISM; TRANCE
P 930.105 SAA

0220 Lewis-Williams, James David
UPPER PALAEOLITHIC ART IN THE 1990'S: A SOUTHERN AFRICAN PERSPECTIVE
South African Journal of Science, Vol.87, Sept., 1991, ill. refs., pp.422–429.
The paper looks at Upper Palaeolithic cave art, comparing its possible meaning and significance with that of San rock art. Notes that methodologies earlier employed in the attempt to explicate this art were inadequate and explains why. Concludes that just as San rock art has been found to be largely shamanistic in origin, the same may well be true of European cave art. Explains the model used to identify the stages that occur when an altered state of consciousness is experienced by a shaman in trance and shows that many symbols and apparently inexplicable animal forms can be linked to the trance experience. Suggests directions for future research which should use new insights from both neuropsychology and ethology.
EUROPE; SOUTHERN AFRICA; ARCHAEOLOGY; BELIEFS; RELIGION; RESEARCH; ROCK ART; SHAMANISM; TRANCE
99/754

0221 Lewis-Williams, James David
ETHNOGRAPHIC EVIDENCE RELATING TO TRANCE, AND SHAMANS AMONG NORTHERN AND SOUTHERN BUSHMEN
South African Archaeological Bulletin, Vol.32 No.155, 1992, refs., pp.56–60.
The paper presents 19th and 20th century Bushman ethnography to show that these people entered an altered state of consciousness, which most researchers call "trance", to heal the sick, go on out-of-the body journeys, make rain, and transform themselves into animals. Notes that the combination of trance experience with these "supernatural" activities suggests that whatever social differences exist between these Bushman ritual practitioners and those in certain Asian and north American societies, it is appropriate to term them "shamans". Shows that the ethnographic material outlined in this paper forms part of the basis for the further argument, not developed here, that South African rock art was at least in some measure associated with the work of Bushmen shamans.
SOUTH AFRICA; ANTHROPOLOGY; BELIEFS; HEALING; RELI-

GION; RESEARCH; ROCK ART; SHAMANISM; TRANCE
P 930.105 SAA

0222 Lewis-Williams, James David
QUANTO? THE ISSUE OF MANY MEANINGS IN SOUTHERN AFRICAN SAN ROCK RESEARCH
Southern African Archaeological Bulletin, Vol.53, 1998, pp86–97.
The article gives a brief outline of the shamanistic explanation of rock art and discusses other explanations (gender negotiation, fertility statements and approaches from art history) in the light of the shamanistic explanation. Notes that part of the question of how much San art rock art was shamanistic, is resolved by distinctions between polysemy, focussed polysemy and multivocality. Draws further distinctions between eland antelopes, the abstract eland symbol, and specifically contextualised rock paintings of eland. Argues that depictions of eland antelopes are contextualised and therefore focused manifestations of the eland symbol. Concludes that the context of the depictions (rock face and associated images) seen in the light of San ethnography and cosmology, suggest that the art was principally shamanistic; other associations were penumbral and contributed to the affective power of the images.
SOUTHERN AFRICA; ANIMALS; ANTHROPOLOGY; BELIEFS; COSMOLOGY; DANCE; RELIGION; RESEARCH; ROCK ART; SHAMANISM; TRANCE
P 930.105 SAA

0223 Lewis-Williams, James David; Bannister, Anthony
BUSHMEN: A CHANGING WAY OF LIFE
Cape Town: Struik Publishers, 1991, ill., 80pp.
The book contains a brief introduction relating to the history of the Bushmen, their current situation and their traditional hunting and gathering life-style. Links beliefs with the rock paintings and gives details about the religious beliefs of modern Kalahari Bushmen. Shows the effect upon the Bushmen of the misrepresentations about them on the part of outsiders. The bulk of the work is devoted to photographs of every aspect of Bushman life.
BOTSWANA; ANTHROPOLOGY; BELIEFS; PHOTOS; RELIGION; SHAMANISM; TRANCE; ROCK ART
R/B 305.8096872 BUS

0224 Lewis-Williams, James David; Blundell, Geoffrey
FRAGILE HERITAGE: A ROCK ART FIELDGUIDE
Johannesburg: Witwatersrand University Press, 1998, ill., vii, 224pp.
The book is a field-guide to rock art sites in all the provinces of South Africa. Gives details about how to reach the sites and illustrates the outstanding features with explanations as to the possible meaning of the art. Also provides information on the museums which have collections of rock art. The introduction gives the background to rock art in order to make it meaningful to the uninitiated viewer. Shows its ritual significance and how it was produced. Outlines the way of life and history of the artists, and gives details of the research which has thrown light on the art.
SOUTH AFRICA; ANIMALS; BELIEFS; HEALING; RELIGION; RESEARCH; ROCK ART; SHAMANISM; SOCIAL ORGANIZATION; TRANCE
709.01130968 LEW

0225 Lewis-Williams, James David; Dawson, Thomas A.
ART AS A WINDOW TO OTHER WORLDS
S.A. Journal of Science, Vol. 83, 1987, 245pp.
The paper describes the rock art research which has taken place since the 1970s and by means of which new light has been thrown on the meaning and significance of the paintings and engravings. Explains that this art is now considered to be religious and symbolic in nature. Many paintings are believed to represent the experiences of shamans who in the trance state experienced hallucinations and were believed to be capable of harnessing supernatural power. Describes the work of the Rock Art Research Unit at the University of the Witwatersrand where a volume of unpublished sections of the Bleek collection from the Jagger Library in Cape Town is being used to link mythology and rock art. Explains the techniques employed to copy paintings.
SOUTH AFRICA; DANCE; MYTHOLOGY; RELIGION; RESEARCH; ROCK ART; SHAMANISM; TRANCE
99/758

0226 Liebenberg, Louis
A GOOD TRACK RECORD
Geographical Magazine, Vol.71 No.6, 1999, ill., pp.86–87.
The article describes the use of a device (the Cyber Tracker) by means of which animals can be tracked and the data regarding their activities can be fed into a geographical information system (GIS). Shows that the data is then used to create a database of great value in conservation, particularly in wildlife reserves. Explains that the inventor of the device, Louis Liebenberg, has worked with Bushmen for many years and realised the value of their vast store of knowledge on all aspects of wildlife. Describes this as a "mental database". Provides details of a training programme for trackers which enables them to improve their skills and obtain diplomas. Explains that the long-term goal is to establish a core of trained trackers who will spread their expertise throughout southern Africa and beyond. Indicates that eight South African national parks are involved in the scheme. Illustrations show the use of the Cyber Tracker by Bushmen in the field.

SOUTH AFRICA; ANIMALS; CONSERVATION; GAME RESERVES; TRACKING; TRAINING
p 910.5 GMA

0227 Louw, J.A.
THE ADAPTATION OF NON-CLICK CONSONANTS IN XHOSA
Traill, A. Khoisan Linguistic Studies 3, 1977. iii, 169pp., pp. 74–92. ISBN 0854944540.
The paper, one of a series on the influence of Khoi on Xhosa, deals with egressive consonants in Khoi and their cognates in Xhosa. Notes that the informant was a Nama-speaking Damara. Refers to the paper by Meinhof, published in 1905, which was the first study of Khoi loans in Xhosa, and made a substantial contribution to the topic although it contained obvious errors.
GRAMMAR; LANGUAGES; LINGUISTICS; KHOEKHOEGOWAB; XHOSA
496.2709 KHO

0228 Lutheran World Federation
LUTHERAN WORLD FEDERATION WORLD SERVICE BOTSWANA ANNUAL REPORT 1978–
Various volumes.
The reports give details of the work done in Botswana by the Lutheran World Federation (LWF). The report for 1990 notes a shift in emphasis from relief work to integrated development and shows the efforts of LWF to reach the poorest and most marginalised groups and to improve social and material structures at local community level. For the years concerned, the priority areas in which the LWF worked in collaboration with both the Botswana Government and other non-governmental organizations included water supply development in RAD settlements, assisting with small-scale horticultural projects, schemes for dryland farming, and activities aimed at self-reliance. Notes that where the borehole water proved to be unfit for human consumption, water desalination equipment was installed and personnel were trained in its running and repair.
BOTSWANA; CHOBOKWANE; KHWA; MONONG; QABO; UKHWI; ZUTSHWA; DEVELOPMENT AID; DESALINATION; FARMING; SELF-DEVELOPMENT; WATER SUPPLY
R/B 368.8705 BOT

0229 Macdonald, Dave; Molamu, Louis
ALCOHOL ABUSE AMONG THE BASARWA AND THE NEED FOR HARM REDUCTION INTERVENTION STRATEGIES: A PRELIMINARY REPORT
Lane, Paul; Hermans, Janet; Molebatsi, Chadzimula. Proceedings from the Basarwa Research Workshop, Gaborone, 24–25 August, 1995. 2001. 106pp. pp. 76–81.
Paper presented at the Basarwa Research Workshop, held on 24–25 August, 1995 at the University of Botswana. This is a brief report representing the findings of a preliminary investigation into alcohol use and abuse among Basarwa living in the Ghanzi and Kgalagadi districts. Articulates the concerns of workers in both the public and voluntary sectors who have worked closely with Basarwa, of the rate of alcohol abuse in many Basarwa communities. Observes that a number of factors like poverty, unemployment and social marginalization and alienation have contributed to alcohol consumption and abuse among Basarwa. Laments the situation of Basarwa in Botswana which he associates with acute deprivation and exploitation that almost negates their citizenship.
BOTSWANA; GHANZI DISTRICT; KGALAGADI DISTRICT; ALCOHOL; POVERTY
R/B 305.8096872 PRO

0230 Madzudzo, Elias
SAN IN ZIMBABWE
Regional Assessment of the San in Southern Africa, No. 2. Robins, Steven; Madzudzo, Elias; Brenzinger, Matthias. An assessment of the status of the San in South Africa, Angola Zambia and Zimbabwe. Windhoek: Legal Assistance Centre, 2001. xiii, 105pp. pp. 78–106. ISBN 9991676546.
The assessment of the status of the San in Zimbabwe focuses on the San in Bulilimamangwe and Tsholotsho districts. Comments that in Zimbabwe San are a minority group living in the marginal areas of the country. Notes that they are socially, economically and politically marginalised as a result of colonial and post-colonial government policies. Sees the San as locked into a cycle of poverty without such essential facilities as draught power and agricultural implements. Considers that access to these facilities would enable them to successfully change to a sedentary life-style. Finds that the attitudes of San are dominated by self-rejection and hopelessness and that relations with dominant groups are characterised by exploitative client relationships. Notes that natural resource management projects have failed to recognise the San as a group with interests that differ from those among whom they live. Considers that as a result the interests of the dominant groups are given priority over those of the San. Makes recommendations which would enhance the ability of San to overcome their marginalization. Emphasises the value to San of exposure to other San groups in the region in order to learn how to improve their status.
BULILIMAMANGWE; TSHOLOTSHO; ZIMBABWE; ATTITUDES; FARMING; FOOD; GOVERNMENT POLICY; INTERGROUP RELATIONS; KALANGA; MATABELE; NATURAL RESOURCES; SELF-DETERMINATION; REGIONAL COOPERATION
R/B 305.80968 ROB

0231 Maingard, L.F.
THE LINGUISTIC APPROACH TO SOUTH AFRICAN PREHISTORY AND ETHNOLOGY

Johannesburg: South African Association for the Advancement of Science, 1934. 143pp.
The presidential address to the South African Association for the Advancement of Science, reprinted from the *South African Journal of Science*, Vol. 31, 1934, is a reflection upon the contribution which language can make to prehistory and ethnology. Shows how language, prehistory and ethnology are interrelated. Looks at language in general, and at the distinction between isolating and inflectional languages. Points out how a study of the development of a language can help to establish its relationships with other languages, and will reveal their common morphological processes. Compares certain grammatical features in Bushman dialects, Hadza and Sanda of Tanzania, and Hottentot, and finds that they share a common morphological tendency. Considers linguistic evidence for a common language from which Bushman, Hottentot and Sandawe are descended and shows how this fits in with archaeological and historical studies of human migration in Africa. Also reports on the influence of Hottentot upon the Xhosa language.
TANZANIA; ANTHROPOLOGY; ARCHAEOLOGY; HADZA; HISTORY; KHOEKHOEGOWAB; LANGUAGES; LINGUISTICS; MORPHOLOGY; SANDAWE; XHOSA
496.01 MAI

0232 Maingard, L.F.
THREE BUSHMAN LANGUAGES: PART I
African Studies, Vol.16 No.1, 1957. pp.37–71.
The article deals with two languages: dzu/?oa:si (Ju/'hoan), a dialect of !khu (!Kung) and ganakwe (G//ana). The third language mentioned in the title is !ko (!Xoo) to be dealt with in a later paper. Explains that the study of the languages is based on recordings made during the Peabody Museum Harvard Smithsonian Institution Kalahari Expedition in 1955. Comments that notes on the phonology of dzu/'oa:si and a detailed exposition of its morphology, together with supporting texts, reveal the instability of its consonantal system, characterised by extensive fluctuation within certain limits. Remarks on the "double verb", the wide range of juxtapositional constructions and the absence of formatives. Raises the question, in the study of //ganakwe, of the relationhsip, phonological, morphological and lexical, of the Central group of Bushman languages to Hottentot. Concludes that these languages must have had a common origin in pre-historic times.
BOTSWANA; G//ANA; JU/'HOANSI; LANGUAGES; LINGUISTICS; PHONOLOGY; RESEARCH
R/B 496.2705 MAI

0233 Maingard, L.F.
THREE BUSHMAN LANGUAGES: PART II: THE THIRD BUSHMAN LANGUAGE
African Studies, Vol.17, 1958, pp.100–115.
The article deals with !ke (!xoo), the most northerly of the Southern Bushman languages. Outlines the phonology, morphology, the sentence structure and use of enclitics. Includes texts transcribed from phonograph records made in the field, and includes English translations of the text.
BOTSWANA; !XOO; GRAMMAR; LANGUAGES; LINGUISTICS; MORPHOLOGY; PHONOLOGY
P 960.05 AST

0234 Maingard, L.F.
THE KORANA DIALECTS
African Studies, Vol.23 No.2, 1964. pp.57–61.
The article looks at the historical and geographic background of the Korana people and shows where they were located when Gordon described them in 1799. Mentions three separate Korana groups: the Orange River tribes, the Gysiqua, a mixed Korana/Tlaping people, and the tribes of the Upper Orange River. Examines two dialect clusters: !kx?am//?oakwa (eastern) and +?oxoku, =naniku and !kaon (western) and provides examples of the vocabulary of these dialects. Concludes that the eastern group (Transvaal-Orange Free State) and the western group (Lower Orange River) represent two distinct dialectical entities. Notes similarities between Lower Orange River dialects and Nama. Shows that the distinguishing feature of Korana phonology is the initial kx? phoneme which is absent from Nama.
SOUTH AFRICA; !ORA; LANGUAGES; LINGUISTICS; RESEARCH
P 960.05 AST

0235 Maingard, L.F.
THE CENTRAL GROUP OF THE CLICK LANGUAGES OF THE KALAHARI
African Studies, Vol.20 No.2, 1961. pp.114–122.
The article deals with the Central group of Bushman languages which includes Naron, Hukwe (spoken in Angola beyond the Okavango River), Ganakwe and Hietso (Hiechware). Looks at word lists collected by David Livingstone, Dorothea Bleek, S.S. Dornan and the author himself. Concludes that the eastern and western dialects differ and may each form their own subgroup within the Central group, though sharing a common lexical foundation and a similar phonological system.
ANGOLA; BOTSWANA; G/UI; G//ANA; HIECHWARE; KHOE; LANGUAGES; LINGUISTICS; MORPHOLOGY; NARO; PHONOLOGY
P 960.05 AST

0236 Maingard, L.F.
A COMPARATIVE STUDY OF NARON, HIETSHWARE AND KORANA
African Studies, Vol.22 No.3, 1963. pp.97–108.
The article provides a comparative analysis of Nama and Hietsware. Also compares these dialects lexically and phoneti-

cally with /Xam and Korana (the most archaic form of Hottentot). Notes that the relationship of Korana with the Central group of click languages is revealed as closer than hitherto expected. Concludes that Hietsware, Naron and Korana are closely related and must at some point have formed a single ancestral language which later split into dialects.
CAPE; SOUTH AFRICA; !ORA; /XAM; HIECHWARE; NARO; LANGUAGES; LINGUISTICS; MORPHOLOGY
P 960.05 AST

0237 Manhire, Anthony
THE ROLE OF HAND PRINTS IN THE ROCK ART OF THE SOUTH-WESTERN CAPE
South African Archaeological Bulletin, Vol.53 No.168, 1998. pp.98–108.
The paper attempts to reconstruct the body heights of the people who made hand prints and to offer reasons why they were made. Notes that although hand prints are a common feature of rock art in parts of southern Africa, their function and relationship to other paintings are not well understood. In particular, the paper brings together two separate lines of enquiry: a field study devoted to the measurement of hand prints in the south-western Cape, and a population study in the Little Karoo. Notes that the results suggest that the majority of handprints in the south-western Cape were in fact made by sub-adults.
CAPE; SOUTH AFRICA; ARCHAEOLOGY; CHILDREN; RESEARCH; ROCK ART
P 930.105 SAA

0238 Marks, Shula
KHOISAN RESISTANCE TO THE DUTCH IN THE SEVENTEENTH AND EIGHTEENTH CENTURIES
Journal of African History, Vol.3 No.1, 1972. pp.55–80.
The article gives a historical account of the interaction between South African Khoikhoi herders, San hunter-gatherers, and the European settlers. Comments that most historians dismiss the European encounters with the Khoisan as being insignificant because in the author's words: "...history tends to be the history of the successful...", and ultimately the Khoisan were not successful. Shows, however, how complex the relationships were and how in fact, at many points in the chronological record, the Khoisan had the upper hand and were the source of great hardship for the European settlers. Disputes the stereotypical view that the pastoral Khoi disintegrated rapidly when confronted by Europeans while the San fought vigorously and says this is an over-simplification. Argues that the extensive violence permeating South Africa, particularly in the eighteenth century, was largely due to Khoisan resistance to European intrusion. Eventually submission did occur, followed by acculturation, so that ethnic identity was submerged and then virtually disappeared.
CAPE; SOUTH AFRICA; CONFLICT; HERDING; HISTORY; HUNTING-GATHERING; INDIGENOUS PEOPLES; INTERGROUP RELATIONS; KHOEKHOE; KHOESAN; POLITICAL LEADERSHIP
93/166

0239 Marks, Shula
"BOLD, THIEVISH AND NOT TO BE TRUSTED"
History Today, Vol. 31, 1981. pp.15–21.
The article examines the complex nature and origin of racial stereotypes in South Africa. The title of the article is taken from the diary of Jan van Riebeeck, the first commander of the Dutch settlement at the Cape in the 17th century and reflects the attitude of the settlers towards the indigenous peoples they encountered. Notes the tendency of writers to telescope 200 years of history and to ignore the inevitable changes experienced by the Khoi during that period. Warns that it is incorrect to assume that the roots of apartheid are to be found in the events and attitudes of the 17th and 18th centuries. Suggests instead that it originated in the conquest of Bantu-speaking societies in the 19th century and their forcible and unequal incorporation into the industrialised economy of modern South Africa.
CAPE; SOUTH AFRICA; COLONIALISM; HISTORY; HUNTING-GATHERING; KHOEKHOE; KHOESAN
P 905 HTO

0240 Marshall, Lorna
MARRIAGE AMONG THE !KUNG BUSHMEN
Africa, Vol.29 No.4, 1959, ill., map. pp.335–365,.
The article describes marriage customs within the !Kung social organization. Notes the expression of the incest taboo in the avoidance relationships. Looks at bride service, family involvement in marriage arrangements, divorce and extra-marital relationships. Notes that the information in the paper is based on fieldwork carried out in 1952 and 1953 in what is now Namibia.
NAMIBIA; !KUNG; CULTURE; MARRIAGE; SOCIAL ORGANISATION; WOMEN
P 960.05 AJI

0241 Marshall, Lorna
!KUNG BUSHMAN BANDS
Africa, Vol.30 No.4 1960. pp.325–355.
The paper describes the band organization of the !Kung Bushmen of the Nyae Nyae area at a time when there were no other inhabitants apart from Bushmen. Notes that a band consisted of groups living together on the basis of cosanguineous and affinal ties. Notes that to be inhabitable the territory of a band needed to contain sufficient veld food and a permanent or semi-permanent water-hole. Deals with family structure,

settlement patterns, naming rules, band membership and the functions of the headman or "owner" of the water and veld food whose main responsibility was to plan the movements of the group in order to utilise the food resources effectively. Comments on methods employed in order to avoid conflict between individual band members, and with other bands.
NAMIBIA; NYAE NYAE; !KUNG; ANTHROPOLOGY; BANDS; CONFLICT; CULTURE; HUNTING-GATHERING; KINSHIP; MARRIAGE; SOCIAL ORGANIZATION
P 960.05 AJI

0242 Mason, R.J.
HUNTING GEMSBOK WITH GWI BUSHMEN, DOBE AREA
1977. 4pp.
The unpublished pages of an archaeologist's journal of a visit to Dobe in June 1976 contain details of the archaeological techniques employed in investigating Bushman camp sites in the area of the Aha Hills in Botswana. Also describes a gemsbok hunt in which the author participated, and describes the subsequent butchering of the animal and distribution of the meat. Describes the plant foods collected and eaten. Investigations of the camp sites included using information gathered from Bushman informants who had used the sites and knew the location of the huts in the past. The presence of European and non-Bushman artefacts suggest the cultural changes taking place in the community.
BOTSWANA; DOBE; ANIMALS; ARCHAEOLOGY; ETHNOBOTANY; G/UI; HERERO; HUNTING-GATHERING; RESEARCH; SEDENTISM
99/189

0243 Mazel, Aron
DIGGING THROUGH DARKNESS: CHRONICLES OF AN ARCHAEOLOGIST BY C. SCHRIRE
South African Archaeological Bulletin, Vol.52 No.165, 1997. pp.76–77.
The reviewer explains that the writer of the book describes it as a "journey" which concerns the history and consequences of racism as seen through the eyes of a colonial archaeologist. Points out that the writer provides historico-fictitious accounts in addition to factual information in order to reveal "deeper messages which can only be read through acts of the imagination." Contains eight chronicles one of which is entitled "Chronicles of a Bushman". The reviewer recommends the book highly and an editorial note congratulates the author for winning the 1997 American Archaeological Book Award.
SOUTH AFRICA; ARCHAEOLOGY; BOOK REVIEWS; POLITICS; RESEARCH
P 930.105 SAA

0244 Mazonde, Isaac N.
SAN PERCEPTIONS
Regional Assessment of the Status of the San in Southern Africa: Report Series, No.3 of 5. Cassidy, Lin; Good, Ken; Mazonde, Isaac; Rivers, Roberta. An assessment of the status of the San in Botswana. Windhoek, Legal Assistance Centre, 2001. xvi, 170pp., pp.59–70. ISBN 999167652X.
The chapter focuses on the perceptions of other Batswana towards the San. Regards attitude as one of the most important aspects of development because the amelioration of the plight of the San in Botswana is largely dependent upon how they are perceived and treated by the dominant non-San communities. Looks at the question of ethnicity and their status as indigenous people who face similar problems to those encountered by such people world wide. Examines the ethnicity question as it arises within Remote Area Dweller Settlements. Considers the educational status of San children. Comments on the great importance of education because only the educated find a place within the structure of modern Botswana. Recommends various interventions which would benefit the San particularly in the field of education. Notes the necessity for a change in attitude on the part of non-San Batswana if San are ever to take their place as equal citizens in modern day Botswana.
BOTSWANA; ADULT EDUCATION; ATTITUDES; CULTURE; DEVELOPMENT POLICY; EDUCATIONAL POLICY; INTERACTION; REMOTE AREA DEVELOPMENT; SETTLEMENTS
R/B 305.8096872 ASS

0245 Mazonde, Isaac N.
THE SAN IN BOTSWANA AND THE ISSUE OF SUBJECTIVITIES: NATIONAL DISINTEGRATION OR CULTURAL DIVERSITY?
Mazonde, Isaac N. Minorities in the millennium: perspectives from Botswana. Gaborone: Lightbooks, 2002. refs., vii, 136pp. pp.57–71. ISBN 9991271244.
The paper focuses on the attitudes of the non-San mainstream majority population in Botswana towards the San. Shows that only a change in attitude towards the San by the majority group will result in their being accorded the basic democratic rights of freedom, autonomy and the right to be different. Finds that the denial of these rights takes place on three levels: those of the individual, the community and the state. Notes that in the past, San were dispossessed of land, cattle and the right to dispose freely of their labour. Notes that these constitute a major factor in the attainment of economic self-sufficiency and self-determination. Examines how, in the current period, denial of their right to education has similar effects on the San. Gives examples of the problems facing San children in the schools of Botswana. Considers that the decision of the Botswana Government to ignore ethnic origins of the Remote Area Dwellers was a crucial error. Shows how domination of San communities in settlements by other ethnic groups has increased their subservience and poverty. Considers that the

Remote Area Development Programme needs to be revamped in order to take into account the special circumstances of the San.
BOTSWANA; ACCESS TO EDUCATION; ASSIMILATION; ECONOMIC DEVELOPMENT; EXPLOITATION; HISTORY; HUMAN RIGHTS; REMOTE AREA DEVELOPMENT
R/B 968.72 MIN

0246 Mazonde, Isaac N.
THE PRACTICE OF ANTHROPOLOGY OUTSIDE THE UNIVERSITY OF BOTSWANA
1989. 18pp.
The paper covers the Remote Areas Development Research and historical overview of anthropological research in Botswana. Points out that the bulk of anthropological research has been focusing on Basarwa dating back as far as the 1920s. Lists academic researchers who have worked among Basarwa in Botswana from the 1920s to the 70s. Notes that the studies conducted among the Basarwa denote a change in emphasis from a static view of them as hunter-gatherers to a group of people undergoing substantial change in their way of life. For example, as boreholes were drilled in the Kalahari and as more people moved into rural areas, the hunting and gathering Basarwa adapted to the changed circumstances. Also recounts that the Basarwa settled on the peripheries of boreholes as well as towns, raising crops and herding livestock. Concludes that many anthropological studies have been done in Botswana since the 1920s. Initial focus was on the Basarwa, but interest developed to other social groups.
BOTSWANA; !KUNG; !XOO; ANTHROPOLOGY; HUNTING-GATHERING; LIVESTOCK; RESEARCH; SOCIAL ORGANIZATION
R/B 301.296872 MAZ

0247 Mazonde, Isaac N.
MINORITIES IN THE MILLENIUM: PERSPECTIVES FROM BOTSWANA
Gaborone: Lightbooks, vii, 136pp. refs., 2002.
The volume presents revised versions of the papers from the conference entitled, "Challenging minorities, differences and tribal citizenship in Botswana" held in May 2000 at the University of Botswana. It is noted in the Introduction that the current debate on minorities arises from a demand for fair representation by the so-called "minor tribes". Topics raised in the papers include the definition of "tribe", the political and historical events leading to the current situation, and the role of the colonial authorities in the drawing of boundaries and their support of the ruling chiefs. Individual papers are abstracted under the names of authors in this bibliography. It should be noted that a Special Issue of the *Journal of Southern African Studies* published in December 2002 continues with the presentation of some of the issues dealt with at the Minorities Conference.
BOTSWANA; BANGWATO; COLONIALISM; CONFERENCE REPORTS; DEMOCRACY; ETHNIC GROUPS; ETHNICITY; HISTORY; MARGINALIZATION; MINORITY RIGHTS
R/B 968.72 MIN

0248 Miers, Suzanne; Crowder, Michael
THE POLITICS OF SLAVERY IN BECHUANALAND: POWER STRUGGLES AND THE PLIGHT OF THE BASARWA IN THE BANGWATO RESERVE, 1926–1940
Miers, Suzanne; Roberts, Richard. The end of slavery in Africa. Wisconsin: University of Wisconsin, 1998. refs., pp.172–200.
The chapter deals with the institution of *bolata* or serfdom as it existed particularly in the Bangwato reserve during the colonial period. Notes that in 1926, 40 years after the establishment of British rule in the Bechuanaland Protectorate, it was alleged that slavery still existed in the country and the issue led to acrimonious debate between the administration, the Bangwato regent and the London Missionary Society for some time. Gives details about how the relationship between Basarwa and Bangwato changed from one of partnership to that in which one party became virtual slaves of the other. Argues that efforts by the colonial administration to allow Basarwa to dispose of their own labour in fact only gave them the option of taking low-paid employment or left them increasingly dependent upon their former masters. Concludes that the steps taken improved neither their material condition nor their social standing.
BOTSWANA; BANGWATO; HISTORY; MISSIONARIES; SERFDOM
PH/B 306.362 END

0249 Miller-Ockhuizen, A.
ISSUES IN JU/'HOANSI ORTHOGRAPHY AND THEIR IMPLICATIONS FOR THE DEVELOPMENT OF ORTHOGRAPHIES FOR OTHER KHOESAN LANGUAGES
Batibo, H.M.; Tsonope, J. The state of Khoesan languages in Botswana. Mogoditshane: Tasalls, 2000. viii, 169pp., ill.. pp.102–124. ISBN 9991295208.
The chapter discusses the current state of Ju/'hoansi orthography and points out the lessons which can be learnt from the history and current problems relating to this. Considers that those involved in developing the orthography of Ju/'hoansi in Botswana could learn from mistakes made in Namibia. Justifies the current orthography and pleads for its adoption. Considers socio-linguistic implications of using International Phonetic Alphabet symbols rather than roman letters for clicks as is done in the Xhosa and Zulu languages. Comments on the criticisms of Dickens' Ju/'hoansi orthography made by Snyman (1998). Discusses some implications of adopting such an orthography for other Khoesan languages. Considers certain

problems relating to orthographic depth and some inconsistencies in the orthography which researchers considering its use for other languages should be aware of. Emphasises the importance of involving Khoisan speakers in the development of the orthography of their own language.
BOTSWANA; NAMIBIA; G/UI; G//ANA; JU/'HOANSI; LANGUAGES; LINGUISTICS; NARO; ORTHOGRAPHY
R/B 496.1 STA

0250 Moesi, M.
MOGAU KILLING LIVESTOCK IN XHABO
Kutlwano, Feb 1998. pp.6–7.
The article describes how livestock, both cattle and goats, are dying in the Xhabo remote area settlement because of the poisonous *mogau* plant. Reports that some residents are leaving the settlement, having lost all their stock. Describes labour intensive public works by means of which the Ghanzi District Council provides employment to remote area dwellers (RADs). Mentions training in tanning, sewing, knitting and craft production provided by the RADP to boost self-sufficiency of Basarwa. Comments that Basarwa have been the main beneficiaries of the Remote Area Dweller Programme and that their school-going children have been assisted with clothing and shoes.
BOTSWANA; XHABO; LIVESTOCK; REMOTE AREA DEVELOPMENT; SELF-DEVELOPMENT; SETTLEMENTS
99/196

0251 Mogwe, A.
HUMAN RIGHTS IN BOTSWANA: FEMINISM, OPPRESSION, AND "INTEGRATION"
1994. pp.189–193.
The paper looks at both the violation of human rights of Botswana's Basarwa people and the ways in which African women have reacted to western feminist ideology. Sees human rights as necessarily holistic and indivisible. Considers that for both indigenous minorities and women, the very structure of society can be an impediment to the creation and maintenance of a human rights ethos and culture. Considers that forced incorporation of minority groups into the ruling culture is a form of "recolonization" and holds this to be similar to the ways in which, at a global level, the South is being pressurised to conform to the priorities of the North. Calls for a re-examination of this approach.
BOTSWANA; GENDER ISSUES; HUMAN RIGHTS; MINORITY RIGHTS; WOMEN
PH/B 341.481096872 MOG

0252 Mogwe, A.
CENTRAL KGALAGADI GAME RESERVE LAND CLAIM: A PRESS RELEASE
Ditshwanelo, 1998. 2pp.
The press release deals with a meeting between the Minister of Local Government, Lands and Housing and the Negotiating Team, held on September 24, 1998. The Negotiating Team represented residents of the Central Kalahari Game Reserve and comprised members of the CKGR Committee, The First Peoples of the Kalahari (FPK), The Working Group of Indigenous Minorities in Southern Africa (WIMSA), Ditshwanelo: Botswana Centre for Human Rights, and the Botswana Christian Council (BCC). States that the Team was mandated to negotiate with the Government of Botswana on land rights for CKGR residents. The meeting was a follow-up of an earlier meeting on July 30, 1998. Sets out the respective positions of the CKGR residents and those of the Botswana Government regarding land rights. Notes the Minister's refusal to recognise that the Team did in fact represent CKGR residents and his decision to visit the villages in the Reserve to ascertain for himself whether the Team was recognised by what he saw as "legitimate structures" in the villages, some of which have no Village Development Committees as yet.
BOTSWANA; CENTRAL KALAHARI GAME RESERVE; GAME RESERVES; GOVERNMENT POLICY; LAND RIGHTS; LEGAL RIGHTS; SETTLEMENT POLICY
99/769

0253 Mokgothi, Archie
THE GOVERNMENT ROLE IN REMOTE AREA DEVELOPMENT EDUCATION
Oussoren, Otto. Education for remote area dwellers in Botswana. Gaborone: University of Botswana, Research and Development Unit; WIMSA, Regional San Education Project, 2001. 107pp. pp.51–52.
The paper examines government's role in the education of the children of remote area dwellers. Explains the role of government as both to provide access to education for all children and to see to it that they all receive quality education. Comments on recommendations made by the National Commission on Education in 1992 regarding provision of education in remote areas. Notes that in spite of high net enrolment in Botswana's Primary Schools, the children of RADs constitute the major proportion of out-of-school youth. Points out that providing hostels for pupils living far from a school has resulted in many problems. Notes the need to provide teachers in remote areas who are both dedicated and compassionate. Considers the need to include cultural elements in the curriculum and points to the success of the methods used by Thirisanyo Catholic Commission and the Bokamoso Pre-School Programme. Notes the willingness of government to learn from such experiments. Concludes by mentioning the UNICEF project looking at hostels with the aim of redesigning the structures and the system as a whole. Notes that aspects of the edu-

cation system require re-evaluation with schools in remote areas receiving special attention.
BOTSWANA; ACCESS TO EDUCATION; CONFERENCE PAPERS; EDUCATION; EDUCATIONAL POLICY; GOVERNMENT POLICY; HOSTELS; PRE-SCHOOL EDUCATION; REMOTE AREA DEVELOPMENT
R/B 372.7096872 WIM

0254 Mokobane, Mosimaneotsile I.
WASTAGE IN PRIMARY SCHOOLS
Oussoren, Otto. Education for remote area dwellers in Botswana. Gaborone: University of Botswana, Research and Development Unit; WIMSA, Regional San Education Project, 2001. 107pp. pp.37–40.
The paper presents the details of a research proposal aimed at conducting a survey in six Remote Area Dweller (RAD) schools in the Kgalagadi District. Gives the background to the proposed study and the reasons why it is necessary. Sets out objectives of the survey as follows: a) to determine drop out patterns at different levels of RAD schools; b) to explain reasons for drop out at different levels at RAD schools; c) to establish relationships between gender, ethnicity, socioecononmic status and school dropout; d) to determine whether school drop-outs re-enter the school system. Mentions the methodology to be employed, who the beneficiaries of the research will be, and to whom it will be circulated.
BOTSWANA; KGALAGADI DISTRICT; ACCESS TO EDUCATION; CONFERENCE PAPERS; EDUCATION; EDUCATIONAL POLICY; HOSTELS; SCHOOL DROP OUTS; SURVEYS
R/B 372.7096872 WIM

0255 Molamu, Louis; Monu E.; Painter, M.
FINDINGS OF A SOCIO-ECONOMIC STUDY OF THE SETTLEMENT OF ZUTSHWA, NORTH KGALAGADI SUB-DISTRICT.
Commerce and Industry, Ministry of; Department of Wildlife and National Parks, Gaborone, Dec 1995. 85pp.
Report of a study designed as part of a monitoring and evaluation system that focuses on changes in the resources to which people have access, the conditions under which access is granted and regulated, and in what ways the conditions of access influence how people use resources. Points out that community-based natural resource management (CBNRM) attempts to change rules of access to resources in ways that create incentives for conservation and sustainable use of nature. Organises information around the axes of gender, ethnicity, and class. Presents major findings focused on: population; crops and livestock; hunting and gathering; employment and other income sources; productive activities and resource use. Points out that the population of Zutshwa relies principally on: a) crop production and livestock; b) hunting and gathering veld products; and c) employment and informal cash-earning activities for its livelihood. Concludes that concentration of people who continue to rely heavily on hunting and foraging in a permanent settlement contributes to depletion of wildlife and veld product resources. Recommends building local capacity to make decisions regarding natural resource management through revitalization of the extended family groups, as units for a natural resource management committee.
BOTSWANA; ZUTSHWA; ECONOMIC DEVELOPMENT; NATURAL RESOURCES; RESOURCES MANAGEMENT; RURAL DEVELOPMENT; SUSTAINABLE DEVELOPMENT
96/447

0256 Molebatsi, Chadzimula
THE REMOTE AREA DEVELOPMENT SETTLEMENTS AND THE INTEGRATION OF THE BASARWA INTO THE MAINSTREAM OF BOTSWANA SOCIETY: THE CASE OF MASIBIKWA AND MANXOTAE – A RESEARCH PROPOSAL
Lane, Paul; Hermans, Janet; Molebatsi, Chadzimula. Proceedings from the Basarwa Research Workshop, Gaborone, 24–25 August, 1995. 2001. 106pp. pp.82–87.
Paper presented at the Basarwa Workshop, held on 24–25 August,1995 at the University of Botswana. Explains that in 1974, as part of its drive towards rural development, the Government of Botswana embarked upon a programme that came to be known as Remote Area Development Programme (RADP). Further explains that this programme was targeted at the country's citizens who resided in the parts of Botswana that were defined as remote. The intended beneficiaries are therefore referred to as Remote Area Dwellers (RADs). As shown in this paper, the definition of the RADP's intended beneficiaries forms the problem of the author's intended study. Shows how two related factors justify the need for the enquiry, namely, the position of Basarwa within Botswana society and the reported plight of Basarwa in some RAD settlements.
BOTSWANA; REMOTE AREA DEVELOPMENT; RESEARCH; RURAL DEVELOPMENT
R/B 305.8096872 PRO

0257 Monageng, Stella
THE BASARWA BIBLIOGRAPHY PROJECT
Lane, Paul; Hermans, Janet; Molebatsi, Chadzimula. Proceedings from the Basarwa Research Workshop, Gaborone, 24–25 August, 1995. 2001. 106pp. pp.74–75.
This is a paper presented at the Basarwa Research Workshop, held on 24–25 August, 1995 at the University of Botswana. The paper creates an awareness of the existence of the Basarwa bibliography database at the Institute of Research and Documentation (NIR) and also requests the Conference participants to assist in the collection of more documents on Basarwa issues for inclusion in the bibliography. Gives a history of the

establishment of this bibliography and notes its objectives and scope. Explains problems encountered by the bibliographers of knowing exactly what has been published on Basarwa. Appeals to researchers to provide them not only with copies of their papers and reports but also with lists of everything they have produced on Basarwa to enable cross-checking of what has been collected and processed.
BOTSWANA; BIBLIOGRAPHIES; CONFERENCE PAPERS; KHOESAN; RESEARCH
R/B 305.8096872 PRO

0258 Motshabi, Kgosi W; Matenge, B.
THE IMPACT OF PRE-SCHOOL EDUCATION IN THE RAD SETTLEMENTS: A RESEARCH PROPOSAL OUTLINE
Oussoren, Otto. Education for remote area dwellers in Botswana. Gaborone: University of Botswana, Research and Development Unit; WIMSA, Regional San Education Project, 2001. 107pp. pp.41–42.
The paper presents a research project to be carried out to assess the impact of pre-school education in Remote Area Dweller settlements and farms in Botswana. Notes that it is intended to carry out a two-phase study to look at the status of pre-school education, the effectiveness of pre-schools, and how the communities and stakeholders benefit from them. Presents a number of preliminary findings and suggests areas requiring further research. Sees the need to create an environment conducive for learning through the medium of child health and by means of culture-specific and child-friendly pre-schools.
BOTSWANA; CONFERENCE PAPERS; EDUCATION; PRE-SCHOOL EDUCATION; REMOTE AREA DEVELOPMENT; RESEARCH
R/B 372.7096872 WIM

0259 Mphinyane, Sethunya T.
THE 'DIRTY' SOCIAL SCIENTIST: WHOSE ADVOCATE, THE DEVIL'S OR THE PEOPLE'S? PROBLEMS OF DOING ANTHROPOLOGY AT 'HOME': THE CASE OF BOTSWANA SOCIAL SCIENTISTS DOING RESEARCH ON THEIR CULTURAL OTHER, THE BASARWA
Barnard, Alan; Kenrick, Justin. Africa's Indigenous Peoples: 'First Peoples or Marginalised Minorities'? Edinburgh: University of Edinburgh, Centre of African Studies, 2001. refs., xv, 322pp., pp.173–189. ISBN 0952791757.
The chapter deals with the dilemmas which confront a local academic when faced with what she/he will automatically tend to regard as prejudice and propaganda against his/her own government. Looks at the issue of the removal of the Basarwa from the Central Kalahari Game Reserve and the protest campaign against their removal by the organization Survival International. Gives both the arguments of the Botswana Government on why it wishes to have the Basarwa vacate the Reserve and the opposing Survival International case. Indicates the possibility of a hidden agenda on the part of the Government. Suggests that in spite of its apparently well-intentioned reasons for wishing the Basarwa to leave the Reserve, in fact the conflict for the Government is whether mining or tourism will prove most profitable in the reserve. Concludes that the non-Western anthropologist needs to approach his/her discipline in a non-Western manner and also to admit the existence of certain prejudices within her/himself.
BOTSWANA; CENTRAL KALAHARI GAME RESERVE; ANTHROPOLOGY; ATTITUDES; CONFERENCE PAPERS; GAME RESERVES; GOVERNMENT POLICY; INTERACTION; MARGINALIZATION; RESEARCH
R/B 305.80968 AFR

0260 Myers, F.R.
CRITICAL TRENDS IN THE STUDY OF HUNTER-GATHERERS
Annual Review of Anthropology, Vol. 17, 1988. pp.261–282.
The paper examines four categories of critique which have emerged in hunter-gatherer studies since the publication in 1968 of Lee and Devore's *Man the hunter* and notes that questioning of the category "hunter-gatherer" itself has been central to much contemporary work. The four categories referred to consist of: a) optimal foraging theory (socioecology); b) historicist (ethnohistorical); c) comparative sociology in the Marxist and structuralist tradition; d) humanistic approaches including advocacy research of political engagement undertaken on behalf of hunter-gatherers and studies emphasising the insider's view. Concludes that the most effective methods of understanding hunter-gatherer social form have been the reflexive approach and the recent advocacy focus which includes a comparative approach.
ADVOCACY; ANTHROPOLOGY; HUNTING-GATHERING; RESEARCH
99/602

0261 Namaseb, Levi
THE PATTERNS OF LANGUAGE USE AND TRANSMISSION AMONG THE KHOEKHOE SPEAKERS IN THE CAPITAL OF NAMIBIA AND FUTURE TRENDS
Batibo, H.M.; Tsonope. J. The state of Khoesan languages in Botswana. Mogoditshane: Tasalls, 2000. viii, 169pp., ill.. pp.57–75. ISBN 9991295208.
The chapter examines language use and transmission among Khoekhoe speakers in Namibia since independence. Provides background information about language policies of the previous South African apartheid-style government. Notes that during this period Afrikaans was the dominating language of government, the media and education. Traces the linguistic developments taking place since independence, when English became the sole official language. Looks at use of Khoekhoe in schools, the media and in churches. Examines reasons why

some parents have not used their right to choose their own language as a medium of instruction for primary school children. Contends that mother-tongue speakers of Khoekhoe wish to retain their language as a cultural heritage but are often unaware of their rights in this regard. Concludes that there is a need for cooperation by all stakeholders regarding the issue of teaching African languages as a subject in secondary schools.
NAMIBIA; CONFERENCE PAPERS; EDUCATION; KHOEKHOEGOWAB; LANGUAGES; LINGUISTICS
R/B 496.1 STA

0262 Naro Language Team, Gantsi, Botswana
NARO NXARA
1997–2000. 4 page magazine.
This magazine written in the Naro language is part of the Naro Language Programme and is used to teach literate Naro speakers to read their own language. It is a monthly publication and contains many illustrations, puzzles, stories and quizzes.
BOTSWANA; LANGUAGES; LINGUISTICS; NARO
R/B 496.1 NAR

0263 Nawa, Karabo Vincent
REMOTE AREA DEVELOPMENT EDUCATION
Oussoren, Otto. Education for remote area dwellers in Botswana. Gaborone: University of Botswana, Research and Development Unit; WIMSA, Regional San Education Project, 2001. 107pp., pp.43–45.
The paper describes the work done by the Tirisanyo Catholic Commission in early childhood care and education in Remote Area Dweller settlements. Describes the strategies used which included: capacity-building; manpower training; appointment of a full-time community mobiliser, pre-school supervisor and counterpart; curriculum development; promotion of community participation; and the promotion of cultural identity through language and other activities. Reports on the opening of pre-schools in the settlements of Make, Monong, Ncaang, Ukhwi and Zutshwa. Comments on support received from the District Council, the Ministry of Local Government and other government departments and donors. Suggests that local authorities need to assist in enlightening parents on the importance of pre-school education for their children.
BOTSWANA; MAAKE; MONONG; NCAANG; UKHWI; ZUTSHWA; CONFERENCE PAPERS; EDUCATION; PRE-SCHOOL EDUCATION; REMOTE AREA DEVELOPMENT; TRAINING
R/B 372.7096872 WIM

0264 Nettleton, Anitra
SAN ROCK ART: IMAGE, FUNCTION AND MEANING: A REPLY TO A.R. WILLCOX
South African Archaeological Bulletin, Vol.39, 1984. refs., pp.67–68.
The article addresses arguments by A.R. Willcox in his attempts to interpret rock art and assess the validity of J.D. Lewis-Williams' approach. Points out the danger of attempting to understand the art of non-Western cultures in the light of such Western concepts as "art for art's sake". Notes that the entire concept of art may be missing from non-Western cultures. Shows that in these cultures some activities interpreted by Westerners as "artistic" frequently have ritual and cosmological significance. Applies the multi-level interpretation of iconography used by art historians to both the metaphorical and mythological interpretation of Bushman art and finds both acceptable according to this criteria. Concludes that southern African rock art will only be understood in terms of San cosmology.
SOUTH AFRICA; BELIEFS; DANCE; MYTHOLOGY; RELIGION; ROCK ART; SHAMANISM; TRANCE
P 930.105 SAA

0265 Ngakaeaja, Mathambo
DEVELOPMENT AND HUMAN RIGHTS
Gaborone: Ditshwanelo: the Botswana Centre for Human Rights, 1998. pp.144–146.
The report deals with socioeconomic conditions in the following seven Remote Area Dweller settlements: Ukhwi, Monong, Zutshwa, Ncaang, Maake, Ngwatle and Inalego. An overview of the settlements as a whole is followed by a survey of each settlement, providing geographical, historical and demographic data and information on households, living conditions, assets (small stock, donkeys, horses arable land), employment structure, household expenditure, health and nutrition, physical and social infrastructure, development projects and local institutions. Documents the involvement of non-governmental organizations in the settlements. Observes that three ethnic groups coexist in the settlements: Bangologo; Balala and Basarwa, and the fact that they do not share common values, needs or problems, and speak different languages, results in a lack of any sense of community. Notes that this results in the failure of local institutions such as Village Development Committees and Kgotlas to function effectively.
BOTSWANA; INALEGO; MAAKE; MONONG; NGWATLE; UKHWI; ZUTSHWA; DEMOGRAPHY; HEALTH; LIVESTOCK; LIVING CONDITIONS; LOCAL GOVERNMENT; REMOTE AREA DEVELOPMENT; SEDENTISM; SOCIAL CHANGE
R/B 321.8096872 DIT

0266 Nienaber, G.S.
DIE VROEGSTE VERSLAE AANGAANDE HOTTENTOTS = THE EARLIEST REPORTS REGARDING HOTTENTOT (LANGUAGE)
African Studies, Vol.5 No.1, 1956. refs., pp.29–35.
The article enquires into attempts, before 1652, at learning the language of the Hottentots. Notes that the information is

drawn from journals by early travellers to the Cape who occasionally included one or two aboriginal words or personal names. Points out that Sir Thomas Herbert, who compiled a short list of common words, including numerals up to 10, figures quite prominently in the survey. Attempts to prove that the Hottentot words for "Bread" and "Cattle" intended for sale to ships, were loan words derived from Dutch and/or English. Examines an interesting aspect of the phonological system of the Hottentot consonants in this connection.
SOUTH AFRICA; CLICKS; KHOEKHOE; KHOEKHOEGOWAB; LANGUAGES; LINGUISTICS
P 960.05 AST

0267 Nienaber, G.S.
'N LYSIE HOTTENTOTSE WOORDE UIT 1626 = A LIST OF HOTTENTOT WORDS FROM 1626
1962, refs., pp.28–39.
The article, in Afrikaans, with a synopsis in English, is a study of all known old glossaria of Khoi-Khoin up to 1815. Deduces certain "consonant laws" and identifies with certainty 28 of the 31 words listed by Sir Thomas Herbert, who in 1626 produced a list of Hottentot words with English equivalents. Compares Herbert's list (the earliest collection of words in Hottentot) with modern Nama, Kora (!ora) and Griqua, and finds some similarities. Notes that Herbert distinguished between the different click sounds and developed a way of writing them.
CAPE; SOUTH AFRICA
P 960.05 AST

0268 Nienaber, G.S.
THE ORIGIN OF THE NAME 'HOTTENTOT'
African Studies, Vol.22 No.2 1963. pp.65–90.
The article provides an extremely detailed account of various explanations of the origin of the name "Hottentot". Examines first the theories relating to the language from which the name is derived and secondly attempts to assess the validity of the arguments upon which the theories are based. Quotes from many early writers from as far back as 1652 up to the 20th century. Concludes that the name originates from the attempt to reproduce sounds used by Hottentot dancers. Claims that "the name Hottentot originates from a jesting carry-over of an incremental-repetitive formula in a typical dancing song".
CAPE; SOUTH AFRICA; HISTORY; KHOEKHOE; KHOEKHOEGOWAB; LANGUAGES; LINGUISTICS
P 960.05 AST

0269 Norborg, Ake
A HANDBOOK OF MUSICAL AND OTHER SOUND-PRODUCING INSTRUMENTS FROM NAMIBIA AND BOTSWANA
Musikmuseets skrifter, 13, Stockholm: Musikmuseets, 1987, ill., xxii, 454pp.
The handbook contains detailed information on musical instruments of Botswana and Namibia. Includes the musical instruments of the San and Nama peoples and illustrates many of them. Provides details on vernacular names, construction, playing technique, uses, distribution and history for the instruments listed. Gives not only bibliographic references but personal details about researchers whose works provided the information used in the book. Includes an annotated discography of recordings known to the author. Provides background information on the geography, history and ethnic groups of the region.
BOTSWANA; NAMIBIA; /'AUNI; !XOO; ETHNIC GROUPS; HISTORY; G//ANA; G/UI; HAI//OM; JU/'HOANSI; MUSIC; NAMA; NARO
R/B 784.19 NOR

0270 Nteta, Doreen; Hermans, Janet
BETWEEN A ROCK AND A HARD PLACE: FARMWORKERS AND FARM OWNERS IN TWO DISTRICTS OF BOTSWANA: A FEASIBILITY STUDY FOR THE PROPOSED SNV FARM LABOURER'S PROJECT
1997, 47pp.
The feasibility study was carried out at the request of the Netherlands Development Organisation (SNV) with the following objectives: a) to identify the most pressing needs as perceived by farm workers themselves; b) to suggest solutions to these problems which would involve the participation of both farm workers and farmers; c) to identify potential partner organizations and a structure that would be ideal for the project implementation. The following problems were identified: low wages; poor housing; non-existent health care; lack of education; lack of any access to information, e.g. through the radio; need for economic empowerment; need for legislation regarding minimum wages and for legislation which would deal with improvement of their lives in general. Recommendations include appointment of a field officer in Ghanzi to initiate a project aimed at improving the lives of farm workers and the identification of a partner organization to carry out the project with SNV. Suggests establishment of a National Steering Committee to look into overall conditions of farm workers and the holding of a workshop involving all the stakeholders.
BOTSWANA; EXPLOITATION; FARM WORKERS; WAGES
R/B 305.563 NTE

0271 Nthomang, Keitseope
THE BASARWA/SAN QUESTION IN BOTSWANA: COMMUNITY ECONOMIC DEVELOPMENT: CREATING AN OPPORTUNITY FOR EMPOWERMENT

Journal of Social Development in Africa, Vol.14 No.16, 1999. refs., pp.53–67.

Basing its argument on the original objectives of the Remote Area Development Programme (RADP) which included improving incomes, generating employment, and improving general quality of life, the paper suggests the need for modification and application of new alternative strategies to suit the prevailing circumstances of the Basarwa. Notes that from its inception, RADP has been undertaken by government with only limited community involvement. Considers that this has contributed to a dependency on government rather than leading to a momentum of self-standing, sustainable improvements. Explains that community economic development proposed in this paper draws lessons from general failures of RADP and builds on its strengths. Argues that it is necessary to continually review approaches to development of Basarwa communities with a view to overcoming past shortcomings and establishing more effective strategies in the future.

BOTSWANA; DEVELOPMENT STRATEGY; DEVELOPMENT POLICY; EMPOWERMENT; GOVERNMENT POLICY; REMOTE AREA DEVELOPMENT; SELF-DEVELOPMENT

P 361.0096 JSD

0272 Nthomang, Keitseope
EXPLORING THE INDIGENOUS/AUTOCHTONOUS MINEFIELD: SOCIAL POLICY AND THE MARGINALIZATION OF INDIGENOUS PEOPLES IN AFRICA
Barnard, Alan; Kenrick, Justin. Africa's Indigenous Peoples: 'First Peoples or Marginalised Minorities'? Edinburgh: University of Edinburgh, Centre of African Studies, 2001. xv, 322pp. refs., pp.127–143. ISBN 0952791757.

The paper examines the current state of social policies in Africa and notes the extent to which they are subordinate to economic policies. Shows how economic policies based on increasing exploitation of natural resources have had devastating effects upon indigenous peoples throughout the continent as their land has been taken from them for various purposes such as wildlife reserves. Uses the example of the Basarwa in Botswana to illustrate this. Notes that in Africa few states will accept that some of their citizens are indigenous and that therefore international efforts to plead their cause only lead to resentment. Considers that negative attitudes towards indigenous peoples are based on deeply held assumptions about their inherent inferiority. Sees the need for a post-nationalist state model to be developed which would overcome the negative effects of current policies and treat indigenous peoples as equal partners in making policies that affect their own lives.

BOTSWANA; ATTITUDES; CONFERENCE PAPERS; ECONOMIC DEVELOPMENT; GOVERNMENT POLICY; INDIGENOUS PEOPLES

R/B 305.80968 AFR

0273 Nthomang, Keitseope; Rankopo, M.J.
INTEGRATED COMMUNITY ECONOMIC DEVELOPMENT IN BOTSWANA: EXPERIENCES FROM THE MARGINS
Quebec: Black Rose Books, 1997. pp.205–232.

The chapter examines two projects aimed at empowering Basarwa in Botswana, namely the Kuru Development Trust in D'Kar and the Maiteko Tshwaragano Development Trust in Zutshwa. Each is examined in the context of Integrated Community Economic Development, a strategy for the empowerment of marginalised communities. Notes that this strategy has social, economic, political, personal and educational objectives, and that both projects examined fulfil these objectives. Concludes that the success of the two projects is linked with the fact that the cultural values of the communities have been respected. Provides an overview of the Remote Area Development Programme and the role played by NGOs in the projects.

BOTSWANA; D'KAR; ZUTSHWA; COMMUNITY DEVELOPMENT; ECONOMIC DEVELOPMENT; EMPOWERMENT; NON-GOVERNMENTAL ORGANISATIONS; REMOTE AREA DEVELOPMENT

98/409

0274 Nurse, G.T.; Jenkins, T.; Beckman, L.; Hauge, M.
HEALTH AND THE HUNTER-GATHERER: BIOMEDICAL STUDIES ON THE HUNTING AND GATHERING POPULATIONS OF SOUTHERN AFRICA
Basel: S. Karger, 1977, refs., ix, 125pp.

The book reports on the health and biological traits of southern African hunter gatherers, San, Khoi and Negro. Describes the habitat and distribution of these groups and pays attention to hunter gatherers who speak Khoisan languages yet who are genetically Negro. Notes that these include the Barakwengo of north-western Botswana and western Caprivi in Namibia. Deals in detail with the morphology of the three population groups, the medical relevance of the genetic polymorphisms and those which have no medical relevance. Examines hunter-gatherer adaptation to the environment, both physical and psychological. Looks at how settlement patterns and economic patterns affect genetic studies of groups as they settle and relate to different neighbours or become remote from genetically similar groups. Considers possible historical trends which may account for peoples reverting to hunting and gathering when they lose their cattle to strangers.

ANGOLA; BOTSWANA; NAMIBIA; SOUTHERN AFRICA; !XOO; !KUNG; BLOOD; DAMARA; DIET; G/UI; G//ANA; HUNTING-GATHERING; KHOEKHOE; KHOESAN; MEDICAL RESEARCH; NAMA; NARO; PASTORALISM; PSYCHOLOGY

R/B 301.2 NUR

0275 N#OAHN: NEWSLETTER OF THE UNIVERSITY OF BOTSWANA: BASARWA RESEARCH COMMITTEE
Gaborone: University of Botswana, Basarwa Research Committee, 1996–
The newsletter reports on recent research being undertaken, conferences and workshops held regionally and world-wide, and book reviews of recent publications. There are occasional papers on topics relevant to Khoe and San studies. Some issues include the network of those involved or interested in the issues presented in the Newsletter.
BOTSWANA; RESEARCH
P/B 305.8096872 NOA

0276 Okhiro, Gary Y.
A REVIEW OF *TESTAMENT TO THE BUSHMEN* BY LAURENS VAN DER POST
International Journal of African Historical Studies, Vol.20 No.3, 1987. pp.549–551.
The review examines the book written to complement a series of six half-hour programmes for television. Notes that the major portion of the book was written by Jane Taylor. Comments appreciatively on the presentation of a well-written text with excellent illustrations but takes issue with what is described as an apolitical portrayal of San victimization. Finds that both Van der Post's contribution, and that of Taylor, gloss over many of the human rights issues which were evident in the living conditions at Chum/kwe and the reasons for its establishment by the South African Defence Force. Notes that the depiction of San life and society is wrenched from its context and meaning and fails to acknowledge the true reality faced by modern-day San.
BOTSWANA; KALAHARI DESERT; NAMIBIA; TSHUMKWE; ANTHROPOLOGY; ARMY; BOOK REVIEWS; CONFLICT; CULTURE; DANCE; HEALING; INTERGROUP RELATIONS; SETTLEMENTS; SOCIAL ORGANISATION
P 960.05 IJA

0277 Oussoren, Otto
EDUCATION FOR REMOTE AREA DWELLERS IN BOTSWANA: PROBLEMS AND PERSPECTIVES
Gaborone: University of Botswana, Research and Development Unit, WIMSA, Regional San Education Project, 2001. 107pp.
The report contains papers presented at the conference, presents findings formulated by groups, and makes recommendations for the solution of problems and improvement of the current situation. Explains the major aims of the conference as the pooling of expertise and exchange of information in preparation for a regional southern African conference to be held in 2001. Mentions pioneering work of the Regional San Education Programme (RSEP) operating under the auspices of the Working Group of Indigenous Minorities in Southern Africa (WIMSA). Presents results under the following headings: current research and projects; RAD education: voices and perspectives; mother-tongue education and literacy. Articles on these and other topics are separately abstracted under name of the author in this bibliography.
BOTSWANA; ACCESS TO EDUCATION; CONFERENCE REPORTS; EDUCATION; FARM WORKERS; GOVERNMENT POLICY; NON-GOVERNMENTAL ORGANISATIONS; SCHOOL DROP OUTS; SCHOOL ENROLMENT
R/B 372.7096872 WIM

0278 Ouzman, Sven
RAIN FROM THE MOUNTAIN OF ZION
The Digging Stick, Vol.11 No.3, 1994. pp.2–4.
The report identifies the rock engraving site of Thaba Sione. Notes that it has at least 559 engravings depicting a wide variety of religious or shamanistic experiences. Explains that rain-making is an example of a religious belief and practice at Thaba Sione which may provide a link between San rock engravers of the past and Setswana speakers. Looks at correspondences in the rain-making beliefs and practices of the /Xam of the central interior and those of Batswana. Identifies another rainmaking practice at Thaba Sione which comprises both Christians and African faith elements. Concludes that Thaba Sione has been a focus for ancient and modern human activity and has been used for one very specific ritual, rain-making, for a very long time.
SOUTH AFRICA; THABA SIONE; /XAM; ANIMALS; BELIEFS; DANCE; INTERACTION; RELIGION; SHAMANISM
P 930.105 DST

0279 Ouzman, Sven
AN ENGRAVED TOUCHSTONE FROM THE FREE STATE
The Digging Stick, Vol.13 No.3, 1996. pp.1–3.
The paper discusses the Boshof engraving site (Free State, South Africa) which covers an area of 7500m2. Notes that it features a wide range of imagery including antelope, eland, elephant, hippopotamus, ostrich, rhinoceros and zebra. Identifies engravings as having visual significance such as the long horns engraved on an antelope. Notes that this indicates that southern African rock engravings like the paintings relate strongly to San religion. Concludes that the Boshof engraving bears evidence of successive visitations, at least five episodes of which left visible marks. Each mark attracted a further mark, the sum of which has left a complex record of rubbing, engraving, hammering and flaking not found elsewhere at the site.
FREE STATE; SOUTH AFRICA; ANIMALS; HUNTING-GATHERING; RELIGION; ROCK ART; VISUAL PERCEPTION
P 930.105 DST

0280 Ouzman, Sven
A PAINTED FRAGMENT OF BUSHMAN HISTORY FROM QWA QWA NATIONAL PARK, SOUTH AFRICA
The Digging Stick, Vol.15 No.2, 1998 refs., pp.4–7.
Gives reflections of research conducted over 120 years on archaeological artefacts as representations of the ways of life of hunter-gatherers of southern Africa's eastern mountains. Fragments of archaeological artefacts like rock paintings, rock shelters, etc. in the Korfshoek of Qwa Qwa National Park are associated with historical events of the Bushmen and are, therefore, used for a better understanding of their ways of life. Describes different painted episodes to depict Bushmen's ways of doing things in the past.
KORFSHOEK; QWA QWA NATIONAL PARK; SOUTH AFRICA; ART; HISTORY; HUNTING-GATHERING; RESEARCH; ROCK ART
P 930.105 DST

0281 Ouzman, Sven
REPLY TO ELSPETH PARRY'S COMMENT ON 'A PAINTED FRAGMENT OF BUSHMAN HISTORY FROM QWA QWA NATIONAL PARK, SOUTH AFRICA' (THE DIGGING STICK, 1998, VOL.15(2) AND 15(3))
The Digging Stick, Vol.16 No.1, 1999. pp.8–10, refs.
This is Sven Ouzman's response to Elspeth Parry's comment on "A painted fragment of Bushman history from Qwa Qwa National Park, South Africa". The author endorses the fact that people are bound to have different interpretations of archaeological phenomena discussed in his article mentioned above. However, he emphasises that although people are going to have these numerous interpretations, it must be noted that some will be more valid than others. Gives interpretations of some artefacts as discussed in his article to provide a better understanding.
QWA QWA NATIONAL PARK; SOUTH AFRICA; HISTORY; ROCK ART
P 930.105 DST

0282 Pager, Harald
SHADED ROCK PAINTINGS IN THE REPUBLIC OF SOUTH AFRICA, LESOTHO, RHODESIA AND BOTSWANA
South African Archaeological Bulletin, Vol.28, 1973. pp.39–48.
The article reports on the presently known distribution of shaded rock-paintings of southern and central Africa, their stylistic affinities and age. Defines shading as "the graded application of one or more colours which produce a variety of softly merging intermediate tones."
BOTSWANA; LESOTHO; SOUTH AFRICA; ZIMBABWE; RESEARCH; ROCK ART
P 930.105 SAA

0283 Pager, Harald
ROCK PAINTINGS DEPICTING FISH TRAPS IN THE LIMPOPO VALLEY
South African Journal of Science, Vol.71, 1975. pp.119–121.
The article suggests that enigmatic Y shapes depicted on rock paintings in the Limpopo Valley could represent fish traps. Evidence to support this is provided by one painting that shows a fish apparently entering a trap. Points out a resemblance to conical basket fish traps widely used in Africa.
SOUTH AFRICA; FISHING; ROCK ART
P 505 SAJ

0284 Pager, Harald
THE RITUAL HUNT: PARALLELS BETWEEN ETHNOLOGICAL AND ARCHAEOLOGICAL DATA
South African Archaeological Bulletin, Vol.38, 1982. Refs. pp.80–87.
The paper recapitulates the procedure of a ritual hunt practised by the Kxoe San of Namibia and documented by Oswin Köhler (1973). Presents specimens of local rock art featuring similar elements and suggesting underlying beliefs of this kind. Suggests that such rites as this, although extremely rare at present, were more ubiquitous formerly. Notes that the main evidence comprises compositions of severed animal heads reminiscent of those at the sacrificial sites of the Kxoe. Concludes that other elements of the Kxoe rites, namely the application of ritual body paint and the utilization of animal tails and animal legs for magico-religious purposes, also have their parallels in the rock paintings of southern Africa.
NAMIBIA; ANIMALS; BELIEFS; HUNTING; KHWE; RELIGION; RITUALS; ROCK ART
P 930.105 SAA

0285 Pakleppa, Richard
CIVIL RIGHTS IN LEGISLATION AND PRACTICE: A CASE STUDY FROM TSUMKWE DISTRICT WEST, NAMIBIA
2001. 11pp.
The case study examines government actions, community and NGO responses and the surrounding legal context of the Namibian Government's plan to resettle 20,000 refugees to a site in Tsumkwe District West, in Namibia. Notes that the San population of Tsumkwe West consists of !Kung, Vasakela and Mpunga groups, and that the land is the ancestral dwelling place of !Kung while the other two groups were resettled there during the 1980s. Notes that in spite of the fact that the !Kung and Ju/'hoan Traditional Authorities were formally recognised under the Traditional Authorities Acts of 1995 and 2000, government consistently ignores their leaders and has not consulted them even over such a vital issue as the resettlement of refugees in their area. Notes that the struggle of the San in East and West Tsumkwe to protect their land has assisted the communities in the understanding of their rights, the functioning of the legal system and the powers of the State. The Epilogue states that in view of changed circumstances regard-

ing refugees, the government has suspended its relocation plans but has neither negotiated with traditional authorities nor withdrawn the original resettlement plan.
NAMIBIA; !KUNG; GOVERNMENT POLICY; JU/'HOANSI; LAND RIGHTS; LAW; LEGAL RIGHTS; NATURAL RESOURCES
PH/B 306 CIV

0286 Parkington, John
SOAQUA: HUNTER-FISHER-GATHERERS OF THE OLIFANTS RIVER VALLEY, WESTERN CAPE
Southern African Archaeological Bulletin, Vol.32 No.126, 1977, pp.150–157.
The article uses both historical written records from early Dutch travellers in the Olifants River Valley and evidence from archaeological research in the area to suggest seasonal changes in the population of the valley at the time of contact between Soaqua (Bushmen) inhabitants of the valley and Europeans. Records comments of early Dutch travellers to provide evidence of the relationships between Soaqua and Hottentots, and gives details regarding their diet. Shows that archaeological evidence confirms their use of bulbs, fish and small animals, obtained by means of trapping and hunting. Shows the need for seasonal movement which would exploit these resources and suggests that further research on this should be undertaken.
CAPE; SOUTH AFRICA; ARCHAEOLOGY; FISHING; HISTORY; HUNTING-GATHERING; INTERGROUP RELATIONS; KHOEKHOE
P 930.105 SAA

0287 Parkington, John
WOMEN LIKE MEAT BY MEGAN BIESELE: A REVIEW
Social Dynamics, Vol.19 No.2, 1993. pp.149–150.
The review examines Biesele's book in some detail, explaining the play on words in the title in which the word "like" has two meanings – it refers to the fact that the Ju/'hoansi women both enjoy meat and are "meat" in their sexual encounters with men. Points out that the main thesis of the book is that folklore reflects the complementary and competitive relationship between men and women. Commends the rendering of the Bushman folktales into English. Notes two related issues which do not appear in Biesele's book. Although the issue of the revisionist debate is not touched upon, the book seems to suggest that the author considered Bushmen as residual hunter-gatherers. Secondly notes that the issues of metaphor and gender as pervasive forces in Ju/'hoansi expressive life are not dealt with but would help in the understanding of rock art. Suggests alternative readings as to the meaning of some therianthropic rock paintings based on the "women like meat" metaphor.
BOTSWANA; BOOK REVIEWS; FOLKLORE; MYTHOLOGY; ROCK ART
P 300.5 SDY

0288 Parkington, John
RESOLVING THE PAST: GENDER IN THE STONE AGE ARCHAEOLOGICAL RECORD OF THE WESTERN CAPE
Altamira Press, 1998. pp.25–37.
The chapter describes work being done on the history of Stone Age precolonial people in the western Cape of South Africa. Illustrates an approach to seeing men and women in the distant past as actors in a social as well as an environmental arena. Argues that there is a consistency among very different kinds of evidence, written and material, about gender relations among southern African hunter gatherers (San, Basarwa, or Bushmen) for the past few millennia, but that this becomes elusive when we look as far back as the terminal Pleistocene. Suggests three sources from which men and women are clearly visible: ethnographic texts, rock art images, and buried human skeletons. Other archaeological records such as stone tools and faunal remains are described, but the author concludes that evidence from these sources does not provide conclusive evidence of gendered space.
CAPE; SOUTH AFRICA; ANTHROPOLOGY; ARCHAEOLOGY; GENDER ISSUES; HISTORY; PREHISTORY; ROCK ART
98/389

0289 Parry, Elspeth
COMMENT ON "A PAINTED FRAGMENT OF BUSHMAN HISTORY FROM QWAQWA NATIONAL PARK, SOUTH AFRICA" BY SVEN OUZMAN
The Digging Stick, Vol.15 No.3, 1998. p.12.
This is Elspeth Parry's comment on Sven Ouzman's article entitled "A painted fragment of Bushman history from Qwaqwa National Park, South Africa" which appeared in the *The Digging Stick*, Vol. 15 No. 2, 1998. Elspeth Parry questions Sven Ousman's description of some paintings presented in his article. Raises concern that such paintings could be interpreted differently by different people. Offers an interpretation that she hopes will assist in making an accurate analysis of those artefacts.
QWA QWA NATIONAL PARK; AFRICA; HISTORY; ROCK ART
P 930.105 DST

0290 Parsons, Neil
EDWIN N. WILMSEN: *LAND FILLED WITH FLIES: A POLITICAL ECONOMY OF THE KALAHARI*: A REVIEW
Journal of Southern African Studies, Vol.19 No.3, 1993. pp.524–525.
The review shows that Wilmsen's book provides a fresh approach to the peoples of the Kalahari and to the anthropological research by means of which they have become known to the outside world. Notes that in reducing the Kalahari communities to a group without a history and thus outside the normal categories of modern humanity, anthropologists have

failed to realise that the current impoverishment of the Kalahari peoples arose from their subordination to the encroaching farming and mining societies, both black and white. Notes that the second half of the book re-evaluates the anthropology of the Zhu/'oasi or !Kung, looking at them in a regional context. The book is commended for the challenges it poses to both anthropologists and historians to approach their study of the Kalahari in new ways.
BOTSWANA; KALAHARI DESERT; !KUNG; ANTHROPOLOGY; BOOK REVIEWS; HISTORY; INTERGROUP RELATIONS; RESEARCH
P 968.05 ISA

0291 Pfaffe, Joachim Friedrich
LEARNING TO HAVE SENSE: THE JU/'HOANSI WAY OF MAKING SCHOOL: TEXTBOOK PRODUCTION FOR JU/'HOAN LEARNERS BY JU/'HOAN STUDENT TEACHERS
Texts and images of people, politics and power: representing the Bushman people of Southern Africa. Johannesburg. 4th – 7th August, 1994, Johannesburg: University of the Witwatersrand. 1994. 15pp.
The paper describes the aim and outcomes of the Village Schools Project in Eastern Bushmanland, Namibia. Explains that the Nyae Nyae Development Foundation of Namibia and the Nyae Nyae Farmer's Cooperative organise programmes for Ju/'hoansi, one of which is the Village Schools Programme. Gives reasons why such a programme is essential in view of the high drop-out rate of Ju/'hoansi at Government schools and the 90% illiteracy rate in the community as a whole. States that the programme aims to provide basic education for Grades 1 to 3 at community level in Eastern Bushmanland, using mother tongue education, training Ju'/hoansi teachers who will educate their own people, developing a relevant curriculum and teaching material in collaboration with communities. Notes that school facilities built within the communities will allow pupils to be in their home environment but ready to join government schools in Grade 4. Sets out the various stages of the training programme which will utilise a multi-dimensional approach targeting teachers and communities.
NAMIBIA; NYAE NYAE; EDUCATION; LITERACY; NON-GOVERNMENTAL ORGANISATIONS
PH/B 373.96881 PFA

0292 Pfaffe, Joachim Friedrich
FEAR AND HELP IN THE PEDALOGICAL CONTEXT OF DEVELOPMENT OVER EMPOWERING THE NOT-SO-POWERLESS
Lane, Paul; Hermans, Janet; Molebatsi, Chadzimula. Proceedings from the Basarwa Research Workshop, Gaborone, 24–25 August, 1995. 2001, 106pp. pp.36–40.
The paper, presented at the Basarwa Research Workshop held at the University of Botswana from 24–25 August 1995, describes the purpose and organization of the Village Schools Project in Eastern Bushmanland and some insights which arose as the project got underway. Looks at the difficulties faced by young, inexperienced teachers in the context of issues of discipline and corporal punishment of pupils. Examines the situation in terms of two concepts: Holistic empowerment leading to liberating and participatory methodology (HELP), or Forced empowerment leading to antagonistic and repressive behaviour (FEAR). Discusses these approaches in the context of both the Village Schools Project and of the new developments taking place within the Nyae Nyae communities.
NAMIBIA; NYAE NYAE; EDUCATION; EMPOWERMENT; TEACHING; TRAINING
R/B 305.8096872 PRO

0293 Phaladi, Salalenna G.G.
HUNTER GATHERERS AND NON-HUNTER-GATHERERS: A LITHIC ANALYSIS FROM N!OMA, TSODILO HILLS, BOTSWANA
Dissertation (M.A.). Michigan State University, East Lansing, 1991. ill., refs., x, 163pp.
Describes the lithic variability of the site of N!oma, Tsodilo Hills in Botswana. Explains interaction between hunter-gatherers and their neighbours. Points out that N!oma is an agropastoralist site dating from AD 700 to AD 1000. Notes lithic and iron, copper, wild and domestic plant and animal remains. Suggests that shells indicate regional trade. Notes tools and activity areas at the site and that artefacts are made of locally available quartz. Explains that data is insufficient to conclude that lithic artefacts were made by pure hunter-gatherers, agropastoralists or both.
BOTSWANA; N!OMA; TSODILO HILLS; ARCHAEOLOGY; HUNTING-GATHERING; INTERACTION; PASTORALISM; PREHISTORY
TH 305.80968 PHA

0294 Platvoet, Jan G.
AT WAR WITH GOD: JU/'HOAN CURING DANCES
Journal of Religion in Africa, Vol.29 No.1, 1999. pp.2–61.
The article discusses the religion of the Ju/'hoansi of the northwestern Kalahari. Points out that their central rite was the frequently practised curing dance, an all-night ritual. Shows how the dance served as the major means of maintaining solidarity within the egalitarian bands, and of removing conflict, while another means was the sharing of food. Notes that solidarity was maintained through the healing dance, partly because the healing dance itself was a process of sharing, of *n/um*, "curing power", and partly because it served as a ritual of exclusion. God and the deceased were blamed for evil present in the group and were declared *personae non gratae* and refused admission to the dances as unwelcome aliens. Highlights the interest in this religion and ritual for the comparative study of religion by examining the link between the anthropological study of the curing dances and recent anthropological research

on San rock paintings which are now interpreted as reflecting a tradition of San curing dances dating back for many centuries.
BOTSWANA; NAMIBIA; !KUNG; DANCE; HEALING; JU/'HOANSI; RELIGION; ROCK ART; SHAMANISM; TRANCE
P 200.965 JRA

0295 Prins, Frans
RIGHTS OF THE SAN
The Digging Stick, Vol.16 No.2, 1999. pp.5–6.
The paper discusses the handover of almost 40,000 hectares of the Kalahari to the formerly dispossessed Khomani San and the current position of descendants of Drakensberg San. Notes the official opening of San rock paintings at Main Caves in Giant's Castle. Observes that Natal Drakensberg Park has been nominated as a World Heritage Site because it has more than 500 rock painting sites. Explains that the Drakensberg San trekked to the Ermelo area of the present Mpumalanga province. Identifies two communities, though small in number, of Drakensberg San descendants alive today. Summarises the tremendous social change since their departure from the Drakensberg. Looks at the treatment of these people by government officials, which is regarded by them as an ongoing form of colonialism and appropriation of their own heritage. Concludes that the rights of the descendants of the Drakensberg San also need recognition.
DRAKENSBERG; KWAZULU-NATAL; SOUTH AFRICA; COLONIALISM; CULTURE; ROCK ART; SOCIAL CHANGE; TOURISM
P 930.105 DST

0296 Qàè khoèm samaria di ba
CAPE TOWN: BIBLE SOCIETY OF SOUTH AFRICA, 2001.
A Bible story in Naro.
BIBLE; LANGUAGES; LINGUISTICS; NARO
PH/B 496.1 QÀE

0297 Ramore, L.
WOMEN IN DEVELOPMENT IN SOUTHERN AFRICA (BOTSWANA, LESOTHO, AND ZAMBIA): AN ANNOTATED BIBLIOGRAPHY, VOLUME 1: BOTSWANA
1991. 89pp.
The annotated bibliography updates the bibliography on women and development commissioned by the Women's Affairs Unit and published in 1985. The arrangement and coverage differs from that of its predecessor as it follows guidelines set out by the Technical Centre for Agricultural and Rural Co-operation. Subject areas include: agriculture; commerce; economic development; education; employment; health; welfare; legal rights; migration and urbanization; San women and social customs. The bibliography is provided with author and subject indices and contains references to both published and unpublished materials. Items cited are stated to be available in various Botswana institutions but entries are not provided with location indicators.
BOTSWANA; BIBLIOGRAPHIES; ECONOMIC DEVELOPMENT; MIGRATION; WOMEN
92/216

0298 Rampadi, Mama
THE WORK OF THE FIRST PEOPLE OF THE KALAHARI
Oussoren, Otto. Education for remote area dwellers in Botswana. Gaborone: University of Botswana, Research and Development Unit; WIMSA, Regional San Education Project, 2001. 107pp. pp.57–59.
The paper deals with the work of the First People of the Kalahari, a non-governmental organization established in 1992 for the purposes of lobbying and advocacy for the Bushmen of Botswana. Explains that the FPK represents the following groups: Naro, T/oakwena, G//anakwe, G/wikwe and Au/ai. Uses the name N/oakwe for San in Botswana. Indicates that the vision of the organization involves: education of the young generation; participation by the N/oakwe in their own development; enabling N/oakwe to reach high positions in local and central government and their participation in decision-making; recognition of the N/oakwe as a tribe like any other in Botswana; overseeing of all aspects of their human rights; making the organization known world wide. Sets out detailed objectives and suggests how these may be met. Emphasises the importance of education for the N/oakwe if they are to develop their potential. Shows the problems that N/oakwe children face in school and how these may be overcome. Challenges the Remote Area Development Programme to help with placements for school-leavers.
BOTSWANA; ACCESS TO EDUCATION; CONFERENCE PAPERS; ADVOCACY; EDUCATION; LAND RIGHTS; NON-GOVERNMENTAL ORGANISATIONS; REMOTE AREA DEVELOPMENT; SELF-DETERMINATION
R/B 372.7096872 WIM

0299 Rasebotsa, Nobantu
MARU AND BESSIE HEAD'S PLACE IN BOTSWANA
Current Writing, Vol.5 No.1, 1993, refs. pp.25–35.
The article considers the situation of Bessie Head, an English-speaking "coloured" exile living in Botswana who, because of her inability to speak Setswana, was unable to participate fully in the culture of those around her. Deals with the similar situation of Margaret, the deracinated, English-speaking Mosarwa who is one of the chief characters in the book *Maru*. Considers that Head's concern is with the relationship between Batswana and the Basarwa, a people living on the periphery of Tswana society and whose culture is despised and denied. Shows that Head's conclusion is that in the current situation pertaining in Botswana, for a Mosarwa to take her place at the

"finishing line" in the great race for social status and cultural acceptance, she would have to lose all aspects of her own culture as Margaret Cadmore has done.
BOTSWANA; INTERGROUP RELATIONS; LITERATURE
P 820.05 CWR

0300 Reuning, Helmut; Wortley, Wendy
PSYCHOLOGICAL STUDIES OF THE BUSHMEN
Psychologica Africana. Journal of the National Institute for Scientific and Industrial Research, Johannesburg, South Africa. Monograph Supplement No. 7, 1973. 113pp.
The book presents results of psychological testing carried out on several groups of Kalahari Bushmen between 1958 and 1966. Discusses the value of experimental psychological studies on subjects such as the Bushmen. Discusses subjective observations on Bushman psychology recorded in the literature. Contrasts the weakness of such evidence with that provided by means of controlled, experimental methods. Reviews earlier psychological experiments on Bushman carried out by Porteus and MacCrone. Comments that rock art research is a fruitful field which could lead to a deeper understanding of Bushman psychology. Pays considerable attention to methodological questions relating to test design, test development and application. Reports on results of the tests on Kalahari Bushmen which included, inter alia, perceptual tests, tests of intellectual ability, and tests of interests, preferences and creativity. Comments that the resulting data provide little evidence that living in a "limited environment" has had negative effects on the intelligence of the Bushmen. Considers that the meaningful response of the Bushmen to these strange tests given to them in the absence of any formal education or contact with modern technological civilization is "truly amazing."
BOTSWANA; !KUNG; G//ANA; G/UI; NARO; PSYCHOLOGY; RESEARCH
R/B 155.84961 REU

0301 Richard, Phanuel
BASARWA SUBORDINATION AMONG THE BAKGATLA: THE CASE OF THE KGAKOLE FAMILY IN NORTHWESTERN KGATLENG 1920–1979
Project Report (B.A.): University of Botswana. Department of History, Gaborone, 1980. Various pagings.
The thesis discusses relationship between Bakgatla and Basarwa at the Kgomodiatshaba cattle post of the Kgakole family located in the Kweneng District, Botswana. Explains that around 200 Basarwa lived in Kgomodiatshaba before the 1920s. Points out that between 1949 and 1960 the cattle-based economy of the Bakgatla weakened Basarwa reliance on hunting and gathering. Therefore, Basarwa herded and ploughed for the Bakgatla and became dependent upon them for their livelihood. Considers that since independence, Basarwa have not improved economically. Notes that Basarwa cannot plough because they have neither land nor any access to boreholes. Concludes that as a result Basarwa continue to rely on the relief programmes for foodstuffs, clothing and schooling for their children.
BOTSWANA; KGATLENG DISTRICT; KGOMODIATSHABA; KWENENG DISTRICT; BAKGATLA; BANGWATO; FARMING; HISTORY; INTERACTION; POVERTY
TH 323.1096872 RIC

0302 Riches, D.
HUNTER-GATHER STRUCTURAL TRANSFORMATION
The Journal of the Royal Anthropological Institute (incorporating Man), New Series, Vol. 1. 1995. pp. 679–701.
The paper illustrates a methodology for addressing structural transformations using material from hunting-gathering societies. Shows that a proper account of the transformation between types of social structure is in three basic steps and sets out these steps in detail. Uses three types of hunting-gathering social structure to highlight the contrasting principles of structuring that pertain to the Eskimo/Bushman, Northwest Coast Indian and Australian. Shows that the Eskimo/Bushman institutions are informed by information structuring while Northwest Coast Indian and Australian are informed more by "authority structuring" and that in terms of legitimacy this is a radical difference.
BOTSWANA; ANTHROPOLOGY; HUNTING-GATHERING; RESEARCH; SOCIAL ORGANISATION
98/1132

0303 Richter, L.M.
INFANT GROWTH IN TWO SAN (BUSHMAN) TRIBES
South African Journal of Science, Vol. 84 No. 9, 1988. pp. 763–765.
The paper reports on research carried out in 1985 on infants of two Bushman groups, Kxoe and Kwengo, or Sekele, who were living in the Camp Omega military base. Notes that the weights and lengths of 52 San infants from two tribes were measured. Observes that birth dates were taken from hospital records and that from a very early age, the children were significantly shorter than American reference values and remained at a constant low level until the end of the second year. Reports that the children were also lighter than the reference group, although not significantly so. Finds that there was a definite trend for weight to deviate increasingly from expected values, indicating a much slower rate of weight gain. Concludes that the smallness of the inputs was interpreted as being consistent with long-term growth adaptation to adverse environmental conditions.
NAMIBIA; !KUNG; CHILDREN; KHWE; MEDICAL RESEARCH
P 505 SAJ

0304 Ritchie, C.
UPDATE ON THE STATUS OF BUSHMANLAND
Cultural Survival Quarterly, Vol. 12 No.3, n.d. pp.34–39.
The update focuses on the uncertain position of the Ju/wasi in their traditional area in pre-Independence Namibia. Notes that the problem stems from the lack of definition on the status of Bushmanland and the conflict of interests between the Department of Nature Conservation and the Department of Agriculture. Comments that restrictions have been placed on cattle farming in some areas of the district. Concludes that the only answer to the problems faced by the Ju/wasi seems to be for those who have moved back to their traditional lands from the overcrowded Tshumkwi settlement to occupy and farm their land as soon as possible. The paper also includes a tribute to =Toma, a well known Ju/wasi elder and one of the informants of the Marshall family when they visited the area.
NAMIBIA; NYAE NYAE; TSHUMKWE; FARMING; GOVERNMENT POLICY; JU/'HOANSI; LIFE STORIES; NATURE CONSERVATION
99/181

0305 Rivers, Roberta
THE POLITICAL STATUS OF SAN IN BOTSWANA
Regional Assessment of the Status of San in Southern Africa: Report Series, No.3 of 5. Cassidy, Lin; Good, Ken; Mazonde, Isaac; Rivers, Roberta. An assessment of the status of the San in Botswana. Windhoek, Legal Assistant Centre, 2001. xvi, 170pp. pp.41–58. ISBN 999167652X.
The chapter on the political status of the San in Botswana commences with a historical review in which key reports of the 1970s to 1990s are discussed. Considers the issue of San access to natural resources, the establishment of projects based on the sustainable use of natural resources, and tourism, as a source of income. Notes that though some San may have been elected onto the Ghanzi District Council, their efforts to speak on behalf of their communities often meet with hostility from other Batswana. Observes that outspoken representatives have been removed from office and replaced with more submissive ones. Concludes that the political position of San in Botswana remains weak. Considers that such advocacy groups as the Working Group of Indigenous Minorities in Southern Africa and the First People of the Kalahari are doing valuable work. Makes recommendations which would assist the San in enhancing their political status and empowering their communities.
BOTSWANA; GHANZI DISTRICT; ATTITUDES; GOVERNMENT POLICY; INTERACTION; LAND RIGHTS; LOCAL GOVERNMENT; NATURAL RESOURCES; NON-GOVERNMENTAL ORGANISATIONS; POLITICAL LEADERSHIP; POLITICS; TOURISM
R/B 305.8096872 ASS

0306 Robins, Steven
NGOS, 'BUSHMEN' AND DOUBLE VISION: THE NOT EQUAL KHOMANI SAN LAND CLAIM AND THE CULTURAL POLITICS OF 'COMMUNITY' AND 'DEVELOPMENT' IN THE KALAHARI
Journal of Southern African Studies, Vol.27 No.4, 2001, pp.833–853.
The article focuses on the ambiguities and contradictions of donor and NGO development discourses in relation to local constructions of "community", cultural authenticity and San identity. Deals specifically with the cultural politics of the successful 1999 Khomani San land claim in the Northern Cape Province of South Africa. Investigates local responses to state, NGO and donor discourses on indigenous identity and "cultural survival". Shows how strategic narratives of community solidarity, social cohesion, and cultural continuity were produced by claimants and their lawyers during this process. Notes however, that in the post-settlement period, social fragmentation and intra-community conflict between "traditionalists" and "Western Bushmen" became increasingly evident. Suggests that these divisions were also a product of the contradictory objectives of NGOs and donors to provide support for traditional leadership, San language and "cultural survival", and to inculcate modern/Western ideas and democratic practices. Furthermore, despite the thoroughly hybridised character of contemporary San identity, knowledge and practices, San traditionalists appeared to stabilise "Bushman" identity by recourse to notions of a "detribalised Other" – the "Western Bushmen" living in their midst. Points out that the "traditionalist" versus "western bushman" dichotomy is itself at the heart of donor and NGO development agendas. Consequently, the donor double vision of the San – as both "First Peoples" and modern citizens-in-the-making – contributed to these intra-community divisions and conflicts.
NORTHERN CAPE; SOUTH AFRICA; KHOMANI; INDIGENOUS PEOPLES; LAND RIGHTS; LANGUAGES; LEADERSHIP; POVERTY
P 968.05 JSA

0307 Robins, Steven
AN ASSESSMENT OF THE STATUS OF THE SAN IN SOUTH AFRICA, ANGOLA, ZAMBIA AND ZIMBABWE
Regional assessment of the San in southern Africa, No.2. Robins, Steven; Madzudzo, Elias; Brenzinger, Matthias. An assessment of the status of the San in South Africa, Angola, Zambia and Zimbabwe. Windhoek: Legal Assistance Centre, 2001. xiii, 105pp.
The volume contains information on each of the countries listed in the title. These reports are separately abstracted under the authors. The volume also contains summaries of the information on South Africa, Angola and Zambia and notes the dearth of any current information on the situation of San in Angola owing to the war there. Reports on interviews conducted with refugees from Angola who had fled to Namibia and Zambia in 1999 which resulted in the recording of oral history.

ANGOLA; SOUTH AFRICA; ZAMBIA; ZIMBABWE; HISTORY; ORAL HISTORY
R/B 305.80968 ROB

0308 Robins, Steven
SAN IN SOUTH AFRICA
Regional assessment of the San in aoutbern Africa, No.2. Robins, Steven; Madzudzo, Elias; Brenzinger, Matthias. An assessment of the status of the San in South Africa, Angola, Zambia and Zimbabwe. Windhoek: Legal Assistance Centre, 2001. xiii, 105pp. pp.1–5.1. ISBN 9991676546.
The assessment of the status of the San in South Africa focuses on the two major communities; the !Xu and Khwe, living near Kimberley and the =Khomani located on the outskirts of the Kalahari Gemsbok National Park Aims to provide baseline information on the socio-economic and political situation of the South African San. Also gives a historical outline of the communities described. Examines the nature of the problems facing these communities, and in the case of the =Khomani, of the role being played by the South African San Institute (SASI) to assist them. Notes key programmes of SASI as advocacy, provision of legal resources, research and development, cultural programmes and tourism. Recommendations include addressing socio-economic issues by the San themselves, and confronting dependency and paternalism. Outlines the community development challenges confronting both groups of San.
SCHMIDTSDRIFT; SOUTH AFRICA; =KHOMANI; !XUN; COMMUNITY DEVELOPMENT; KHWE; LAND RIGHTS; NON-GOVERNMENTAL ORGANISATIONS; POLITICS; REGIONAL COOPERATION; SELF-DETERMINATION
R/B 305.80968 ROB

0309 Robins, Steven
WHOSE 'CULTURE'/WHOSE 'SURVIVAL'? THE =KHOMANI LAND CLAIM AND THE CULTURAL POLITICS OF 'COMMUNITY' AND 'DEVELOPMENT' IN THE KALAHARI
Barnard, Alan; Kenrick, Justin. Africa's Indigenous Peoples: 'First Peoples or Marginalised Minorities'? Edinburgh: University of Edinburgh, Centre of African Studies, 2001. xv, 322pp. pp.229–253. ISBN 0952791757.
The paper examines a series of issues which have arisen in relation to the land claims process by means of which =Khomani San successfully negotiated return of their ancestral land in the mid 1990s. Situates the discussion within the framework of the current unhappy socio-economic situation of the community. Notes that this is in strong contrast to earlier descriptions of a harmonious and culturally unified group. Focuses on how the land claim process contributed to leadership struggles and divisions between "traditional" and "Western" San. Notes that the markers of San authenticity insisted on by "traditional" =Khomani actually applies to few of the group. Examines the roles of international donors and local NGOs in the promotion of San as "First Peoples". Considers that South African NGOs are challenged to seek the empowerment of all marginalised rural communities irrespective of their ethnic background.
KALAHARI GEMSBOK NATIONAL PARK; SOUTH AFRICA; =KHOMANI; ADVOCACY; ATTITUDES; CONFERENCE PAPERS; EMPOWERMENT; LAND RIGHTS; NON-GOVERNMENTAL ORGANISATIONS; POVERTY; SELF-DETERMINATION; SOCIAL CHANGE
R/B 305.80968 AFR

0310 Rogers David
A TALE OF THREE CAVES
Getaway, Vol. 6 No.5, Aug 1994, ill. pp.103–110.
The article describes the rock paintings in three Drakensberg caves: Battle Cave, near Injasuti, Main Caves, Giant's Castle and Game Pass Shelter. Explains the widely recognised relationship between trance dances, shamans and Bushman paintings which has been revealed as a result of research by David Lewis-Williams and Thomas Dowson. Looks at the paintings in the three caves in the light of these insights.
DRAKENSBERG; KWAZULU-NATAL; SOUTH AFRICA; BELIEFS; DANCE; HEALING; RELIGION; RESEARCH; ROCK ART; SHAMANISM
98/764

0311 Ross, Robert
ALAN BARNARD – HUNTERS AND HERDERS OF SOUTH AFRICA: A COMPARATIVE ETHNOGRAPHY OF THE KHOISAN PEOPLES; ROBERT GORDON – THE BUSHMAN MYTH: THE MAKING OF A NAMIBIAN UNDERCLASS: REVIEWS
African Affairs: the Journal of the Royal African Society, Vol.92 No.368, 1993. pp.468–470.
Reviews two books on the Khoisan, both published in 1992. Describes Barnard's book as both "an encyclopaedic compendium of Khoisan ethnography and an attempt at structuralist comparison between the various ethnographies". Notes this author's use of comparative, structuralist arguments to assume the existence of a Khoisan cultural system coinciding with the Khoisan language area. Commends the book for its immense value in providing description and comparison of Khoisan ethnography. With regard to Gordon's book, shows how myths come about and that stereotypes of the Bushmen were partly the cause and partly the justification for their oppression and murder in Namibia. Reveals how these myths changed during the colonial period.
NAMIBIA; SOUTHERN AFRICA; ANTHROPOLOGY; BOOK REVIEWS; CULTURE; HISTORY; KHOESAN; INTERACTION; RESEARCH
P 960.05 AAF

0312 Rudner, Jalmar
THE USE OF STONE ARTEFACTS AND POTTERY AMONG THE KHOISAN PEOPLES IN HISTORIC AND PROTOHISTORIC TIMES
South African Archaeological Bulletin, Vol.34, 1979. pp.3–17.
The paper attempts to trace the use of both stone artefacts and pottery among Khoisan in historic and protohistoric times and to show their use of either Smithfield or late Wilton tool kits. Looks at the distribution of Khoisan groups throughout the region as indicated from historical records. Examines historical and ethnological evidence for use of stone tools by Bushman and some Hottentot groups, as well as the use of pottery by both groups. Concludes that eastern Bushmen used a Late Smithfield tool kit and made grass-tempered and stamp-decorated pottery up till the end of the 19th century while early Hottentots of the southern and western Cape, Gordonia, Griqualand West and Namibia used a Final Wilton tool-kit and made well-fired, thin-walled pottery with a stone temper. Considers that contemporary Hottentot-speaking Bushmen of Botswana and Namibia may be descended from hunter-gatherer proto-Hottentot ancestors of pastoral Hottentots.
BOTSWANA; NAMIBIA; ARCHAEOLOGY; MATERIAL CULTURE; PASTORALISM; PREHISTORY
P 930.015 SAA

0313 Rudner, Jalmar
"BELIEVING AND SEEING: SYMBOLIC MEANINGS IN SOUTHERN SAN ROCK PAINTINGS": A REVIEW. JAMES DAVID LEWIS-WILLIAMS
South African Archaeological Bulletin, Vol.37, 1982. p.48.
This review of James David Lewis-Williams' revised Ph.D. thesis shows the value of work on material in the Bleek and Lloyd collection and the paper by J.M. Orpen on the meaning of Bushman rock art. Notes that these studies led to the surmise about its symbolic meaning. Points out that use of both historical writings and current ethnography led to the realization that there is a close relationship between findings which could also be applied to rock art. Notes that the book examines and dismisses earlier theories on the significance of rock art and that the second part deals with the importance of the eland in the belief system of the Bushmen.
SOUTHERN AFRICA; ANIMALS; BELIEFS; BOOK REVIEWS; DANCE; RELIGION; ROCK ART; SHAMANISM; TRANCE
P 930.105 SAA

0314 Rudner, Jalmar; Rudner, Ione
THE HUNTER AND HIS ART: A SURVEY OF ROCK ART IN SOUTHERN AFRICA
Pasadena: Munger Africana Library, 1974, ill., maps, 60 col. Plates, refs. xi, 278pp.
The book provides a detailed survey of the rock art of southern Africa and is lavishly illustrated. Commences with the rock art of Europe, comparing it with that of Africa and indicating the geographical distribution of rock art throughout Africa. Explains methodology employed in attempting to date both rock paintings and engravings. Discusses the problem of the relationship between painters and engravers and provides evidence that in some areas both forms of rock art were carried out at the same time. Notes that the use of either painting or engraving was often related to the availability of suitable surfaces. Looks at the techniques employed by both painters and engravers, pigments used in painting, and the most common subjects depicted. Concludes that the art may have had a number of purposes which can no longer be deduced. Attempts to establish the race of the people shown in paintings and finds that while Bushmanoid types are most common, Negroid, Bergdama and Caucasoid types are also depicted. Reports on linguistic research on Hottentot and Bushman languages which indicates the relationship between peoples and their movements and geographical distribution.
ANGOLA; BOTSWANA; LESOTHO; NAMIBIA; SOUTH AFRICA; ZAMBIA; ARCHAEOLOGY; HISTORY; RESEARCH; ROCK ART
R/B 759.0113 RUD

0315 SASI (South African San Institute) Annual Review, 2001–2002
2001. 64pp.
The review documents the work carried out by the South African San Institute during the period under review. Defines the mission of SASI as being a non-governmental organization which mobilises resources for the San people of South Africa as mandated by WIMSA, the Working Group of Indigenous Minorities in Southern Africa and other San organizations. Notes as a milestone the establishment in 2002 of the San Council, a body focussing on issues of heritage, economic and social and communication. Also reports on the culture and heritage programme, legal programme and the tourism management programme. Notes that SASI has contacts with indigenous bodies and with the UN Permanent Forum on Indigenous Issues and membership of the Indigenous Peoples of Africa Co-ordinating Committee (IPAC).
SOUTH AFRICA; SOUTHERN AFRICA; CULTURE; DEVELOPMENT PROJECTS; EDUCATION; KHWEDAM; SELF-DETERMINATION; TRAINING
R/B 305.80968 SAS

0316 Sadler, Katherine
GENDER AMBIGUITY IN PRIMARY SOURCE MATERIAL: THE USE OF SOUTHERN AFRICAN ROCK ART
Ufahamu, Vol.19 No.15, 1990/91. refs. pp.112–129.
The paper looks at rock art as a primary historical source for understanding San culture. Uses the controversial "White Lady of the Brandberg" as a prime example of how Western research-

ers may see cultural productions of other races from their own perspective. Shows that the questioning of the Abbe Beuil's interpretation of this figure as female because she carries a bow, exemplifies attempts to apply Western notions of labour and gender roles to the art of non-Western peoples. Provides other examples of this tendency and indicates that San women who were expert trackers could provide useful information to male hunters about whereabouts of prey animals and were equally involved with men in the shamanistic role. Considers that regarding any rock art painting of a human being carrying a bow as automatically depicting a male denies the role of women in the above activities.
NAMIBIA; SOUTHERN AFRICA; ARCHAEOLOGY; BELIEFS; CULTURE; DANCE; HUNTING-GATHERING; RELIGION; RITUALS; ROCK ART; TRANCE; WOMEN
P 960.05 UFA

0317 Sadr, Karim
KALAHARI ARCHAEOLOGY AND THE BUSHMEN DEBATE
Current Anthropology, Vol. 38 No 1, Feb 1997. pp.104–112.
The paper deals with the "Kalahari Debate" and questions the conclusions reached by its main proponents, Denbow and Wilmsen. Considers that the claim that from the 6th to 11th centuries the Bushmen were in contact with an Early Iron Age cattle herding hierarchy and encapsulated within it, is doubtful. Notes the evidence supporting this hypothesis: a) Bushman materials found in Iron Age sites; b) Iron Age items found in Bushman sites, and the Tsodilo Hills rock paintings which are said to depict cattle being herded by Bushmen. Concludes that close examination of the archaeological evidence does not provide conclusive proof of Bushman encapsulation within an Early Iron Age society, nor do comparisons with similar sites in the Western Cape. Suggests also that the many depictions of Bushmen herding cattle at Tsodilo are open to many different interpretations.
BOTSWANA; TSODILO HILLS; ARCHAEOLOGY; CATTLE; EARLY IRON AGE; PASTORALISM; REVISIONISM
99/807

0318 Sadr, Karim
BASARWA ARCHAEOLOGY
Lane, Paul; Hermans, Janet; Molebatsi Chadzimula Proceedings from the Basarwa Research Workshop, Gaborone, 24–25 August, 1995. 2001. refs. 106pp. pp.21–25.
The article explains that ethnological research in the Kalahari since the 1950s portrayed Basarwa as hunter-gatherers who had not changed since palaeolithic times. Notes that during the 70s and 80s the image of the Basarwa was revised, producing instead a picture of the Basarwa as encapsulated herder-hunter clients in the Iron Age political economy of southern Africa. Discusses the idea that this model of Basarwa encapsulation rests upon three lines of archaeological evidence which are: a) rock paintings in the Tsodilo Hills which support the idea of Basarwa as herder-clients; b) wild game remains and stone tools found at some of the iron age centres, indicative of Kalahari commodities extracted from the Basarwa; c) metal, pottery, and remains of cattle found in Late Stone Age sites representing presentations offered by the Iron Age centres in return for the sandveld commodities. Concludes that 1500 years ago the erstwhile Late Stone Age Basarwa hunter-gatherers of the Kalahari became herder-hunter clients of the Iron Age polities.
BOTSWANA; TSODILO HILLS; ANIMALS; ECONOMY; HERDING; HUNTING-GATHERING; IRON AGE; POLITICAL SYSTEMS; ROCK ART
R/B 305.8096872 PRO

0319 Sampson, Clavil Garth
STYLISTIC BOUNDARIES AMONG MOBILE HUNTER-FORAGERS
Smithsonian series in archaeological inquiry. Washington: Smithsonian Institution, c1988. ill., refs. 186pp.
The book reports on archaeological research conducted in the Seacow Valley area of the Northern Cape. Provides information on the valley wide distribution of Bushman decorative pottery over an area of 2,000 sq. kilometres. Presents a methodology for tracing band territories by examining the archaeological surface trace left by mobile hunter-forager societies. Notes that the large area involved, taken as a single sample, provides a database permitting innovative modelling of prehistoric hunter-forager organization and the exploration of the role of decorative style as a means of establishing group identity of hunter-foragers.
NORTHERN CAPE; SOUTH AFRICA; ARCHAEOLOGY; CULTURE; HUNTING-GATHERING; MATERIAL CULTURE; PREHISTORY
968.004961 SAM

0320 Sampson, Clavil Garth
TAPHONOMY OF TORTOISES DEPOSITED BY BIRDS AND BUSHMEN
Journal of Archaeological Science, Vol.27 No.9, 2000. pp.779–788.
The article explains that in the semi-arid Karoo of South Africa's central plateau, tortoises are commonly preyed upon by raptors, some of which roost on ledges in the backs of small rock shelters. In the past, any suitable ledge could be occupied if the shelter was not in use by Bushman hunter-gatherers. Thus, both agents could have contributed tortoise elements to the faunal deposits which accumulated in the shelter fills over the past two millennia. Element survival and breakage rates of tortoise remains in a recent shelter roost accumulation show reversed frequencies to those for tortoise carcasses left at raptor kill sites: what is abundant at the roost (skeletal

elements, particularly from the neck and head) are scarce at the kills. When the roost sample is compared with the Bushman foodwaste sample beneath it, the two are readily distinguished by their element composition and condition. A surface sample from a neighbouring shelter without roosting ledges is also rich in skeletals, but lacks the characteristic cranials and vertebrae. Small carnivores are the suspected non-human agents. Although radiocarbon dates indicate an earlier hiatus in this sequence, no such raptor-like tortoise assemblages are detectable at this level.
SOUTH AFRICA; ARCHAEOLOGY; FOOD
P 930.105 JAS

0321 Sanders, A.J.G.M.
THE BUSHMEN OF BOTSWANA: FROM DESERT DWELLERS TO WORLD CITIZENS
Africa Insight, Vol.19 No.3, 1989. ill., map, refs. pp.174–182.
The article surveys the current situation of Bushmen in Botswana. Looks at the major features of their traditional life-style. Notes how this has been affected by the incursion of Tswana-speaking cattle-owners and white farmers into the areas previously inhabited solely by Bushmen. Looks at aspects of Bushman social life which can be defined as "law" and at their position both under the national law of Botswana and under international law. Concludes that only by consultation with the people concerned will their special needs and concerns be equitably addressed.
BOTSWANA; LAW; RESETTLEMENT; SOCIAL CHANGE; SOCIAL ORGANISATION
PH/B 305.8096872 SAN

0322 Sands, Bonny E.
COMPARISON AND CLASSIFICATION OF KHOISAN LANGUAGES
Language history and linguistic description in Africa. Trenton: Africa World Press, Inc., 1998. x, 316pp. pp.75–85, ISBN 0865436320.
The paper examines the hypothesis that there is a shared set of noun class markers which can account for similarities in root formation between !Xoo, Naro, !Xu and Sandawe. Suggests that initial analysis of these languages indicates that all coda vowels and consonants and second syllables of vowels may have once been separate morphemes. Notes that there is less data available on Hadza and Sandawe, so that apparent differences in relatedness may be due to lack of data and not to a difference in degree of relatedness. Considers that additional initial analysis of verbs and nouns may provide evidence of an earlier shared system.
SOUTH AFRICA; TANZANIA; !XOO; !XUN; GRAMMAR; HADZA; KHOEKHOEGOWAB; KHOESAN; LANGUAGES; LINGUISTICS; NAMA
R/B 496 LAN

0323 Saugestad, Sidsel
THE NEED FOR STANDARDISATION OF REFERENCES TO KHOESAN LANGUAGES: A USER'S PERSPECTIVE
Batibo, H.M.; Tsonope, J. The state of Khoesan languages in Botswana. Mogoditshane: Tasalls, 2000. viii, 169pp. refs., ill. pp.163–169. ISBN 9991295208.
The paper outlines problems encountered when attempting to indicate the correct name of a Khoesan language. Suggests the urgent need for a proper mapping of Khoesan languages and dialects, and for the development of a simple, standardised taxonomy and orthography. Notes that such a project would have to provide both an overview of this whole language area and attempt to trace the interwoven patterns and minute details of the language groups and dialects. Illustrates the difficulties of correctly assigning language names by describing the problems encountered by the compilers of *The Khoe and San: an annotated bibliography*. Gives details about the Bibliography Project and its associated collection in the University of Botswana Library. Records the decisions taken in the attempt to standardise the terminology and orthography employed for the Subject Keywords used in the Bibliography. Provides details of the working terminology developed for this purpose.
BOTSWANA; BIBLIOGRAPHIES; CLICKS; CONFERENCE PAPERS; KHOESAN; LANGUAGES; LINGUISTICS; ORTHOGRAPHY; RESEARCH; TERMINOLOGY
R/B 496.1 STA

0324 Saugestad, Sidsel
BACKGROUND TO THE BASARWA RESEARCH PROGRAMME
Lane, Paul; Hermans, Jane; Molebatsi, Chadzimula. Proceedings from the Basarwa research workshop, Gaborone. 24–25 August, 1995. 2001. 106pp. pp58–63.
This is a paper on Basarwa Research Programme presented by Sidsel Saugestad at the Basarwa Research Workshop held at the University of Botswana from 24–25 August, 1995. Paper gives a full description of the history of how the Basarwa Research Programme started, and its development and status at the University of Botswana. Notes research challenges that they have been faced with. Refutes allegations that Basarwa are among the most researched on and best known people of the world noting that, this would mean that there is no need for the Basarwa Research Programme. Sees these allegations as exaggerations of what is exactly happening.
BOTSWANA; CONFERENCE PAPERS; RESEARCH
R/B 305.8096872 PRO

0325 Saugestad, Sidsel
CONTESTED IMAGES: 'FIRST PEOPLES' OR 'MARGINALISED MINORITIES' IN AFRICA
Barnard, Alan; Kenrick, Justin. Africa's Indigenous Peoples:

'First Peoples or Marginalised Minorities'? Edinburgh: University of Edinburgh, Centre of African Studies, 2001. xv, 322pp. refs. pp.299–322. ISBN 0952791757.
The paper deals with the controversy surrounding the term "indigenous" and the recent emergence of African indigenous organizations. Points out that the debate as to the meaning of the word "indigenous" attempts to clarify the ambiguous relationship between a modern sovereign state and a special type of traditional community which does not constitute a political entity. Suggests that the following definition highlights the salient features of an indigenous group: a) priority in time; b) the voluntary perpetuation of cultural distinctiveness; c) an experience of subjugation, marginalization and dispossession; d) self-identification as "indigenous". Notes that African governments often do not accept the validity of the concept. Also regards the term "marginalised" as unhelpful as a blanket description since it may lead to programmes which do not address the need for empowerment. Sees the requirement for a change in the dominant political discourse and the need to challenge the current rules of society. Traces the history of international indigenous organizations. Points out that in the African context, such organizations have often developed without time in which to establish grass-roots support. Lists major international indigenous organizations in Africa and highlights the multiplicity of challenges they face.
BOTSWANA; NAMIBIA; CONFERENCE PAPERS; EMPOWERMENT; INDIGENOUS PEOPLES; MARGINALIZATION; NON-GOVERNMENTAL ORGANISATIONS; POVERTY; SELF-DEVELOPMENT
R/B 305.80968 CON

0326 Schadeberg, Jurgen
THE KALAHARI BUSHMEN DANCE
London: Wildwood House, 1982. ill.
The book contains photographs taken in 1959 and a short essay on the lifestyle of the Kalahari Bushmen at that period. Describes hunting practices, gathering and ecobotanical knowledge, land use, social life and customs. The section entitled "The dance of exorcism" provides unique photographs of the healing dance and the healing work of the trance dancer.
BOTSWANA; BELIEFS; DANCE; FORAGING; HEALING; HISTORY; HUNTING-GATHERING; LAND USE; PHOTOS; RELIGION; TRANCE
306.4 SCH

0327 Schapera, Isaac
THE TRIBAL DIVISIONS OF THE BUSHMEN
Man, No. 47, 1927, pp.68—73.
The article comments on an article by E.H.L. Schwarz published in *Science Progress*, No. 81, 1926, and entitled "The Bushmen of the Kalahari". Finds that the article contains many inaccuracies, particularly with regard to the author's criteria of race and language to distinguish Bushman groups. Prefers to present a classification of Bushman tribes based on recent research while commenting on Schwartz's findings in passing. Notes the criteria used in classifying peoples i.e. culture, race and language and contends that in the case of the Bushmen, a classification based on language is the most profitable. Uses the terms Southern, Central and Northern to identify the main groupings of Bushman languages as outlined by Dorothea F. Bleek. Comments on the various languages in each group and gives their geographic location.
ANGOLA; BOTSWANA; LESOTHO; NAMIBIA; SOUTH AFRICA; /'AUNI; /XAM; !XOO; HAI//OM; HIECHWARE; JU; KHOEKHOEGOWAB; LANGUAGES; LINGUISTICS; NAMA; NARO; SOUTHERN
99/194

0328 Schapera, Isaac
A SURVEY OF THE BUSHMAN QUESTION
Race Relations, Vol.6 No.2, 1939, pp.68–83.
The article notes that information regarding the Bushmen people of the Union of South Africa, Bechuanaland Protectorate and South West Africa was inadequate for any decision regarding their future because conditions under which they lived, their numbers and their mode of life were not known. Points out that in 1937 a committee was formed in Cape Town to ensure the presentation of the Bushmen as a separate race. The standing committee investigated the following: a) definition of Bushman regarding the physical, cultural and linguistic characteristics of the race; b) enumeration of Bushman tribes and mapping of their distribution; c) mode of life, means of subsistence, health and diet, geographical conditions and resources; d) relationships with other tribes, historical and present evidence of adjustability to new conditions. Concludes that there is no single criterion by which we can nowadays characterise all the people commonly called "Bushmen".
BOTSWANA; NAMIBIA; SOUTH AFRICA; CULTURE; DECISION-MAKING; DIET; LANGUAGES; SOCIAL ORGANIZATION
PH/B 305.80968 SCH

0329 Schapera, Isaac; Farrington, E.
THE EARLY CAPE HOTTENTOTS: DESCRIBED IN THE WRITINGS OF OLFERT DAPPER (1668), WILLEM TEN RHYNE (1686) AND JOHANNES GULIELMUS DE GREVENBROEK (1695)
Westport: Negro Universities Press, [1970], xv, 309pp. ill., facsims., refs.
The book contains three seventeenth century accounts of the early Cape Hottentots in the original Dutch or Latin with English translations. Each section is provided with a brief foreword giving the biography of the author and the source of his information. In addition, the editor's general introduction

summarises what was known of Hottentot tribal groups, way of life, language and beliefs as a result of the accounts in these and other early writings. Notes that though some of the details are incorrect, the three accounts are of value when attempting to reconstruct the main aspects of Hottentot culture before it was overwhelmed through contact with western culture.
CAPE; SOUTH AFRICA; BELIEFS; CULTURE; HISTORY; KHOEKHOE; LANGUAGES; LINGUISTICS; RELIGION; SOCIAL ORGANISATION
301.2968 SCH

0330 Schladt, Mathias
A MULTIPURPOSE ORTHOGRAPHY FOR KXOE: DEVELOPMENT AND CHANGES
Batibo, H.M.; Tsonope, J. The state of Khoesan languages in Botswana. Mogoditshane: Tasalls, 2000. viii, 169pp., ill., pp.125–130. ISBN 9991295208.
The paper describes the development of a multi-purpose orthography for Kxoe, a member of the non-Khoekhoe sub-group of the Khoe languages. Lists the following Kxoe dialects: Bumakxoe, //Xomkxoe, //Xokxoe and Bugakxoe. Notes that there is no language data on Bugakxoe, spoken in Botswana but there is information on the other three dialects. Explains that the current orthography is based on the work of Oswin Köhler. Notes that before commencing their field work, the researchers from the Institute of African Studies in Cologne compiled a preliminary Kxoe–English/English–Kxoe dictionary based on Köhler's documents, and made some pragmatic decisions on the orthography to be used. Reports on the revised Köhler orthography, pointing out why it continued to be too complex and almost unusable. Comments on two workshops held with Kxoe-speakers in West Caprivi and a conference in Germany on Khoesan languages. Deals with the following features of the orthography: tone, vowels, consonants and the problems of representing velar and aspirated sounds and nasalization. Sets out the underlying principles of the Kxoe orthography in the broad context of Khoesan studies.
NAMIBIA; CLICKS; KHWEDAM; LANGUAGES; LINGUISTICS; ORTHOGRAPHY; RESEARCH
R/B 496.1 STA

0331 Schladt, Mathias
A PRELIMINARY LIST OF KXOE WILD PLANTS. KHOISAN FORUM WORKING PAPER, NO.4
Cologne: University of Cologne, 2000. 47pp. ISSN 14331306.
The book provides a preliminary list of wild plants of the Western Caprivi region of northern Namibia as identified by the Kxoe. The list gives the botanical identification and the corresponding Kxoe name for the plant. The editor's introduction provides information on the Kxoe at the present time, the orthographic conventions employed, details on the informants, a note on the taxonomy and the abbreviations used.
NAMIBIA; WESTERN CAPRIVI; BOTANY; ETHNOBOTANY; KHWE; KHWEDAM; RESEARCH
PH/B 581.9419 SCH

0332 Schmidt, Sigrid
KHOISAN FOLKTALES: ORIGINAL SOURCES AND REPUBLICATIONS
African Studies, No. 41, 1982. pp.203–212.
This list of sources of Khoisan (San, Khoekhoe, Damara) folktales provides two-way cross references to original and secondary sources. Notes that many of these sources were compiled in the nineteenth century for leisure reading rather than being intended as examples of serious scholarship. Provides details of author, title and information about the source of the tales recorded.
NAMIBIA; BIBLIOGRAPHIES; DAMARA; FOLKLORE; KHOEKHOE; RESEARCH
98/786

0333 Schmidt, Sigrid
SOME BELIEFS OF THE /KHOBESIN (WITBOOIS) CONCERNING FISHING
Khoisan Special Interest Group Newsletter 2, 1984. refs. pp.9–13.
The paper shows that the beliefs and customs of the /Khobesin (Witboois), a Nama-speaking group living along the Namibian coast, were similar to those of !Kung hunters. In the case of Khobesin the "prey" consisted of fish rather than game and similar customs regarding the "first-kill" of the young men were observed for both groups.
NAMIBIA; !KUNG; CUSTOMS; HUNTING; NAMA
PH/B 496.1 KHO

0334 Schmidt, Sigrid
THE RELATIONS OF NAMA AND DAMA WOMEN TO HUNTING
Bernd Heine. Sprach und Geschichte in Afrika, Vol.7 No.1. Hamburg: Helmut Buske, 1986. 457pp. pp.329–350. ISBN 3871187593.
The paper deals with beliefs of the Nama and Dama peoples regarding the ways in which the behaviour of women relates to hunting. Explains that both groups speak Nama but that the Nama are ethnically Khoi while the Dama are of negro origin and were formally hunter-gatherers. Notes that the beliefs described relate to an earlier life-style which no longer exists but is still remembered by members of the two groups. Shows that among the Dama there is an analogy between women and game, so that while the husband hunts the wife must behave in ways symbolising behaviour of the prey. Con-

versely, among the Nama the woman must guard the fire which symbolises the husband's strength. Notes the existence of similar beliefs among African groups who have been in contact with Khoisan peoples.
NAMIBIA; BELIEFS; CULTURE; DAMARA; HUNTING; KHOEKHOEGOWAB; NAMA
95/825

0335 Shanefelt, Robert
A REVIEW OF *BUSHMAN FOLKTALES: ORAL TRADITIONS OF THE NHARO OF BOTSWANA AND THE /XAM* BY MATHIAS GUENTHER
Canadian Journal of African Studies, Vol.25 No.3, 1991, pp.497–499.
The reviewer considers that the collection of stories includes much that is "oral literature" rather than folklore. Criticises the arrangement or "packaging" of the book, its lack of an index and of original language texts plus the number of typographical errors. Suggests that it does not deal adequately with conceptual issues. Points out that the idea of a pan-Bushman/Hottentot religious system was first suggested by Schapera 50 years ago. Concludes that despite these weaknesses, its readers will learn much about Nharo and /Xam literature and the cross-cultural setting of southern Africa.
BOTSWANA; CAPE; /XAM; BELIEFS; BOOK REVIEWS; FOLKLORE; NARO; RELIGION
P 300.5 CJA

0336 Silberbauer, George B.
NEITHER ARE MY WAYS YOUR WAYS
Kent, Susan. Cultural diversity among twentieth-century foragers: an African perspective. Cambridge, Cambridge University Press, 1996. xiii, 344pp., ill., maps, pp.21–64. ISBN 0521482372.
The paper looks at the concept of "hunter-gatherer" and enquires what the characteristics of such a society are. Concludes that, to the people concerned, no matter how they obtain their food either by traditional means or from wage labour, the tradition of hunting and gathering continues to provide them with significant social and cultural meanings. Compares the G/wi and the !Kung in order to indicate the similarities and diversity characteristic of their social organization and beliefs. Shows the effect of the new technology of deep-well boring techniques on the life-style of the G/wi at Xade. Concludes that Wilmsen's hypothesis that the hunting-gathering lifestyle resulted from dispossession by outsiders is disproved by the fact that many Basarwa chose to return to their territories and an autonomous existence despite the hardships of such a life.
BOTSWANA; XADE; !KUNG; ANTHROPOLOGY; BELIEFS; DANCE; FARMING; FOOD; G/UI; HUNTING-GATHERING; RELIGION; SEDENTISM; SOCIAL ORGANISATION; TRANCE
306.364 CUL

0337 Silberbauer, George B.
A SENSE OF PLACE
Burch, Ernest S.; Ellanna, Linda J. Key issues in hunter-gatherer research. Oxford: Berg, x, 534pp., 1994. pp.119–134. ISBN 0854963758.
The article discusses and compares the attitudes of the Australian Pitjantjatjara with those of the central Kalahari G/wi regarding the relationships of humans to their land. Also considers the role of anthropology as it seeks to explain human social and cultural behaviour. Emphasises the necessity for an understanding of a people's construction of reality to be integrated into the effort to comprehend social behaviour. Considers that the G/wi concept of human relationships with the land can be characterised as "human-in-society on the land" while the Pitjantjatjara consider themselves as part of the very existence and functioning of the land. Discusses the external and internal relations of both peoples arising from these conceptions.
AUSTRALIA; BOTSWANA; BELIEFS; G/UI; INDIGENOUS PEOPLES; LAND RIGHTS; RELIGION; TERRITORIALITY
306.3 KEY

0338 Singer, R.; Kimura, K.
BODY HEIGHT, WEIGHT AND SKELETAL MATURATION IN HOTTENTOT (KHOIKHOI) CHILDREN
American Journal of Physical Anthropology, Vol. 54, 1981, pp.401–413.
The paper discusses growth of body height and weight and skeletal maturation of Hottentot and Rehoboth Baster children from Namibia and Cape Coloured children from Cape Town. Notes that the related populations, Rehoboth Basters and Cape Coloureds are taller and heavier than Hottentots and have almost the same body height as black and white Americans after the age of 18 years. Finds that the mean TW2 skeletal age in the Rehoboth Basters and Hottentots is always less than the British standard by one or two years in both sexes. Notes that in general the Rehoboth Baster children have a skeletal age which is intermediate between Hottentot and British children. Finds that in both Hottentots and Rehoboth Basters, the increase in body height shows a linear relation to the skeletal age and the regression curves are almost parallel in both sexes. Comments that the differences in body height and weight between Hottentots and Rehoboth Basters become greater after the skeletal ages of 15 years for boys and 13 years for girls.
NAMIBIA; SOUTH AFRICA; KHOEKHOE; MEDICAL RESEARCH
98/1152

0339 Sixpence, Hunter Qace
KURU DEVELOPMENT TRUST
Lane, Paul; Hermans, Janet; Molebatsi, Chadzimula. Proceedings from the Basarwa Research Workshop, Gaborone, 24–25 August, 1995. 2001. 106pp. p.33.
The report is one of those presentations that highlighted the establishment of Kuru Development Trust in 1986. Its aim is self development of the Basarwa people. The Board of Kuru is chosen by the participants and fully represents the Basarwa people involved in Kuru. The presenter informed the conference that people work to change their lives generating income like sewing, tanning, leather work and pre-school education. Also they have educational activities (including cultural awareness programmes) and contemporary art. Points out that Kuru Development Trust is writing the Naro language. This is very important for them because it makes the Basarwa proud and realise that they are equal to all other people.
D'KAR; BOTSWANA; COMMUNITY DEVELOPMENT; ECONOMIC DEVELOPMENT; CONFERENCE PAPERS; SELF-DETERMINATION
R/B 305.8096872 PRO

0340 Skotnes, Pippa
HEAVEN'S THINGS: A STORY OF THE /XAM
LLAREC Series in Visual History, Cape Town: LLAREC, 1999. 56pp.
The book employs both text and visual images to celebrate the collaboration between members of the Bleek family and their /Xam informants. Narrates the history of the dispossession and destruction of the Cape /Xam. Includes legends told by //Xabbo, /Han#kasso and Dia!wain taken from the unpublished notebooks of Lucy Lloyd and photographs from various sources, as well as reproductions of water colours by the author.
CAPE; SOUTH AFRICA; /XAM; ART; HISTORY
R/B 305.80968 SKO

0341 Smith, Andrew B.
PASTORALISM IN AFRICA: ORIGINS AND DEVELOPMENT ECOLOGY
London: Hurst, 1992. xv, 288pp. ill., refs.
The book provides a historical survey of the development of pastoralism in Africa and how it was adapted to the open grasslands of the continent. Uses ecological evidence from prehistory to enlarge understanding of the difficult situation now facing African herders. The chapter entitled "Reconstructing Africa's pastoral past: southern Africa" looks at adaptive strategies in the Kalahari and pastoral strategies in Namibia. Suggests there were early contacts between pastoral and hunting communities both inland and in the Western Cape. Provides a short description of Khoikhoi social organization and hypothesises on the reasons for the rapid disintegration of Khoikhoi society at the Cape after the arrival of white settlers. Examines the effects of the Tribal Grazing Land Policy upon Basarwa formerly inhabiting areas now opened up for cattle rearing in Botswana with the drilling of deep boreholes.
BOTSWANA; CAPE; NAMIBIA; SOUTH AFRICA; CATTLE; COLONIALISM; CULTURE; ECOLOGY; ENVIRONMENT; HISTORY; KHOEKHOE; PASTORALISM
304.2096 SMI

0342 Smith, A.B.
'THINGS FROM THE BUSH': A CONTEMPORARY HISTORY OF THE OMAHEKE BUSHMEN
Journal of Southern African Studies, Vol.28 No.1, 2002. pp.214–216.
The review looks at two recently published studies on Namibian Bushmen: *Things from the Bush: a contemporary history of the Omaheke Bushmen* by James Suzman and *Living on Mangetti* by Thomas Widlok. Shows that the two books deal with similar themes, the problem of how the identity of Omaheke Ju/'hoansi and the =Akhoe Hai=om from north-central Namibia is in both cases created in terms of their association with outsiders, and even the construction of self-identity is dominated by others. Points out that the two books form part of a new trend in ethnography which seeks to examine identity among those hunter-gatherers previously regarded by anthropologists as not representing the "pure" Bushman culture, owing to their association with farming neighbours. Reports cultural and economic changes that have affected the two groups, and considers that the publication of these books represents a breakthrough in Bushman ethnography which can now be said to have "come of age".
NAMIBIA; ATTITUDES; BOOK REVIEWS; CULTURE; CULTURAL CHANGE
P 968.05 JSA

0343 Smits, Lucas
ROCK PAINTINGS IN LESOTHO: SITE CHARACTERISTICS
South African Archaeological Bulletin, Vol.38 No.138, 1983, refs. pp.62–76.
The article examines rock painting sites that have been recorded by the Analysis Rock Art Lesotho project in four areas in Lesotho. Correlates site distribution with aspects of the physical environment such as altitude, geology and distance from water. Investigates preferences with respect to exposure, location, aspect, dimensions and spacing. Notes occurrence of other cultural remains at the sites, and assesses relative importance of sites in terms of paintings per site. Analyses differences in subject matter between the four study areas and draws attention to the resulting contrast in eastern and western Lesotho.
LESOTHO; RESEARCH; ROCK ART
930.105 SAA

0344 Snyman, J.W.
PALATALISATION IN THE TSOWA AND G/UI LANGUAGES OF CENTRAL BOTSWANA
Batibo, H.M.; Tsonope, J. The state of Khoesan languages in Botswana. Mogoditshane: Tasalls, 2000. viii, 169pp., refs. ill.. pp.33–43. ISBN 9991295208.
The paper presents data on palatalization in the eastern, non-Khoesan languages Tsowa and G//anakhoe. Demonstrates, by means of maps and word-lists, the sound changes occurring in both the languages discussed. Considers that sound changes from "velar to palatal-like" sounds form part of an extensive change of non-palatals to palatals which has not been observed by other researchers.
BOTSWANA; G//ANA; CONFERENCE PAPERS; LANGUAGES; LINGUISTICS; PHONOLOGY; TSUA
R/B 496.1 STA

0345 Snyman, J.W.
BUSHMAN LANGUAGES: *THE COMPLEAT GUIDE TO THE KOON* BY A. TRAILL
South African Journal of Science, Vol.71, 1971. pp.251–252.
The review provides a detailed analysis of Traill's account of the !Xo language and comments that the report uses earlier published material to offer plausible explanations for the present linguistic situation in the !Xo area. Notes that the study of Khoisan languages can bring new insights and new dimensions to linguistic science, and that it contains many stimulating facts that will serve as an embarkation point for students of the !Xo language.
BOTSWANA; !XOO; LANGUAGES; LINGUISTICS; RESEARCH
P 505 SAJ

0346 Snyman, J.W.
THE BUSHMAN AND HOTTENTOT LANGUAGES OF SOUTHERN AFRICA
Limi, Vol. 2 No. 2, 1974. pp.28–44.
The article summarises available data on the subject of the classification of Bushman and Hottentot languages by referring to lexical, phonological and grammatical information collected by Westphal and other investigators. Uses the Bushman language Zu/'hoasi and the Hottentot language Nama as the basis of comparison, noting that they represent the most comprehensively documented examples of the languages under discussion.
SOUTHERN AFRICA; GRAMMAR; JU; JU/'HOANSI; KHOE; KHOEKHOEGOWAB; LANGUAGES; LINGUISTICS; PHONOLOGY; SOUTHERN
98/902

0347 Snyman, J.W.
THE INTERRUPTED JUXTAPOSED VOWELS OF ZU/'HOASI
Traill, A. Khoisan Linguistic Studies 3, 1977. pp93–106. ISBN 0854944540.
The paper provides a descriptive study of the spectrographic patterns of juxtaposed vowels in Zu/'hoasi. Explains that the term describes a sequence of two like or unlike vowels separated auditorily by a tightening of the vocal cords with a resulting low frequency breathy vowel. Notes that Vedder and Doke were aware of juxtaposed vowels but did not describe them.
BOTSWANA; GRAMMAR; JU/'HOANSI; LANGUAGES; LINGUISTICS
496.2709 KHO

0348 Snyman, J.W.
THE CLICKS OF ZU/'HOASI
Tweede Afrikatale-kongres van UNISA = Ssecond Africa languages congress of UNISA. Pretoria: University of South Africa, 1978. pp.144–168. ISBN 0869811134.
The paper introduces the Zu/'hoasi click system. Gives examples which are representative of the various clicks and explains the articulation of clicks by interpreting their spectrograms. Suggests a new click classification based on the number of airstreams involved in the articulation of a click. Gives as examples monogressive, bigressive and trigressive clicks. Each of the categories are again subdivided according to the means of articulation. Compares the Zu/'hoasi click system with that of the Hottentot languages. Finds that the Zu/'hoasi click system is more complex and contains more click combinations than do the Hottentot languages.
CLICKS; JU/'HOANSI; KHOEKHOEGOWAB; LANGUAGES; LINGUISTICS
496 AFR

0349 Snyman, J.W.
DOKE'S CONTRIBUTION TO !XUU
Khoisan identities and cultural heritage conference. Cape Town. 12–16 July, 1997. 32pp.
The paper, presented at the Khoisan Identities and Cultural Heritage Conference of 12–16 July 1997 does not appear in the published proceedings. Points out that Doke's paper: "An outline of the phonetics of the language of the Chu Bushmen" which appeared in *Bantu Studies* Vol. 2, 1925 is a record of the speech of the Southern dialect of the Omatako Zu/'hoasi. Compares Doke's findings with those presented in Snyman's "A preliminary classification of the !Xuu and Zu/hoasi dialects" (1977) and pays tribute to the excellence of Doke's work. Uses Doke's headings to discuss vowels, emitted consonants, reversed consonants or clicks, and vocabulary.
NAMIBIA; !XUN; CLICKS; JU/'HOANSI; LANGUAGES; LINGUISTICS; PHONETICS; RESEARCH
98/949

0350 Solomon, Anne
REPRESENTATIONS AND THE AESTHETIC IN SAN ART
Critical Arts: a Journal of Cultural Studies, Vol.9 No.2, 1995. pp.49–64. ISSN 02560046.
The paper focuses on aspects of the non-visual aesthetic and its operation in rock art research. Notes that the depiction of San art and culture has become a contentious issue which emerges across a number of disciplines. Indicates that the shamanistic explanation of rock art has tended to overlook the complexity of the art and can lead to the emergence of new stereotypes. Considers that contemporary theoretical and philosophical problems are vital when looking at questions of aesthetics in the presentation of San history.
ART; RESEARCH; ROCK ART; SHAMANISM
PH/B 305.80968 CRI

0351 Solomon, Anne
THE MYTH OF RITUAL ORIGINS? ETHNOGRAPHY, MYTHOLOGY AND INTERPRETATION OF SAN ROCK ART
South African archaeological Bulletin, Vol.52 No.165, 1997. pp.3–13
The paper presents an interpretation of San rock art which reconsiders the importance of San mythology in relation to rock paintings. Suggests that figures with both animal and human features are not trancers or shamans as the dominant model suggests but are better understood in relation to San myths and to beliefs about the spirits of the dead. Outlines a model which focuses on myth, history and the spatio-temporal schemata of San cosmology and culture. Notes that this model addresses problems of the "ethnographic method" and of interpretations which assign priorities to the role of the shaman and the production of San visual imagery.
ARCHAEOLOGY; COSMOLOGY; CULTURE; HISTORY; MYTHOLOGY; RESEARCH; ROCK ART
P 930.105 SAA

0352 Solway, Jacqueline S.
NAVIGATING THE "NEUTRAL" STATE: "MINORITY RIGHTS" IN BOTSWANA
Journal of Southern African Studies, Vol.28 No.4, 2002. refs. pp.711–729. ISSN 03057070.
This article analyses the rise of minority struggles in Botswana. Traces the development of these struggles from the relatively isolated and muted complaints of non-Tswana to the organised, sophisticated and effective political movements that are seeking to render the state more inclusive. Notes that this transition, occurring over approximately one decade, culminated in a Presidential Commission and a White Paper proposing constitutional change as well as the redrawing and renaming of internal geographic units. Comments that the issue has provoked intense media coverage and open discussion. Traces the roots of these struggles and analyses the conditions that enabled their development. Argues that in the Botswana case, state institutions fostered the development of minority activism, not by their failings, but rather by their effectiveness. Highlights citizens' abstract trust in rationalised bureaucratic structures as laying the basis for minority self-identification and empowerment. Finds that in creating effective institutions, the state produced the conditions for its own challenge and provided an orderly means by which dissenting parties could proceed. Presents the various ways minority groups have agitated for change and provides case material. Raises questions regarding the capacity of liberal states to grant rights simultaneously to both individuals and collectives. Asks to what extent states can recognise and grant rights to both while promoting social justice on the one hand, and maintaining their own integrity, on the other.
BOTSWANA; BAKGALAGADI; GOVERNMENT POLICY; KHOESAN; LAW; MINORITY RIGHTS
P 968.05 JSA

0353 South West Africa. Department of National Education
ZJUC'HOA ORTHOGRAPHY
Windhoek: South West Africa, Department of National Education, 1987. 57pp.
This orthography replaces "The !Xu orthography No.1" published by the Administration of South West Africa in 1969. Contains an outline of the phonetics of Zjuc'hoa (Ju/'hoan) in both English and Afrikaans, a wordlist and a sample text in both the old and new orthographies. Explains in the Foreword the justification for a new and more practical orthography as the Bible Society required it to enable the Bible to be translated into the language, and developments in Bushmanland also made a more standardised orthography necessary. Points out that major changes include use of only letters of the Roman alphabet, avoidance wherever practical of diacritics, and sound representations wherever possible from Afrikaans. Emphasises substitution of the letters c,x,q and c cedilla for International Phonetic Alphabet symbols.
NAMIBIA; CLICKS; JU/'HOAN; LANGUAGES; LINGUISTICS; ORTHOGRAPHY; PHONETICS
R/B 496.1 SOU

0354 Spohr, Otto H.
WILHELM HENDRICH IMMANUEL BLEEK: A BIO-BIBLIOGRAPHICAL SKETCH
Varia, No.6. Cape Town: University of Cape Town Libraries, 1962. viii, 77pp.
The book contains a biography of W.H.I. Bleek and a bibliography of his unpublished correspondence; manuscripts; published works and a number of references to his work appearing in books

and periodicals. Includes posthumous works completed by L.C. Lloyd and D.F. Bleek but based on his own researches. The section entitled "Bleek, authority on Bushman language and folklore, 1870–1875" provides details on Bleek's studies of the language including the methods used to learn it from the Bushman prisoners who lived at his home for several years. Reports that his initial information on click sounds came from H. Tindall, author of "Grammar and vocabulary of the Namaqua Hottentot language" and that he received help from missionaries working in Damaraland among the Hottentot people. Records Bleek's work on the proposed "Bushman-English Dictionary" which was eventually published in 1956 having been completed by his daughter, Dorothea F. Bleek. Quotes from letters and other documents which explain the reasons why Bleek felt it so essential to record the folklore of the Cape Bushmen.
SOUTH AFRICA; /XAM; BIBLIOGRAPHIES; FOLKLORE; KHOEKHOEGOWAB; LANGUAGES; LIFE STORIES; LINGUISTICS; RESEARCH
R/B 808.06692 SPO

0355 Steyn, H.P.
ASPECTS OF THE ECONOMIC LIFE OF SOME NOMADIC NHARO BUSHMAN GROUPS
Annals of the South African Museum, Volume 56 No. 6, 1971, pp.275–322.
The paper describes the economic life of Nharo Bushmen in the Western Kalahari and is based on fieldwork carried out between 1967 and 1971. The material is part of the author's MA thesis entitled "The social structure and organization and economic life of the Nharo Bushmen" (University of Stellenbosch, 1971). Notes that while Nharo were in touch with other Bushman groups, the main acculturative influence was the establishment of farming areas in Namibia and Botswana. Comments on the existence of three broad categories among modern-day Nharo: a) those permanently living on the farms; b) those living in the veld but who associate with Bantu at waterholes in times of scarcity; c) those not permanently associated with Bushmen in either of the above categories, but who may squat on farms while visiting friends and relations and who hunt seasonally, though none are now full-time hunters and gatherers. Describes: settlement patterns; daily activities of men and women; hunting and trapping methods, including use of steel traps and dogs. Lists plants used and notes their importance as sources of liquid when there is no surface water. Comments on economic interaction between Nharo and Bakgalagadi and the fact that healing powers of Nharo dancers are respected by their Bantu neighbours.
BOTSWANA; NAMIBIA; BAKGALAGADI; CULTURE; DANCE; HUNTING-GATHERING; INTERACTION; NARO; SEDENTISM; SOCIAL ORGANISATION
93/069

0356 Steyn, H.P.
'THE ART OF TRACKING' BY LOUIS LIEBENBERG
South African Archaeological Bulletin, Vol.45, 1990. pp.137–138.
The book review discusses the book on tracking by Louis Liebenberg. Notes that the book is presented in three parts. The first covers the evolution of hunter-gatherer subsistence. The second summarises data on living hunter-gatherers of the Kalahari. The third part concerns the fundamentals of tracking. Observes that tracking evolved in arid and/or cold areas. Speculates that tracking problems in a changing environment may have contributed to the decline of the Neanderthalers. Discusses themes such as the age of spoor, distance, direction and knowledge of animal behaviour. Examples of creative speculative thinking of !Xo and other trackers are presented.
SOUTHERN AFRICA; !XOO; BOOK REVIEWS; EVOLUTION; HUNTING
R/B 305.0896883 LIE

0357 Steyn, H.P.
SOUTHERN KALAHARI SAN SUBSISTENCE ECOLOGY: A RECONSTRUCTION
South African Archaeological Bulletin, Vol.39, 1993. refs. pp.117–124.
The paper formed part of a study of early Cape herders and hunter-gatherers. Records information from three San couples from the Southern Kalahari who were interviewed during 1982 and 1983. Reconstructs their subsistence ecology in the region. Notes that it shared a focus on the gemsbok and other non-migratory game animals, a relatively small range of dependable plant foods and a reliance on moisture-bearing plants in particular the *tsamma* melon. Comments that these individuals were no longer hunter-gatherers and that they were descendants of the Cape San taken by Donald Bain to be exhibited at the Empire Exhibition in Johannesburg in 1937 and who were subsequently studied by Rheinallt-Jones and Doke.
KALAHARI DESERT; SOUTH AFRICA; =KHOMANI; /'AUNI; ECOLOGY; ETHNOBOTANY; FOOD; FORAGING; HUNTING-GATHERING
P 930.105 SAA

0358 Steyn, H.P.; Pisani, E. du
GRASS-SEEDS, GAME AND GOATS: AN OVERVIEW OF DAMA SUBSISTENCE
SWA Wissenschaftliche Gesellschaft, Journal XXXIX. 1984/85. pp.37–52.
The paper describes the subsistence patterns of the Dama of the Lower Ugab River Valley in the vicinity of the Brandberg, Namibia. Provides historical information on the first contacts between white travellers and the Dama people in the nineteenth century. Notes that although present-day Dama no

longer make as great a use of plant foods, owing to their increasing integration into the money economy, they do continue to know a variety of plants used for food and for other purposes. Lists the plant foods currently in use and reports on the hunting methods employed both in the past and currently and mentions the species hunted.
NAMIBIA; DAMARA; ETHNOBOTANY; FOOD; FORAGING; HISTORY; HUNTING-GATHERING
98/1158

0359 Story, R.
SOME PLANTS USED BY THE BUSHMEN IN OBTAINING FOOD AND WATER
Pretoria: Union of South Africa. Department of Agriculture. 62 plates. 1958. 115pp.
The book lists edible plants used by Kalahari Bushmen of Namibia and Botswana. Provides the botanical name and the Bushman names in addition to information as to the preparation and use of the plants listed. Mentions that the languages represented in the paper are as follows: !khu, //ganakwe, /Gikwe, Naron and Auen.
BOTSWANA; NAMIBIA; /'AUO; !KUNG; BOTANY; ETHNOBOTANY; FOOD; G/UI; G//ANA; LANGUAGES; LINGUISTICS; NARO
R/B 581.632 STO

0360 Stow, George W.; Theal, George McCall
THE NATIVE RACES OF SOUTH AFRICA: A HISTORY OF THE INTRUSION OF THE HOTTENTOTS AND BANTU INTO THE HUNTING GROUNDS OF THE BUSHMEN, THE ABORIGINES OF THE COUNTRY
London: London Swan Sonnenschien. ill. 1910, xii, 561pp.
The book represents one of the earliest attempts to trace the history and demise of the Bushmen of South Africa and of their conflict with the invaders of their hunting territories. Contains 13 chapters dealing with the Bushmen and an equal number on the Griquas, Bastards and Bantu-speaking tribes. Considers that the Bushmen were divided into two groups, sculptors and painters. Believes that both groups originated in North Africa and moved southwards long before the arrival of the Bantu-speaking peoples. Points out as typical characteristics the loyalty of the Bushmen, their unselfishness in sharing of food, unflinching courage and love of freedom. Describes implements, weapons, medicines, hunting methods, social customs, music and musical instruments, dances, folklore and religious beliefs.
SOUTHERN AFRICA; BELIEFS; CULTURE; FOLKLORE; HISTORY; HUNTING-GATHERING; MATERIAL CULTURE; RELIGION; ROCK ART; SOCIAL ORGANIZATION
R/B 301.2968 STO

0361 Strydom, J.L.C.
IKHANA HÀ ABAROS XA
Windhoek: Gamsberg Macmillan, 1994. 65pp.
This school textbook in Khoekhoegowab is included in the bibliography to illustrate the orthography used for the writing of this language in Namibia.
NAMIBIA; KHOEKHOEGOWAB; LANGUAGES; LINGUISTICS
R/B 496.1 STR

0362 Suzman, James
AN INTRODUCTION TO THE REGIONAL ASSESSMENT OF THE STATUS OF THE SAN IN SOUTHERN AFRICA
Regional assessment of the status of the San in Southern Africa: Report Series, No.1 of 5. Windhoek: Legal Assistance Centre, 2001. refs. v, 88pp.
This introductory volume of a five-part series explains that the study was initiated at the request of the ACP–EU Joint Assembly held in Windhoek, Namibia on March 22, 1996. Outlines the following objectives of the assessment: a) strengthening the opportunity for San people in Botswana, Namibia, South Africa, Angola, Zambia and Zimbabwe to define and achieve their own development objectives; b) increasing the participation of San people in political decision-making; c) providing comprehensive and up-to-date information for use by the main stakeholders in San matters (politicians, governments, NGOs, parastatals etc); d) enhancing the potential beneficial impact of the various international declarations and conventions on human rights and indigenous people in the region. Recommends the establishment of special programmes to address the unarguable marginalization of the San while not explicitly referring to their indigenous status because of the reluctance of governments in the region to recognise this as an issue. Notes that without such commitment the San may become increasingly dependent upon welfare and further alienated from their respective nation states. Examines issues relating to government, policy, NGOs and community organizations. Makes recommendations on the priority issues of food and poverty, land and access to land, education, community-based natural resource management and health issues.
ANGOLA; BOTSWANA; NAMIBIA; SOUTH AFRICA; ZAMBIA; ZIMBABWE; ADVOCACY; ALCOHOLISM; CULTURE; EDUCATION; GOVERNMENT POLICY; HEALTH; HUMAN RIGHTS; LAND RIGHTS; NON-GOVERNMENTAL ORGANISATIONS; POVERTY
R/B 305.80968 SUZ

0363 Suzman, James
AN ASSESSMENT OF THE STATUS OF THE SAN IN NAMIBIA
Regional assessment of the status of the San in southern Africa: Report Series, No.4 of 5. Windhoek: Legal Assistance Centre. refs. 2001. xxii, 163pp.
The volume examines, in considerable detail, the situation of San in Namibia. Provides a brief historical overview which indicates the factors that have led to most of these people lack-

ing land rights, being materially dependent upon others, desperately poor and having little or no access to channels of empowerment. Finds that at independence, San fell into five distinct but fluid socio-spatial categories: a) living in commercial farming areas; b) living in resettlement areas; c) living as minority populations in communal areas; d) living as majority populations in communal areas (i.e. former Bushmanland); e) living in game reserves (i.e. West Caprivi). Estimates San population as between 30,000 and 35,000 which represents 2% of the national population of Namibia. Considers the following factors which result in the continuing marginalization of San: a) landlessness; b) lack of education; c) social stigmatization; d) high mobility; e) extreme poverty and dependency. Looks at these problems as they exist in each of the above-mentioned areas and makes recommendations in all cases. Examines the roles of both the Government of Namibia and of NGOs *vis à vis* the position of the San. Considers the land question, resettlement of San communities, and the concomitant problems. Describes the health and educational situation of San and recommends ways of improving both. Looks at community based natural resource management and tourism in the light of the possibility of there being a source of income for San communities. Concludes by making recommendations on the key areas requiring intervention if the position of Namibian San is to be ameliorated.
NAMIBIA; DECISION-MAKING; DEMOGRAPHY; DEVELOPMENT PLANNING; EDUCATION; GOVERNMENT POLICY; INTERACTION; LAND RIGHTS; NATURAL RESOURCES; POLITICAL LEADERSHIP; POVERTY; RURAL DEVELOPMENT; SELF-DETERMINATION
R/B 306.809688 SUZ

0364 Suzman, James
INDIGENOUS WRONGS AND HUMAN RIGHTS: NATIONAL POLICY INTERNATIONAL RESOLUTIONS AND THE STATUS OF THE SAN OF SOUTHERN AFRICA
Barnard, Alan; Kenrick, Justin. *Africa's Indigenous Peoples: 'First Peoples or Marginalised Minorities'?* Edinburgh: University of Edinburgh, Centre of African Studies, 2001. xv, 322pp. pp.273–297. ISBN 0952791757.
The paper considers the main issues raised in *The Regional assessment of the status of the San in southern Africa*, published in 2001 and carried out at the request of the ACP–EU Joint Assembly. Lists the following common markers of San marginalization: a) lack of land rights; b) extreme poverty and dependency on welfare programmes; c) low levels of literacy, poor school attendance and high drop-out rates; d) poor health care, squalid living conditions, a high incidence of social problems and a lower than average life expectancy; e) weak representation in political or administrative structures and a limited capacity to advocate their own interests at national, regional or local level; f) a sense of sometimes extreme social and political alienation. Considers that stressing the indigenous status of San is counterproductive when southern African governments do not accept this status as a reality. Prefers the use of the UN Covenant on Civil and Political Rights to allow governments and San organizations to focus on the above-mentioned problems.
BOTSWANA; NAMIBIA; SOUTH AFRICA; ATTITUDES; CONFERENCE PAPERS; EDUCATION; INTERACTION; HUMAN RIGHTS; INDIGENOUS PEOPLES; LAND RIGHTS; LEGAL RIGHTS; POVERTY; MARGINALIZATION
R/B 305.80968 AFR

0365 Suzman, James
MINORITIES IN INDEPENDENT NAMIBIA
London: Minority Rights Group International, 2002. refs. 36pp.
The book considers the extent to which SWAPO's attempts at nation-building have favoured some communities over others. Documents the constitutional and legal safeguards for minorities in Namibia. Discusses the Government's human rights record. Covers many of Namibia's minority communities and topical concerns, including: the crackdown on secessionists in Caprivi, the potential impact on Himba of a proposed dam on the Kunene River, the extreme marginality of the San, the role of traditional authorities and leaders, and women's equality.
NAMIBIA; !XOO; GAME RESERVES; GOVERNMENT POLICY; HAI/'OM; JU/'HOANSI; LAND RIGHTS; LOCAL GOVERNMENT; MARGINALIZATION; MINORITY GROUPS; POVERTY
PH/B 306.809688 SUZ

0366 Sylvain, Renee
BUSHMEN, BOERS AND BAASSKAP: PATRIARCHY AND PATERNALISM ON AFRIKANER FARMS IN THE OMAHEKE REGION, NAMIBIA
Journal of South African Studies, Vol.24 No.4, 2001. pp.717–737.
Examines the paternalistic and patriarchal components inherent in the institution of *baasskap* (an Afrikaans word meaning "boss-ship") on Afrikaner farms in the Omaheke Region of Namibia, where farm labourers and domestic servants are largely Ju/'hoansi. Starts by examining the development of baasskap from the top down, focusing on macro-level political economic trends, and the farmers' reactions to those trends that helped to create an ambiguous class status for the Ju/'hoansi. Then examines the dialectics of coercion, collusion and consent between farmers and the Ju/'hoansi in the maintenance of *baasskap* by outlining two important features of Afrikaner-Ju/'hoan interactions: first, the pseudo-familial relations between farmers and farm workers, as these are perceived by both farmers and Ju/'hoansi. Argues that the conflation of the farmers' role as *baas* and "father figure" es-

tablishes the patriarchal family as the model for race and class relations on the farms. Observes that, while the paternalistic attitudes of the farmer are openly expressed, and therefore easily challenged, and manipulated, by the Ju/'hoansi', unequal gender relations are largely unnoticed.
NAMIBIA; AFRIKANERS; FARM WORKERS; GENDER ISSUES; HISTORY; JU/'HOANSI
P 968.05 JSA

0367 Sylvain, Renee
AFTER FORAGING: THE OMAHEKE SAN
Cultural Survival Quarterly, Vol.26 No.1, 2002. pp.17–18.
The report shows that the Ju/'hoansi San working on white-owned farms in the Omaheke District of Namibia receive very low wages and are exploited by their employers. Notes that resettlement camps established for the indigent in the area are inhabited mainly by pensioners and the sick and disabled, most of whom rely on pension payments as a source of income. Describes the Omaheke San as the most impoverished, stigmatised and marginalised community in the country. Points out that in spite of their problems the Omaheke San continue to speak their own languages and to carry out such aspects of their culture as healing dances and intitiation ceremonies. Finds that the San kinship and naming systems continue to be used and provide a basis for mutual support and as a means for ordering social relations. Reports on the advocacy and training schemes initiated by the Working Group of Indigenous Minorities in Southern Africa (WIMSA) and the Omaheke San Trust (CST) to address the socio-economic and political problems of the San community in the area.
NAMIBIA; OMAHEKE DISTRICT; ADVOCACY; DEVELOPMENT PROJECTS; EXPLOITATION; FARM WORKERS; HEALING; JU/'HOANSI; MARGINALIZATION; NON-GOVERNMENTAL ORGANISATIONS; POVERTY
R/B 305.8096872 CUL

0368 Szalay, Miklos
THE SAN AND THE COLONIZATION OF THE CAPE, 1771–1879
Research in Khoisan Studies, No.11, Cologne: Rüdiger Köppe. refs. 1995. 151pp.
The book shows that, contrary to the usual assumption, the disappearance of the San from the Cape did not result from their extermination. Traces the history of the conflict between the white settlers and the San, showing that a need for farm labour was a contributing factor even when commandos were mounted to pursue San bands. Points out that those who capitulated would be captured and taken to work on the farms. Notes that here they gradually adapted to a new way of life and after a few generations became known as "Hottentots" rather than as "Bushmen" and they would then be subject to the same laws and regulations as the former. Points out that some San farm labourers escaped to form marauding bands which robbed and attacked their former employers often in revenge for the cruelty practised against them. Gives details of the attempted pacification of the San from around 1795, when authorities, in an effort to civilise them and persuade them to settle and become pastoralists, provided them with livestock. Notes that by 1830, although some San had become successful pastoralists, the areas where this occurred were taken over by settlers and the San were forced into labour service. Describes the various efforts to establish Christian missions among the San, all of which were unsuccessful because the hostility of the settlers forced them to close. Notes that the notion that the San were totally unable to change from a hunting-gathering life-style is disproved by the fact they had made a number of adaptations during the period under review, and were eventually incorporated into the group known as "coloured", some of whom are also prepared to admit to their San ancestry.
CAPE; SOUTH AFRICA; COLONIALISM; CONFLICT; CULTURAL CHANGE; HISTORY; HUNTING-GATHERING; KHOEKHOE; PASTORALISM
R/B 305.80968 SZA

0369 The Penduka Declaration on the Standardization of Ju and Khoe Languages
Penduka Declaration. Windhoek, Namibia. 20–22 April, 2001.
The paper presents the main recommendations made at a conference held at the Penduka Training Centre, Windhoek, from April 20–22, 2001 to study the issue of alphabet standardization in certain Ju and Khoe languages. Notes that the participants were specialists on language, oral history and education from three countries. Emphasises the importance of the conference as the first occasion on which San speakers themselves were involved in vital decisions regarding the orthography to be adopted for their own languages. Also notes that representatives of language groups already having standardised orthographies worked with those whose language is not yet written down. Calls upon governments, the media and the public to have greater awareness and respect for San people's languages and cultures. Appendices list the names of conference delegates, their affiliations and language speciality, and also give reasons why San speakers wish to write their own languages.
NAMIBIA; JU/'HOANSI; KHOEKHOEGOWAB; KHWE; KHWEDAM; NON-GOVERNMENTAL ORGANISATIONS; N/U
PH/B 496.1 PEN

0370 The University of Botswana and the University of Tromsø Collaborative Programme for Basarwa Research and Basarwa Studies
Lane, Paul; Hermans, Janet; Molebatsi, Chadzimula. Proceedings from the Basarwa Research Workshop, Gaborone, 24–25

August, 1995. 2001. 106pp. pp.64–73.
Paper presented at the Basarwa Research Workshop, held on 24–25 August, 1995 at the University of Botswana. The paper records the details of the joint application from the two Universities to the Norwegian Universities Committee for development Research and Education (NUFU). The proposal is to seek support from NUFU for launching a fully fledged programme of research and studies relating to the Khoesan peoples of Botswana, locally designated as the Basarwa, San or Bushmen. Notes that the main aim of launching such a programme would be to promote Basarwa research as it was realised that although research has been conducted on this group, the problem is that it has been conducted by foreign scholars. Justifies the need for such a research programme which would assist in bringing in local academics who are familiar with Basarwa issues. Gives a history of this research programme, partnership between the University of Botswana and the University of Tromsø, and outlines the objectives of the programme.
BOTSWANA; CONFERENCE PAPERS; KHOESAN; RESEARCH
R/B 305.8096872 PRO

0371 Tagart, E.S.B.
REPORT ON THE MASARWA AND ON CORPORAL PUNISHMENT AMONG NATIVES IN THE BAMANGWATO RESERVE OF THE BECHUANALAND PROTECTORATE
Dominions, No. 136, London: Dominions Office, 1931. 29pp.
The report on the Masarwa was made in response to the proclamation of the High Commissioner for South Africa in July 1931 requesting enquiry to be made on various issues relating to the Masarwa in the Bamangwato Reserve. These included the following: employment conditions and remuneration; the extent to which they are free to engage in any occupation or transfer their services from one employer to another, or move from one place to another, and their ability to exercise such freedom; their general conditions of life including their status in rights of person and property; and the circumstances which have led to the present subject position of these people. Investigates all the issues listed above and reports thereon. Lists points about which general agreement was expressed by those consulted. These included the following: a) regular remuneration to be paid by Bamangwato masters and no compulsory labour permitted; b) Masarwa to be free to offer their services freely without reference to their Bamangwato masters; c) Basarwa should be expected to pay taxes; d) land should be made available to Basarwa wishing to live independently. Notes that a declaration covering similar points was made by the British High Commissioner in the Serowe Kgotla in 1926 but was never enforced. Considers the most important recommendations to be the suggestion for further study on the Masarwa and the suggestion that there be closer contact between the European Officers and the Masarwa.
BOTSWANA; SEROWE; BANGWATO; EXPLOITATION; GOVERNMENT POLICY; HISTORY; INTERACTION; LABOUR; SERFDOM
R/B 306.3 TAG

0372 Tanaka, Jiro
THE ECOLOGY AND SOCIAL STRUCTURE OF CENTRAL KALAHARI BUSHMEN: A PRELIMINARY REPORT
26pp.
The report consists of a preliminary study of two Central Kalahari Bushman groups, the G/ui and G//ana. Explains that the research was carried out over seven months in 1967 and 1968 in the !Xade area. Includes information on the natural environment, hunting methods employed and major species hunted but comments that in fact, plant foods formed the basis of G/ui and G//ana diet. Notes that camps moved according to seasonal changes in food supply in an area where no surface water exists for most of the year and people were dependent on plants for liquid. Looks at the mechanisms within Bushman society by means of which social tensions are relieved and a stable social life maintained. Concludes that the controlling principle in Bushman life is sharing and cooperation based upon kinship ties. Describes Bushman religious ideas and the role of the healing dance. Regards the hunting-gathering society as providing a key to the formation of human society from sub-human primate society and to the evolution of more complex human societies.
BOTSWANA; CENTRAL KALAHARI GAME RESERVE; XADE; ANIMALS; ANTHROPOLOGY; DANCE; ECOLOGY; G/UI; G//ANA; HEALING; HUNTING-GATHERING; KINSHIP; PLANT ECOLOGY; SHAMANISM; TRANCE; SOCIAL ORGANISATION
PH/B 305.8096872 TAN

0373 Tanaka, Jiro; Sugawara, Kazuyoshi
/GUI AND //GANA
Lee, Richard; Daly, Richard. The Cambridge encyclopedia of hunters and gatherers. Cambridge, Cambridge University Press, 1999. xx, 511pp., ill, maps. pp.195–199. ISBN 052157109X.
The article provides information on the /Gui and //Gana formerly resident in the Xade area of the Central Kalahari Game Reserve but who have now mostly been relocated to Kxoenhakene, a settlement 70 km west of Xade outside the CKGR. The ethnological present of the article is the 1960s and 1970s when research was carried out by a team of Japanese researchers. Topics presented include: history of the /Gui and //Gana in the Xade area; ecological setting; economy; settlement; mobility and land use; domestic and political organization; religion and spirituality. Notes the profound changes in all aspects of /Gui and //Gana life which took place with sedentarization around the borehole, introduction of stock

rearing and agriculture, introduction of new hunting methods and the entry of the community into the cash economy.
BOTSWANA; CENTRAL KALAHARI GAME RESERVE; XADE; ANTHROPOLOGY; CULTURE; ECOLOGY; ECONOMY; G/UI; G//ANA; HUNTING; LAND USE; SEDENTISM; SETTLEMENTS; SOCIAL CHANGE
R 306.36403 CAM

0374 Taylor, Michael
"YOU CANNOT PUT A TIE ON A BUFFALO AND SAY THAT IS DEVELOPMENT": DIFFERING PRIORITIES IN COMMUNITY CONSERVATION, BOTSWANA
refs. n.d. 15pp.
The paper deals with community-based natural resource management (CBNRM) as it is being carried out in three Basarwa villages around the Okavango Delta, and poses questions as to how committed CBNRM in Botswana is to truly empowering local communities, and what factors need to be considered to make it relevant and useful to the people it is supposed to serve. Observes that though CBNRM is intended to involve local people in managing and benefiting from local resources, many Basarwa (San) feel that elements of the programme do not take into account their specific circumstances, priorities, values and local understandings of resource elements. Argues that the implementation of CBNRM in these communities has overlooked the specific historical, political and social contexts of the inhabitants of this area who, as indigenous people have a history of being marginalised from political decision-making processes and also see themselves as having a different relationship to the land and the resources on it. Believes that these narratives of difference define how they see themselves as well as their priorities for "development" and involvement in conservation and tourism. Concludes that while claiming to empower local communities to manage their own development, CBNRM in Botswana has instead fuelled resentment and undermined its own potential effectiveness.
BOTSWANA; NGAMILAND; OKAVANGO DELTA; CONSERVATION; GOVERNMENT POLICY; LAND USE; NATURAL RESOURCES
PH/B 333.7096872 TAY

0375 Taylor, Michael
NARRATIVES OF IDENTITY AND ASSERTIONS OF LEGITIMACY: BASARWA IN NORTHERN BOTSWANA
Senri ethnological Studies, No.59. Anderson, David; Ikeya, Kazunobu. Parks, property and power: managing hunting practice and identity within state policy regimes. Osaka: National Museum of Ethnology, 2001. refs., i, 203pp., pp.157–182. ISSN 03876004.
The paper explores how Basarwa in Ngamiland often represent themselves in terms of their hunting and gathering heritage and their current material poverty and attempt to utilise such expressions of identity to assert their rights. Discusses the theoretical issues pertaining to Basarwa identity in Botswana. Examines such expressions of identity as a means of asserting their rights against government policies and the dominant values of mainstream society. Finally, explores the ambiguity existing in social action and the relationship between dominant and subordinate groups and the methods by means of which Basarwa negotiate these dichotomies.
BOTSWANA; NGAMILAND
R/B 363.68 PAR

0376 Taylor, Michael
LIFE, LAND AND POWER: CONTESTING DEVELOPMENT IN NORTHERN BOTSWANA
Thesis (PhD). University of Edinburgh, 2000, ill., maps, photos, refs. xix, 323pp.
This thesis, based on 15 months of fieldwork in three Basarwa (San) villages on the northern periphery of the Okavango Delta, Botswana, is a study of the indeterminate yet universally powerful notion of "development". Explores the dynamics, meanings and implications of different local and national conceptions of what "development" in this area should entail, and focuses on efforts by Basarwa to fashion a better "life" for themselves, as well as on the policies and programmes of various agencies of the Botswana government. Basarwa have attracted much anthropological interest, which had been based on assumptions as to their status as "hunter-gatherers". Instead, this author views their ethnicity as a key set of symbols and practices, which have structured the nature of their participation in official development programmes. Contextualises contemporary development interventions within the framework of a much longer historical process of alienation from political and economic processes in the region. Considers that their loss of control over land and wildlife, central markers of their ethnicity, has been of particular importance. Explores these themes principally within the context of the community based natural resource management (CBNRM) programme, an initiative increasingly common to African governments. Notes that CBNRM claims to decentralise management of natural resources to rural residents. Shows that despite these aims, in practice CBNRM on the Okavango fringe has so far served in certain ways to achieve exactly the opposite. Points out that nonetheless, many Basarwa have taken the introduction of CBNRM as an opportunity to reverse the trend of alienation by asserting their rights to land and the resources on it, as well as the power to manage them according to their own priorities. In bringing the themes of ethnicity and development together, concludes by suggesting means by which CBNRM could better accommodate local-level diversity, and be used to meet the overlapping goals of government, tourism, conservation, and Basarwa themselves.

BOTSWANA; NGAMILAND; BUGAKHWE; CONSERVATION; DEVELOPMENT POLICY; ETHNICITY; GOVERNMENT POLICY; HUNTING; LAND RIGHTS; NATURAL RESOURCES; RURAL DEVELOPMENT; TOURISM; TS'IXA
TH 333.72096872 TAY

0377 Thackeray, Francis
AARDVARK, ROAN ANTELOPE AND AGRICULTURE IN AFRICA: AN EXPLORATORY STUDY IN THE FIELD OF "LINGUISTIC PALEONTOLOGY"
The Digging Stick, Vol.15 No.3, 1998. refs. pp.3–4.
The paper notes that the aardvark and roan antelope have similar distributions in Africa and that this coincides with the distribution of sorghum. Observes that the transmission of sorghum to southern Africa is associated with the migration of Iron Age populations within the last 2000 years. Explains that in West Africa, roan and aardvark are known to have been important in agricultural rituals and beliefs held by the Bambara in Mali. Discusses the fact that cultivation of sorghum is linked to beliefs associated with fertility, productivity, endurance and a "working animal". Concludes that certain examples of African art deserve to be exploited further in the context of linguistics.
AFRICA; BAMBARA; LESOTHO; MALI; WEST AFRICA; ANIMALS; ARCHAEOLOGY; AGRICULTURE; BEHAVIOUR; BELIEFS; FERTILITY; IRON AGE; LANGUAGES; LINGUISTICS; MIGRATION
P 930.105 DST

0378 Thackeray, J.F.
DISGUISES, ANIMAL BEHAVIOUR AND CONCEPTS OF CONTROL IN RELATION TO ROCK ART OF SOUTHERN AFRICA
South African Archaeological Society, Goodwin Series, No. 4, 1983. pp.38–43.
The paper attempts to discover what evidence there is for the use of disguises by Bushman hunters and whether concepts of control over game were associated with shamans using animal skin disguises. Considers whether such concepts of control were identifiable with animal behaviour patterns and could be identified in the rock art. Concludes that the use of animal skin disguises provides a means of taking advantage of "curiosity" behaviour in antelope, ostriches and other animals. Uses ethnographic accounts to suggest that concepts of game controlling powers developed in part from the use of animal skin disguises. Discusses examples of rock art in relation to ethnographic data concerning animal behaviour, skin costumes and controlling powers attributed to shamans.
SOUTHERN AFRICA; ANIMALS; ANTHROPOLOGY; BELIEFS; HUNTING; RELIGION; ROCK ART
99/728

0379 Theal, George McCall
THE YELLOW AND DARK SKINNED PEOPLE OF AFRICA SOUTH OF THE ZAMBEZI: A DESCRIPTION OF THE BUSHMEN, THE HOTTENTOTS, AND PARTICULARLY THE BANTU, WITH FIFTEEN PLATES AND NUMEROUS FOLKLORE TALES OF THESE PEOPLE
New York: Negro Universities Press, 1969. xiv, 397pp.
The reprint of a book published in 1910 by an early South African historiographer, covers aspects of the history, customs and folklore of the various peoples of South Africa. Considers that the Bushmen originated in Central Asia, and show similarities to Semang in the Malay Peninsula and to the Andamanese who were seen as equally intellectually limited. Comments on the Bushman language and the work of the traveller Lichtenstein and the missionary Arbousset in collecting vocabularies. Commends the linguistic work of W.H.I. Bleek and Lucy Lloyd and quotes from publications by Bleek on the language. Provides brief details on customs, dance, hunting methods, rock art, beliefs and diet. Includes three Bushman folktales. Regards the place of origin of the Hottentots as Somaliland, with light-skinned Hamites intermarrying with Bushman females. Suggests that Hottentot is related to Hamitic languages of North Africa but includes clicks adopted from the Bushman language. Discusses the Hottentot language which by the time of writing was only spoken by Griqua and Nama. Describes the formation of Hottentot tribes and their internecine wars and conflict with the Bushmen encountered as they moved south. Describes customs, clothing, food and cooking methods, care and training of cattle, and general life style.
SOUTH AFRICA; SOUTHERN AFRICA; ANTHROPOLOGY; FOLKLORE; HISTORY; KHOEKHOEGOWAB; KHOESAN; LANGUAGES; LINGUISTICS; SOCIAL ORGANISATION
R/B 301.296872 THE

0380 Thupe, Gaolatlhe
THE BOKAMOSO PRE-SCHOOL TRAINING PROGRAMME OF KURU DEVELOPMENT TRUST
Oussoren, Otto. Education for remote area dwellers in Botswana. Gaborone: University of Botswana, Research and Development Unit; WIMSA, Regional San Education Project, 2001. 107pp., pp.54–56.
The paper, based on personal experience both of teaching in Ghanzi District Primary schools and working in the Bokamoso Pre-school Training Programme, describes the Bokamoso Programme and discusses the problems relating to remote area dweller education. Notes as major problems the following: a) lack of communication between children and their teachers because there is no common language and the same applies to parents and teachers; b) too little cooperation between stakeholders and lack of respect for each other's cultures; c) lack of involvement by parents in school activities or participation by them in parent-teacher associations; d) reluctance on the part of teachers to be transferred to remote areas re-

sulting in their demotivation. Provides no solutions to the problems outlined above but asks pertinent questions which require answers.
BOTSWANA; GHANZI DISTRICT; ACCESS TO EDUCATION; ATTITUDES; CONFERENCE PAPERS; EDUCATION; PRE-SCHOOL EDUCATION; PRIMARY EDUCATION; TEACHER TRAINING; TEACHING
R/B 372.7096872 WIM

0381 Tobias, Phillip V.
PROFILE OF A HUNTER-GATHERER PEOPLE: THE BUSHMEN OF THE KALAHARI
South African Journal of Science, Vol.74, 1978. pp.3–7 and 71–72.
The article summarises the main contributions made at a symposium on Bushman research held on June 15–16, 1973, in Johannesburg and organised by the Institute for the Study of Man in Africa. Notes results of tests given to Bushmen subjects to discover their physical endurance capacity and investigate their vision and hearing, dentition and genetic structure. Also reports on research on nutrition, physical size and female genitalia. Provides details of archaeological research on Late Stone Age sites in the Transvaal and Orange Free State which suggest the possibility of a continuous sequence from approximately 19,000 B.C. to the modern period. Notes the results of psychological testing of Bushmen. Gives details of the botanical knowledge of !xo Bushmen of the Lone tree/Takatokwane region. Details the current situation regarding linguistic research on non-Bantu click languages and on hitherto unreported aspects of !xo grammar.
BOTSWANA; LONE TREE; TAKATOKWANE; !XOO; ARCHAEOLOGY; ETHNOBOTANY; GENETICS; LANGUAGES; LINGUISTICS; MEDICAL RESEARCH; PSYCHOLOGY
P 505 SAJ

0382 Tomaselli, Keyan G.
MYTHS, RACISM AND OPPORTUNISM: FILM AND TV REPRESENTATIONS OF THE SAN
Crawford, P.; Turtan, D. Politics, ethics and indigenous imagery. London: Manchester University Press. 1992. pp.204–221.
The chapter deals with films and television programmes depicting the San. Includes origins and effects of critical responses to both ethnographic and entertainment films. Regards the central dynamic between film-makers and subject-communities as one of power, and notes that questions of accountability regarding production and distribution practices seldom arise with regard to ethnographic films. Deals with ciriticism of *People of the Great Sandface* (Myburgh, 1985), *The Hunters* (Marshall, 1956), *Lost World of the Kalahari* (Van der Post, 1959), *Testament to the Bushmen* (Van der Post, 1982), and *The Gods Must Be Crazy* (Uys 1980 and 1989).
SOUTH AFRICA; ANTHROPOLOGY; FILMS; INDIGENOUS PEOPLES
PH/B 305.80968 TOM

0383 Tomaselli, Keyan G.
THE CINEMA OF JAMIE UYS
Blignaut, Johan; Botha, Martin. Movies–moguls–mavericks: South African cinema 1979–1991. Cape Town: Showdata. 1992. pp.191–231.
The chapter deals in some detail with the career of Jamie Uys, South African film director and producer. Looks at his early career and pioneering of humorous, stereotypical films in Afrikaans. Secondly analyses the later films in which blacks and San "Bushmen" are depicted. Notes that the release of the first *Gods Must Be Crazy* (1978) film unleashed a storm of criticism and debate in academic and popular forums about whether or not it was racist. Points out that in spite of Uys' repeated denials that his films contained any "message" his viewers thought otherwise. Those supporting apartheid regarded them as an affirmation of their beliefs while the opponents regarded the depiction of blacks and "Bushmen" as demeaning and racist. Gives background information on the fantasised version of the life story of Xi, the chief actor in *Gods I* and its use for publicity purposes. Comments that Uys provided an unrealistic picture of the life of modern "Bushmen" as innocent primitives living in splendid isolation while being well aware of their actual conditions at places like Tshumkwe in Namibia at the time.
NAMIBIA; TSHUMKWE; ANTHROPOLOGISTS; FILMS; INTERACTION; LIVING CONDITIONS; POVERTY
PH/B 791.4372 TOM

0384 Tomaselli, Keyan G.
INTRODUCTION: MEDIA RECUPERATION OF THE SAN
Critical Arts: a Journal of Cultural Studies, Vol.9 No.2, 1995. refs. pp.i– xxi, ISSN 02560046.
The Introduction to a special edition of *Critical Arts* traces the themes presented in the volume. Points out that in the "New South Africa" there has been a proliferation of written and visual material on the San but few attempts to correlate these various insights. Notes that the underlying thread has been an effort to rehabilitate the image of the San and provide a more positive and dynamic view of this community, even seeing the San as a bridge between past and future. The Introduction also analyses critical insights provided by Ntongela Masilela (1987) inspired by the ideas of Laurens van der Post. Stresses the importance of myth in these interpretations, both the semiotic and Jungian definitions thereof. Considers that films on the San may represent an attempt by film-makers to depict the essential "soul" or "spirit" of the San while also attempting to explore their own consciousness.

SOUTH AFRICA; FILMS; LITERATURE; MYTHOLOGY
PH/B 305.80968 CRI

0385 Traill, Anthony
AGREEMENT SYSTEMS IN !XO
Limi, Vol.2, 1974. refs. pp.12–28
The article examines agreement systems in !xo. Notes earlier studies on the language by W.H.I. Bleek, J.F. Maingard, H-J Heinz, D. Ziervogel and E.O.J. Westphal. Shows that !xo exhibits a partial harmonic concordial system in sentences and a non-harmonic one across sentences. Examines the problems of formalising these systems as well as a number agreement system within the context of a generative theory.
BOTSWANA; !XOO; GRAMMAR; LANGUAGES; LINGUISTICS; RESEARCH
PH/496.2705 TRA

0386 Traill, Anthony
A HISTORICAL !XOO-G/UI CONTACT ZONE: LINGUISTIC AND OTHER RELATIONS
Batibo, H.M.; Tsonope, J. The state of Khoesan languages in Botswana. Mogoditshane: Tasalls, 2000. viii, 169pp., ill.. pp.1–17. ISBN 9991295208.
The paper discusses the typological features of the southern African Khoesan languages which differentiate them from other African languages. Shows that archaeological evidence suggests a time depth of 100 centuries for Khoesan-related languages. Regards these languages as occupying a "residual zone" and indicates the special features of such a zone. Contrasts "residual zones" occupied by Khoesan languages with the "spread zones" characterising Bantu language areas. Uses the known historical contact situation in western Botswana, between the mutually unintelligible languages !Xoo and /Gui as a model for similar interactions which probably took place in prehistoric times. Points out that other contact situations have been identified between Khoesan languages in Botswana. Concludes that at an early stage in the linguistic prehistory of southern Africa a situation of radical linguistic diversity evolved. Notes that in order for communication to take place between Khoesan groups bilingualism would be necessary. Suggests that though language shift did not occur a process of diffusion took place leading to the spread of words and phonological features across different languages.
BOTSWANA; !XOO; G/UI; LANGUAGES; LINGUISTICS
R/B 496.1 STA

0387 Traill, Anthony
ANOTHER CLICK ACCOMPANIMENT IN !XOO
Khoisan Linguistic Studies, No.5, Johannesburg: University of the Witwatersrand, 1975. ill. pp.22–29.
The paper reports on the existence of a hitherto undetected click accompaniment. Notes that the sound is also found in the /Gwi language. Emphasises the necessity of distinguishing, at the systematic level, between two types of ejective accompaniment; click+ kx? and click+q?. Observes that the dialect of !Xoo spoken at Lone Tree shows a contrast between the two types of ejective accompaniment, a plain ejective and a sequence of ejective stops (kq?) which, in rapid speech is realised as an ejective affricate. A table lists the complete range of click accompaniments in !Xoo.
BOTSWANA; !XOO; CLICKS; G/UI; LANGUAGES; LINGUISTICS
496.1 KHO

0388 Traill, Anthony
THE PHONOLOGICAL STATUS OF !XOO CLICKS
Traill, Anthony. Khoisan Linguistic Studies 3. 1977. pp.107–131. ISBN 0854944540.
The paper discusses the claim by S.R. Anderson in his paper "On the description of multiple articulated consonants" (1976) that these can only be analysed into primary and secondary articulation. Considers evidence in support of the analysis of clicks as underlying velarised consonants. Finds that the analysis cannot be sustained because the arguments used are unable to discriminate satisfactorily between primary and secondary closure. Notes that this result supports the view of clicks as underlying double segments. Comments that this conclusion is based on phonological not phonetic arguments. Concludes that primacy in multiply articulated consonants cannot always be decided on phonological grounds.
!XOO; CLICKS; GRAMMAR; LANGUAGES; LINGUISTICS; PHONETICS
496.2709 KHO

0389 Traill, Anthony
A CONFUSION OF SOUNDS: THE PHONETIC DESCRIPTION OF !XU CLICKS
Gowlett, Derek F. African linguistic contribution. Pretoria, Via Afrika, 1992. 388pp., pp.345–362. ISBN 0799412759.
The paper looks at the problems faced by both early and recent researchers of the !Xu language when attempting to describe and transcribe the plain and aspirated clicks. Identifies five click types in !Xu as follows: plain (!), nasal (n!), voiced (g!), aspirated with silent velar release (n!'h), and prevoicing with aspiration (g!h). Describes an experimental investigation designed to explore the mechanism responsible for the difference between the audible and silent release of the velar closure. Concludes that changes are needed in the transcription of clicks so that they accord with the phonetic facts and provides a table showing a revised phonological classification of clicks. Points out how an experimental approach to specific phonetic problems can identify the sources of recurrent confusion between sounds and provide an objective basis for their description.

NAMIBIA; !XUN; CLICKS; LANGUAGES; LINGUISTICS; PHONETICS
R/B 496 WES

0390 Traill, Anthony
A !XOÕ DICTIONARY
Quellen zur Khoisan-Forschung = Research in Khoisan Studies, Vol.9. Cologne: Rüdiger Köppe, 1994. 292pp.
The dictionary of the !Xoo language, the last remaining member of the Southern language group of Bushman languages, covers the dialect spoken in the Lone Tree — Kacgae area of Botswana. Apart from the dictionary proper which contains a larger !Xoo-English and a shorter English-!Xoo section, the work includes a note on the orthography and detailed information on the grammar. Acknowledges the contribution of the !Xoo-speakers who so patiently and efficiently taught the compiler their language. Notes the inclusion of such unusual features as names of pans, birds, animals and personal names which provide valuable lexical material.
BOTSWANA; SOUTHERN; !XOO; DICTIONARIES; GRAMMAR; LANGUAGES; LINGUISTICS; ORTHOGRAPHY
R/B 496.1 TRA

0391 Tributsch, Helmut
DOES MIRAGE-DERIVED MYTHOLOGY GIVE ACCESS TO SAN ROCK ART?
South African Archaeological Bulletin, Vol.55 No.171, 2000. pp.71–76.
The paper suggests that the environment inhabited by many Bushmen was one where optical mirage phenomena were part of their environment. Considers that mirage elements are reflected in their rock art in various forms: flying antelopes, double antelopes, flying creatures (rain animals). Since mirages were interpreted as encounters with another world, San mythology may have been inspired by these phenomena. Suggests that this would permit a tentative new interpretation of San rock art and confirm that San were realistic observers of nature. Gives examples of various types of mirages and shows how they may have been interpreted as "rain animals" or "water snakes" on which the Bushmen tried to exert spiritual power. Analyses some of the key symbols of rock art to demonstrate how the transcendental world of the San may have worked within the concept of simulating the inverted world of the mirage.
SOUTH AFRICA; ANIMALS; BELIEFS; MYTHOLOGY; RELIGION; RESEARCH; ROCK ART
P 930.105 SAA

0392 Tshireletso, Lucky
THE SIGNIFICANCE OF LANGUAGE AND CULTURE IN THE CLASSROOM
Oussoren, Otto. Education for remote area dwellers in Botswana. Gaborone: University of Botswana, Research and Development Unit; WIMSA, Regional San Education Project, 2001. 107pp., pp.77–81.
The paper considers how the personal experiences of teachers can affect their attitudes towards students from a different cultural background. Notes certain advantages enjoyed by members of the Tswana-speaking mainstream but not shared by those from minority groups. Also observes that part of their socialization has often included the inculcation of mistaken assumptions about Basarwa as a people and how they view themselves. Notes that the inadequate preparation of teachers during their training has not done away with such misconceptions. Presents examples of various methods used in the classroom situation, some of which allowed students more participation in the learning situation. Summarises common experiences of Basarwa children entering the classroom with existing disadvantages related to their minority status, marginal culture and language background and coming from a situation of poverty and servitude. Notes that even when they attempt to deny their own cultural background in order to conform to the mainstream identity, minority children continue to be harassed and stigmatised.
BOTSWANA; ACCESS TO EDUCATION; CONFERENCE PAPERS; EDUCATION; INEQUALITY; SCHOOLS; TEACHER TRAINING; TEACHING
R/B 372.7096872 WIM

0393 Tucker, A.N.
REVIEW OF J.W. SNYMAN'S ZU/'HOANSI FONOLOGIE EN WOORDEBOEK
Journal of African Languages and Linguistics, Vol.1 No.1, 1979. refs. pp.133–135.
The reviewer recommends the book highly, stating that it supersedes previous studies of the Zu/'hoasi language by Vedder, Dorothea Bleek, C.M. Doke and J.F Maingard. Explains the theoretical basis of the phonology and deals in some detail with the arrangement of the dictionary. Notes that one aim of the book is to make it possible for the student to transcribe and docket any hitherto unrecorded item. Concludes that the dictionary is likely to remain "the standard and authoritative work for a long time".
BOTSWANA; DICTIONARIES; JU/'HOANSI; LANGUAGES; LINGUISTICS; ORTHOGRAPHY; PHONOLOGY
P 496.05 JAL

0394 University of Botswana; Lane, P.; Hermans, Janet; Molebatsi, Chadzimula
BASARWA RESEARCH WORKSHOP – UNIVERSITY OF BOTSWANA, 24–25 AUGUST, 1995
Gaborone: University of Botswana. 2001. (various pagings).

The volume presents the papers delivered at the Workshop held at the University of Botswana in August 1995. The workshop had the following aims: a) to take stock of the current position regarding research on Basarwa; b) to discuss the direction Basarwa research should follow and translate this into plans and projects; c) to establish a regional network of Basarwa/San researchers and people interested in promoting Basarwa studies. The Preface reports on the successful establishment of the UB/Tromsø Collaborative Programme funded by the Norwegian Universities Committee for Development, Research and Education.(NUFU). Papers presented include information on the various local regional advocacy bodies set up to speak for the San and help to develop self-help projects. Papers on a variety of topics are abstracted in this bibliography under the names of the authors.
BOTSWANA; CONFERENCE REPORTS; RESEARCH
R/B 305.8096872 BOT

0395 Van Rijssen, W.J.
A REVIEW OF *THE RAIN AND ITS CREATURES AS THE BUSHMEN PAINTED THEM* BY BERT WOODHOUSE
South African Archaeological Bulletin, Vol.48 No.157, 1993. p.56.
The review describes the book as "an incomparable volume" dealing with all aspects of rain and its associated myths. Points out the importance of rain to the Bushmen and their prey animals and shows how their attempts to control the rain are depicted in rock art. Considers that while some of the ideas presented are documented in the literature, others may cause controversy as they are unsupported by any evidence.
SOUTH AFRICA; BELIEFS; BOOK REVIEWS; DANCE; RELIGION; ROCK ART
P 930.105 SAA

0396 Van der Post, Laurens
THE CREATIVE PATTERN IN PRIMITIVE AFRICA
Eranos lectures, 5, Dallas, Spring Publications, c1957. 40pp.
The lecture uses interpretation of Bushman legends and dance to illustrate how primitive man, epitomised by the Bushmen, was in touch with the creative spirit within, from which modern man has become estranged. Calls upon his hearers to encourage and cultivate the creative spirit within themselves and so be renewed.
SOUTHERN AFRICA; BELIEFS; DANCE; FOLKLORE; HEALING; RELIGION; SHAMANISM; TRANCE
299.681 VAN

0397 Van der Post, Laurens
A FAR-OFF PLACE
London: Howarth Press, 1974. 310pp.
The novel and its sequel *A story like the wind* include a Bushman character named Xhabbo (Dream) who epitomises much of what the author believed about the nature and characteristics of the Bushmen. Xhabbo is, in some ways the hero of the story as his knowledge of the bush and extra-sensory perception or "tapping" enable him to lead Francois and his companion Nonnie to safety in spite of danger from the African invaders who destroy Francois' home and kill all its inhabitants.
BELIEFS; FOLKLORE; LITERATURE
823.968 VAN

0398 Van der Post, Laurens
A MANTIS CAROL
London: Hogarth Press, 1975. 165pp.
The book is the life story of a Bushman who, through strange vicissitudes, ended his life in a New York apartment. The author, who claims that this is a true account, attempts to explore, together with the unnamed woman who told him the story of Hans Taaibosch after his death, the meaning of this life. Pursues the thought that throughout history the Bushmen were persecuted and oppressed because to their oppressors they epitomised the hidden part of themselves which they most feared and which like the Bushmen, "could not be tamed." Uses the figure of Mantis the god of the Bushman, the myths in which he figures, and the dance by means of which the Bushman shows forth his deepest feelings about life, to express a revelation of the power of love, epitomised in Hans Taaibosch.
BELIEFS; DANCE; LIFE STORIES; LITERATURE; MYTHOLOGY; RELIGION; TRANCE
823.9968 VAN

0399 Vierich, Helga; Hitchcock, Robert K.
KUA: FARMER/FORAGERS OF THE EASTERN KALAHARI, BOTSWANA
Kent, Susan. Cultural diversity among twentieth-century foragers: an African perspective. Cambridge: Cambridge University Press, 1996. xiii, 344 p., ill., maps. pp.108–124. ISBN 0521482372.
The chapter assesses the adaptive strategies of the Kua of the eastern and south-eastern Kalahari Desert. Points out that they have moved in and out of foraging activities for centuries. Concludes that in response to major developments affecting the region, such as the establishment of new water points, changes in land allocation, commercialization of livestock farming and increased labour migration to towns and villages in the east and to South African mines, the Kua have continued to survive. Notes that their strategy for survival has depended upon participating in a mixed economic system involving livestock production, farming, wage labour, emigration and foraging. Contends, however, that the contemporary political,

economic and environmental context has rendered these strategies less effective in preventing their impoverishment. Notes that cultural diversity is yet another strategy to deal with these changes so that today there is neither a "Kua culture" nor a "foraging culture" but a variety of responses to current social problems.
BOTSWANA; CULTURAL CHANGE; ECONOMY; FARMING; FORAGING; KUA; SOCIAL CHANGE
306.364 CUL

0400 Viljoen, Hans; MacGaddery, Pauline
PEPIB-PEPSICOLA DOB XA
Windhoek: Gamsberg Macmillan, 1991. 31pp.
This illustrated story book in Nama/Damara is included in the bibliography to demonstrate the orthography employed for the writing of this language in Namibia.
NAMIBIA; KHOEKHOEGOWAB; LANGUAGES; LITERATURE
R/B 496.1 VIL

0401 Viljoen, Russel
MORAVIAN MISSIONARIES, KHOISAN LABOUR AND THE OVERBERG COLONISTS AT THE END OF THE VOC ERA, 1792–5
Bredekamp, Henry; Ross, Robert. Missions and Christianity in South African History. Johannesburg: Witwatersrand University Press, 1995. refs. 270pp., pp.49–64. ISBN 1868142906.
The chapter looks at the relationships between the Moravian missionaries and farmers of the Overberg region east of the Hottentots Holland Mountains in the Cape during the last few years of the Dutch East India Company. Points out how the situation of Khoikhoi, previously an independent people, had changed as white colonists entered the region and took over their grazing lands, giving them the choice of withdrawing into the interior or becoming labourers on the white farms. Shows that the three Moravian missionaries who arrived in 1792 to resume the mission work at Baviaanskloof (later Genadendal) annoyed the farmers by responding to such issues as the encroachment upon the land of the Khoikhoi and the enforcement of pass laws. Focuses on the efforts of the Moravians to change relations between farmers and their Khoihkhoi labour and the resulting conflict between colonists and the mission.
CAPE; SOUTH AFRICA; CONFLICT; HISTORY; INTERGROUP RELATIONS; MISSIONARIES
209.68 MIS

0402 Visser-Wiegel, Coby
LITERACY CAN SAVE LIVES: THE NARO LITERACY PROJECT
Oussoren, Otto. Education for remote area dwellers in Botswana. Gaborone: University of Botswana, Research and Development Unit; WIMSA, Regional San Education Project, 2001. 107pp., pp.68–72.
The paper deals with the importance of literacy to the San community. Discusses the misconceptions of the educated regarding the illiterate and dispels these myths. Notes that in 1992 language development was seen by the San community as essential as they wished to read and write their own language as well as Setswana and English. Shows that the Naro Language Project is a response to this felt need, and has three aspects: a) developmental-helping people to read and write their own language; b) linguistic-describing the grammar and sound system of the Naro language and creating an orthography for it; c) missionary – translating the Bible. Mentions the achievements of the project since its inception, including: publications in Naro; literacy courses at D'Kar and on a cattle post; advanced literacy for literates who cannot yet read their own language. Indicates the necessity for partnership between departments, non-governmental organizations, communities, adult education facilitators, and the adult learners themselves if adult education is to be fully developed.
BOTSWANA; D'KAR; ADULT EDUCATION; CONFERENCE PAPERS; LITERACY; LANGUAGES; LINGUISTICS; NARO; ORAL HISTORY; ORTHOGRAPHY
R/B 372.7096872 WIM

0403 Visser, Hessel
KHOESAN ORTHOGRAPHY REVISITED: ADVANTAGES AND DISADVANTAGES OF USING ROMAN LETTERS FOR CLICK SOUNDS
Batibo, H.M.; Tsonope, J. The state of Khoesan languages in Botswana. Mogoditshane: Tasalls, 2000. viii, 169 p., ill.. pp.140–160. ISBN 9991295208.
The paper looks at the pros and cons of using International Phonetic Alphabet symbols or Roman letters for click sounds in Naro and other Khoesan languages. Points out that the Roman alphabet is not a feasible option for all Khoesan languages when, for example !Xoo has five basic clicks and 17 possible click effluxes. Notes practical reasons for the use of the Roman alphabet when writing Naro. Gives the history of the current Naro orthography. Evaluates arguments for and against employment of Roman letters or IPA symbols by means of a series of tables and concludes that for Naro, the Roman system is preferable. Examines the possibility of a uniform orthographic system for all Khoesan languages. Considers that the IPA system should be employed for all academic publications on Khoesan languages. Notes, however that the arguments for use of a particular orthography for use with a particular language varies from one language to another and complete uniformity is probably neither feasible nor desirable.
BOTSWANA; NAMIBIA; CLICKS; KHOEKHOEGOWAB; LANGUAGES; LINGUISTICS; NARO; ORTHOGRAPHY
R/B 496.1 STA

0404 Visser, Hessel
NARO DICTIONARY: NARO-ENGLISH, ENGLISH-NARO
Gantsi: Naro Language Project, 2001. viii, 240pp.
This is a working document, sharing the lexical information on the Naro language. Words are arranged in alphabetical order in two sections the first section being a translation from Naro to English while the second section contains English to Naro.
BOTSWANA; DICTIONARIES; LANGUAGES; LINGUISTICS; NARO
R/B 496.1 VIS

0405 Vossen, Rainer
THE COMPARATIVE STUDY OF KHOE LANGUAGES
Khoisan Special Interest Group Newsletter 2, 1984. refs. pp.3–5.
The paper reports on a research project aimed at the historical reconstruction of the Khoe languages. The project also aims to examine the cultural-historical and ethno-historical implications of the linguistic reconstructions, focusing on the migratory history of the Khoekhoe-speaking peoples and the problem of early Khoe culture. Notes that this is currently characterised by the dichotomy between hunter-gatherers and pastoralists. Lists two suggested classifications of the Khoe languages by Köhler and Westphal upon which the research is based and reports on modifications. Observes that comparisons based on linguistic proximity and divergence suggest no correlation between geographical distribution and linguistic proximity. Finds the closest relations between Naro and //Anikwe and the weakest between Khoekhoe and the other sub-groups of Khoe languages.
//ANIKHWE; KHOE; KHOEKHOEGOWAB; LANGUAGES; LINGUISTICS
PH/B 496.1 KHO

0406 Vossen, Rainer
Q IN KHOE: BORROWING, SUBSTRATE OR INNOVATION?
Gowlett, Derek F. African linguistic contribution. Pretoria, Via Afrika, 1992. pp.363–388. ISBN 0799412759.
The paper looks at the voiceless uvular stop "q" which occurs both as plain consonant and click accompaniment in Khoe languages: Notes that the sound only occurs in the non-Khoekhoe languages and is more frequent in the western sub-groups, particularly Kxoe. Finds that in the genealogical context "q" seems to be reconstructible only for proto-non-Khoekhoe and subsequent ancestor languages. Notes that in the semantic context words containing "q" mostly belong to the macro-domain of "nature". Presents three hypotheses which might explain the origin of the sound: borrowing, substrate and innovation. Concludes that "q" is probably derived as a result of innovation.
KHOE; LANGUAGES; LINGUISTICS
496 AFR

0407 Voss, A.E.
DIE BUSHIE IS DOOD: LONG LIVE DIE BUSHIE: BLACK SOUTH AFRICAN WRITERS ON THE SAN
African Studies, Vol.49 No.1, 1990. pp.59–69.
The article looks at how South African writers, both black and white have seen the Bushman as "the other" but recently as symbolising resistance to white oppression. Bases the article on the hypothesis that "otherness" is a function of social forces and dependant on the circumstances of the time and is also a matter of inarticulacy on the part of those so regarded. Comments that so far the Bushmen have not written anything themselves about their situation. Examines the work of such early African writers as Thomas Mofolo, S.M. Molema and Sol Plaatje and of historians such as Stow and Macmillan. Comments that the latter regarded the Bushman as models of resistance. Considers that this theme is repeated in both modern historiography and in the representation of Bushmen in contemporary black writing as representing communal resistance against repression. States that the work of black writers about Bushmen includes a mythical element, but this has now been adapted in response to the tensions of recent South African politics.
SOUTH AFRICA; LITERATURE; POLITICS
P 960.05 AST

0408 Wadley, L.
BIG ELEPHANT SHELTER AND ITS ROLE IN THE HOLOCENE PREHISTORY OF CENTRAL SOUTH WEST AFRICA
Cimbebasia, Vol. 3 No. 1, State Museum, 24 Apr 1979. 75pp.
The paper centres round results and implications of archaeological excavations in Big Elephant Shelter in Central South West Africa (Namibia), a site believed to have been inhabited by Dama in prehistoric times. Includes an ethnographic background by means of which the place of the Dama in the history and prehistory of South West Africa is documented. Aims to investigate the adaptations of prehistoric man to the variable landscape of the country. Includes a detailed analysis of faunal and botanical remains from Big Elephant Shelter as well as lithic and non-lithic artefacts. Compares the site with others in central South West Africa, and considers the effects that the arrival of pastoralists in the area would have had on a hunter-gatherer population.
NAMIBIA; ANTHROPOLOGY; ARCHAEOLOGY; DAMARA; PASTORALISM; RESEARCH
99/710

0409 Waldman, Linda
NO RAINBOW BUS FOR US: BUILDING NATIONALISM IN SOUTH AFRICA
Barnard, Alan; Kenrick, Justin. Africa's Indigenous Peoples: 'First Peoples or Marginalised Minorities'? Edinburgh: Uni-

versity of Edinburgh, Centre of African Studies, 2001. refs., xv, 322pp., pp.211–228. ISBN 095279175.
The paper traces the history of the negotiations taking place between 1994 and 1998 on the part of the state on one side and the Griqua on the other, and also between the various Griqua groupings. Demonstrates that questions of Griqua unity and political representation are closely linked to both past events and present circumstances. Believes that the construction of local identities is not a threat to national consciousness. Shows how the establishment of the National Griqua Forum and the possible setting up of a new "directorate of traditional affairs "has brought Griqua groups together in opposition to other minority groups.
SOUTH AFRICA; ADVOCACY; CONFERENCE PAPERS; INTERACTION; GRIQUA; INDIGENOUS PEOPLES; NON-GOVERNMENTAL ORGANISATIONS; POLITICAL LEADERSHIP
R/B 305.80968 AFR

0410 Walker, Nick
IN THE FOOTSTEPS OF THE ANCESTORS: THE MATSIENG CREATION SITE IN BOTSWANA
South African Archaeological Bulletin, Vol.52 No.166, 1997. pp.95–112.
The paper describes the famous Matsieng site and compares it with other footprint petroglyph sites in Botswana and Zimbabwe. Notes that most rock art research in southern Africa has focused on paintings, although more attention has been given of late to naturalistic and abstract petroglyphs. Comments that one category of petroglyph which has, however, been largely ignored is the footprint. Although there are no records as to the meaning or use of these symbols by Bushmen, it is suggested that there is some evidence to link them at least originally with Bushman religious practices and possibly with possessing animals for magic purposes. Observes that it seems that such sites in Botswana were incorporated into Tswana mythology and in the case of Matsieng, this became (or continued to be) an important rainmaking place.
BOTSWANA; MATSIENG; ZIMBABWE; ARCHAEOLOGY; BELIEFS; RELIGION
P 930.105 SAA

0411 Walker, Nick
BOTSWANA'S PRE-HISTORIC ROCK ART
Lane, Paul; Reid, Andrew; Segobye, Alinah. Ditswammung: The archaeology of Botswana. Gaborone: Pula Press, The Botswana Society, 1998. 263pp. refs. ill.(some col.) pp.206–232. ISBN 9991260390.
The chapter looks at research on the rock art of Botswana. Points out that diversity in San art in Botswana has long been recognised and described, but the significance of this diversity remains poorly studied and understood. Explains that archaeologists studying San rock art in Botswana have tended to give general descriptions of specific sites. Notes that the Tsodilo Hills are the one area which has had systematic study. Art historians, in contrast to the approach of archaeologists, emphasise the visuality of the rock art, focusing rather on graphic devices, style and spatiality. San art from elsewhere in southern Africa displays a number of similarities in subject matter such as the predominance of humans and large herbivores, but is far more diverse in terms of form and style than that found in Botswana.
BOTSWANA; TSODILO HILLS; ART; PREHISTORY; RESEARCH; ROCK ART
R/B 930.1096872 DIT

0412 Ward, Valerie
A SURVEY OF THE ROCK ART IN THE NATAL DRAKENSBERG: PRELIMINARY REPORT
Southern African Journal of Science, Vol.75 No.11, 1979. pp.482–485.
The article provides a progress report on a survey of rock art in the Natal Drakensberg carried out under the auspices of the Department of Forestry and the Natal Museum, Pietermaritzberg in 1978/79. The survey aimed to supply data which would enable the Natal Parks Board and the Department of Forestry to: adequately plan for and manage the areas under their jurisdiction; assess the quantity, quality, uniqueness and significance of paintings at each site and assess their condition with regard to natural degradation and vandalism; provide data which would be of use in monitoring effects such as weathering, water seepage, fire and visitor use. Comments that previous to the survey, no site list of rock art in the Drakensberg existed, but after 11 months, 433 rock art sites and 40 other archaeological sites had been recorded.
DRAKENSBERG; KWAZULU-NATAL; SOUTH AFRICA; RESEARCH; ROCK ART
P 505 SAJ

0413 Weich, F.
DIE VERTALING VAN MARKUS IN !XU = THE TRANSLATION OF MARK INTO !XU
Traill, A. Khoisan Linguistic Studies 3, 1977, pp.63–73. ISBN 085494454.
The article in Afrikaans describes the difficulties encountered in the translation of the Gospel of Mark into the !Xu language which was undertaken by the author at Tsumkwe, Namibia. Indicates the difficulties encountered when attempting to find words or descriptive sentences for concepts totally foreign to the !Xu culture. Gives many examples of such concepts and notes the solutions found. Notes cases which arose because of the !Xu kinship system which has separate words, for example for "younger brother" and "older brother". Comments on the

existence a tonal element in !Xu which cannot easily be indicated in writing, but which has a bearing on the meaning of words, particularly in relation to showing that events occurred in the past. Comments that while it would be normal to have native speakers of a language read the translation to test its accuracy, at the time there was only one !Xu-speaker who could read, but it was tested on various Bushman groups and was apparently understood. Includes an Addendum which shows where in Namibia and Botswana the !Kung language could be understood, and provides a map showing where various language groups are located, based on a journey undertaken to establish if it was possible to carry out mission work among the Bushmen.
BOTSWANA; NAMIBIA; !XUN; BIBLE; LANGUAGES; LINGUISTICS; MISSIONARIES
496.2709 KHO

0414 Weinberg, Paul.; Berger, Dhyani J.
ONCE WE WERE HUNTERS: A JOURNEY WITH AFRICA'S INDIGENOUS PEOPLE
Cape Town: D. Philip, Amsterdam: Mets & Schilt, c2000. col. ill. 175pp.
The book describes the current situation of indigenous peoples of six African countries. The chapter entitled "Kalahari, Namibia and Botswana – no respite for the San" records encounters with Ju/'hoansi in the Nyae Nyae area of Namibia, Kxoe inCaprivi, G/ui and G//ana in the Central Kalahari Game Reserve and at New Xade, and Naro at d'Kar and the Dqae Qare Game Farm. Uses a combination of dialogue and photography to document the problems and aspirations for the future of these people. Also reports on the successful land claim of the =Khomani San of the southern Kalahari.
BOTSWANA; CAPRIVI; CENTRAL KALAHARI GAME RESERVE; GEMSBOK NATIONAL PARK; NAMIBIA; NYAE NYAE; SOUTH AFRICA; =KHOMANI; CONSERVATION; EMPOWERMENT; ETHNOBOTANY; GAME RESERVES; GOVERNMENT POLICY; G/UI; G//ANA; JU/'HOANSI; LAND RIGHTS; PHOTOS; SEDENTISM
R/B 306.2 ONC

0415 Wendt, W.E.
"ART MOBILIER" FROM THE APOLLO II CAVE: AFRICA'S OLDEST DATED WORKS OF ART
South African Archaeological Bulletin, Vol.31. 1976. pp.5–11.
The paper gives a resumé of the archaeological research programmes carried out in South West Africa (Namibia) from 1968. Includes an abstract of a paper, written originally in German, explaining the aims of the research programme and detailing the results of work done on the Apollo II cave site. Concludes that painted slabs found at the site date back to between 30,000 and 25,000 years B.P., and thus constitute the oldest known dated rock art so far discovered in Africa. Considers that the discovery of such early rock art cannot be used to postulate the existence of a continuous art tradition which lasted from this early date up till the 19th century.
NAMIBIA; ARCHAEOLOGY; RESEARCH; ROCK ART
P 930.105 SAA

0416 Wessels, Elizabeth
THE SITUATION OF OUT-OF-SCHOOL YOUTH IN GHANZI TOWNSHIP
Oussoren, Otto. Education for remote area dwellers in Botswana. Gaborone: University of Botswana, Research and Development Unit; WIMSA, Regional San Education Project, 2001. 107pp. pp.32–34.
The paper highlights the situation of out of school youth in Ghanzi Township, and the work and aims of the Task Force on out-of-school Youth (operating under the auspices of the Ghanzi Youth Council). Reports on a workshop for parents, community stakeholders and the youth themselves, held in May 2000. Lists recommendations from the workshop and suggests the future tasks of the Task Force.
BOTSWANA; GHANZI; CHILDREN; CONFERENCE PAPERS; EDUCATION; POVERTY; SCHOOL DROP OUTS
R/B 372.7096872 WIM

0417 Wheat, Sue; Amodeo, Chris
BUSHMEN DRIVEN FROM ANCESTRAL HOME
Geographical Magazine, Vol.74 No.5, 2002. p.8.
Describes the action taken by Botswana Government against the G//ana and the G/wi bushmen of the Central Kalahari Game Reserve who are refusing to move from their ancestral land. Explains that, in an effort to force them to move, the Government decided to cut off the water and food supplies.
BOTSWANA; CENTRAL KALAHARI GAME RESERVE; FOOD; G//ANA; GOVERNMENT POLICY; G/UI; INDIGENOUS PEOPLES; LAND RIGHTS; WATER SUPPLY
P 910.5 GMA

0418 Willcox, A.R.
COMMENT ON "SAN ROCK ART: IMAGE, FUNCTION AND MEANING": A REPLY TO A.R. WILLCOX BY ANITRA NETTLETON
South African Archaeological Bulletin, Vol.39, 1984. refs. pp.142–143.
The comment criticises various points in Nettleton's article. Provides the following reasons why the San produced rock paintings: a) to record important or pleasant events in the life of the community; b) to instruct the young or to illustrate folktales; c) to give pleasure to the artist through his work and his re-creation, on the rock, to be seen again, what had pleased him at first view, coupled with the satisfaction of sharing the aesthetic experience and receiving admiration for his skill. Points out that these reasons do not fully cover the reasons for

the non-representational, geometric designs found mainly in engravings.
SOUTH AFRICA; RESEARCH; ROCK ART
p930.105 SAA

0419 Willcox, A.R.
AN ANALYSIS OF THE FUNCTION OF ROCK ART
South African Journal of Science, Vol.74, 1978. pp.59–64.
The paper reviews current theories of motivation with the aid of quantitative data now available, and by adding new evidence to propose a new theory accounting for the art form. Notes that the paper only deals with the Drakensberg area. Explores the theories propounded by P. Vinnicombe and D.J. Lewis-Williams on the motivation for the paintings. Rejects these theories for an alternative one. Contends that Bushmen artists possessed eidetic ability, namely the ability to retain a sharp visual image, relatively accurate in detail and colour, of something seen. Gives a number of reasons to support this theory and suggests that the motivation for Bushman art included the desire of the artists to recapture or "see again" images of what they had enjoyed seeing or doing; the wish to record events of importance to the community, and so share it with others; and the need to depict aspects of their mythology.
DRAKENSBERG; SOUTH AFRICA; DANCE; MYTHOLOGY; RESEARCH; ROCK ART; SHAMANISM; TRANCE
P 505 SAJ

0420 Willcox, A.R.
COMMENTS ON "ELAND, RHEBUCK AND CRANES" BY A.D. MAZEL
South African Archaeological Bulletin, Vol.39, 1984. refs. pp.71–72.
The comment refers to the article by A.D. Mazel in the South African Archaeological Society Goodwin Series no. 4, 1983, pp.34–37, and includes a reply from Mazel. Contends that the details in Mazel's article do not support the contention that Bushmen painted in the summer months. Mazel responds to various points of detail. Denies that these provide a substantive argument showing that a study of eland groups does/does not lend credence to a hypothesis of seasonal timing of paintings in the Drakensberg. Emphasises that the research referred to in the original paper illustrates that certain seasonal features of animal behaviour are discernible in the art.
DRAKENSBERG; KWAZULU-NATAL; SOUTH AFRICA; ANIMALS; ECOLOGY; RESEARCH; ROCK ART
P 930.105 SAA

0421 Willet, Shelagh; Monageng, Stella; Saugestad, Sidsel; Hermans, Janet
THE KHOE AND SAN: AN ANNOTATED BIBLIOGRAPHY, VOLUME 1
Gaborone: Lightbooks, 2002. maps. vii, 248pp.
This bibliography is a result of a project on Basarwa studies, which started in 1993 with the aim of collecting contemporary written materials relating to the Khoe and San peoples of southern Africa. Provides annotations of published and unpublished works on San and Khoe. Main topics include: linguistics, anthropology, rock art, social relations, history, health, music, religion, land tenure, government policy. Notes in the Introduction that the project was inspired by a Norwegian anthropologist from the University of Tromsø, Professor Sidsel Saugestad who originally visited Botswana in 1992 as a research facilitator for the Remote Area Development Programme, on a two-year NORAD contract. Working closely with Stella Monageng, the idea developed and an ongoing collaborative programme for San/Basarwa research between the University of Tromsø and the University of Botswana, funded by the Norwegian Council of Universities' Committee for the Development Research and Education (NUFU), has provided financial support for the project since 1996.
BOTSWANA; NAMIBIA; SOUTHERN AFRICA; BIBLIOGRAPHIES; KHOESAN; LANGUAGES; LINGUISTICS; RESEARCH
R/B 305.8016 KHO

0422 Wilmsen, Edwin N.
SUMMARY REPORT OF RESEARCH ON BASARWA IN WESTERN NGAMILAND
ill. 40pp.
The survey provides information on the history, demography, kinship, nutrition, land use, economy, attitudes and acculturation of Basarwa in the Nxai Nxai community. Notes that the research was carried out from March 1975 to May 1976 for submission to the Ministry of Local Government and Lands. Predicts the possible effects upon the community of the improved water supply and building of a school which may cause changes in population size and increased pressure on resources. Concludes that planning for Basarwa should respect the existing kinship networks and land allocation patterns in order to reduce conflict and promote cooperation.
BOTSWANA; NGAMILAND; NXAI NXAI; ACCULTURATION; CULTURE; DEMOGRAPHY; HERERO; HISTORY; LAND USE; PHYSICAL PLANNING; WATER
PH/B 307.7 WIL

0423 Wilmsen, Edwin N.
HUNTERS AND HERDERS OF SOUTHERN AFRICA: A COMPARATIVE ETHNOLOGY OF THE KHOISAN PEOPLES BY ALAN BARNARD: A REVIEW
Journal of South African Studies, Vol.19 No.3, 1993. pp.530–531.
The review highly commends the book for condensing a large proportion of the information on all Khoisan peoples and

showing both the varieties and commonalities of their economic, political and social lives. Notes that this has the effect of banishing the notion of a homogenous Bushman culture which was thought to be archetypal of a pan-human past. Deals in some detail with the theoretical basis of the book, and offers some criticism of certain aspects of this. Commends the materials on kinship which provide insights into transformations occurring in all Khoisan societies.
SOUTHERN AFRICA; ANTHROPOLOGY; BOOK REVIEWS; KHOESAN; KINSHIP; SOCIAL STRUCTURE
P 968.05 JSA

0424 Wilmsen, Edwin N.
MUTABLE IDENTITIES: MOVING BEYOND ETHNICITY IN BOTSWANA
Journal of Southern African Studies, Vol.28 No.4, 2002. refs. pp.825–841. ISSN 03057070.
The author explains that a focus on minorities suggests a move away from a discourse revolving around notions of ethnicity to one emphasising personal participation in the political arena. This would lead to a devaluation of divisions among peoples demarcated by language, parentage, class or so-called "race" in favour of a concept of citizenship. Argues that ethnic allegiance is a form of cultural capital that is increasingly marginal to social functions of the present. Explains that, not only do such constructions not stand up to historical scrutiny, but they can also be incorporated in a variety of potentially dangerous claims to cultural authenticity and the uniqueness of particular cultural visions. Explains that understanding these constructions and their consequences requires detailed analyses of local ethno-histories, of colonial rule and policy, and of the connection between expansionary capitalism and the processes of social formation. Turns first to the backgrounds of ethnicity in Botswana and then to languages of labour in the nineteenth and twentieth centuries before examining present-day political contention among minority and elite fractions of the country. Concludes that an effective minority discourse would dissolve the surface appearance of ethnic disconnectedness and fragmentation and re-establish historic connections upon which an equality served citizenship could be based.
BOTSWANA; BAKGALAGADI; ETHNICITY; FORAGING; INDIGENOUS PEOPLES; INEQUALITY; KHOESAN; KINSHIP; LANGUAGES
P 968.05 JSA

0425 Wilson, Monica
THE HUNTERS AND HERDERS
Wilson, Monica. The Oxford history of South Africa. London: Oxford University Press, 1969. xiii, 502pp. pp.40–74. ISBN 0198216416.
The chapter provides detailed information for both hunters and herders on the their characteristics and distribution, oral traditions, languages, social structure, economy and the history of their relationships with other ethnic groups in South Africa. Quotes from many early accounts, particularly with reference to the relationships between herders and Dutch settlers and the subsequent history of various groups such as Griqua and Korana.
CAPE; SOUTH AFRICA; !ORA; CONFLICT; GRIQUA; HISTORY; INTERGROUP RELATIONS; KHOEKHOE; KHOESAN; LANGUAGES; LINGUISTICS; SOCIAL STRUCTURE
968 WIL

0426 Wily, Elizabeth
THE BUSHMEN: A BRIEF HISTORICAL PERSPECTIVE
n.d., 5pp.
The unpublished paper provides a brief history of Kalahari Bushmen and introduces the programme set up by the Ministry of Local Government and Lands to assist them. Shows that Bushman isolation and lack of contact with other ethnic groups led to a lack of any strong self-image or sense of cultural identity. Likewise the unchanging nature of their circumstances gave them no mechanisms for dealing with social change. Finds that confronted with the differing life-styles of other groups, they did not adopt them but merely adapted to them but in ways which leave them subservient and dependent. Considers approaches to the Bushmen adopted by British colonial authorities which proved neither helpful nor realistic. Sets out the aims of government programme being set up to assist Bushmen as citizens who are handicapped by historical, economic, social and cultural circumstances.
BOTSWANA; CULTURE; DEVELOPMENT POLICY; INTEGRATION; INTERGROUP RELATIONS; POVERTY; SEDENTISM; SOCIAL CHANGE
PH/B 301.296872 WIL

0427 Winkler, Danny
LAND RIGHTS AND WRONGS
Ecologist, Vol.32 No.4, 2002. p.22.
Focuses on the struggles facing the San Bushmen in the Central Kalahari Game Reserve of Botswana over the relocation issue. Highlights tactics used by the Botswana Government towards Bushmen who refused to relocate, restrictions imposed on the food and water supply of the Bushmen. Includes comments from Robin Hanbury-Tenison, president of Survival International. Reports on concerns of Bushmen over the effect of economic development on their way of life.
BOTSWANA; CENTRAL KALAHARI GAME RESERVE; G//ANA; GOVERNMENT POLICY; G/UI; INDIGENOUS PEOPLES; RESETTLEMENT; LAND RIGHTS
P 301.305 ECO

0428 Winter, J.C.
STRUCTURAL SPECIFICS OF HUNTER-GATHERER KINSHIP NOMENCLATURES: COMPARATIVE AFRICAN EVIDENCE FROM KHOISAN, MBUTI AND DOROBO
Bernd Heine. Sprache und Geschichte in Afrika, Vol.7 No.2. Hamburg: Helmut Buske, 1986. 465pp., pp433–451. ISBN 3871187607.
The paper addresses the question of whether there are semantic structures of kinship terminology systems which may be the correlation of a hunting-gathering life-style. Also attempts to distinguish between correlations which reflect an "original" hunting and gathering economy and those due to "re-primitivisation". Provides detailed background on the kinship theories propounded by Lewis Henry Morgan and Gertrude E. Dole. Provides samples from Northern, Central and Southern Khoisan and from non-Khoisan hunting-gathering groups to show the existence of semantic structures of kinship terminology typical of hunter-gatherer societies.
SOUTHERN AFRICA; /XAM; !XUN; =KX'AU//'EI; CULTURE; KHOEKHOE; KHOESAN; KINSHIP; LANGUAGES; LINGUISTICS; NARO
95/824

0429 Woodburn, James
THE POLITICAL STATUS OF HUNTER-GATHERERS IN PRESENT-DAY AND FUTURE AFRICA
Barnard, Alan; Kenrick, Justin. Africa's Indigenous Peoples: 'First Peoples or Marginalised Minorities'? Edinburgh: University of Edinburgh, Centre of African Studies, 2001. refs. xv, 322pp. pp.1–14. ISBN 0952791757.
The paper deals with the political status of hunter-gatherers and former hunter-gatherers in Africa today. Points out that such people are found in Cameroon, Congo (Brazzaville), The Democratic Republic of the Congo, Rwanda, Burundi, Botswana and Namibia. Notes that the widespread use of the term "Batwa" indicates that they are recognised as a distinctive human category. Finds that they are generally neither disappearing nor assimilating. Shows the extent to which they are symbolically recognised as the first owners of the land even to the extent of being included in the Coat of Arms of the new South Africa. Indicates that in spite of this, they are still discriminated against. Suggests that one possible route towards possible re-evaluation of their status might lie in developing the symbolism of the first ownership of the land into a political one with a strong symbolic component. Recognises the political difficulties of such claims but suggests that only if the land rights of first peoples are recognised will they have a chance of a viable future. Concludes that to make any claim effective, existing discrimination would have to be countered.
BOTSWANA; NAMIBIA; CONFERENCE PAPERS; HUMAN RIGHTS; HUNTING-GATHERING; INTERACTION; INDIGENOUS PEOPLES; LAND RIGHTS; POLITICS
R/B 305.80968 AFR

0430 Woodhouse, H.C.
THEMES IN THE ROCK ART OF SOUTHERN AFRICA
Johannesburg: Institute for the Study of Man in Africa, 1969.
The paper is the text of a lecture delivered at the Institute for the Study of Man in Africa on September 17, 1969 and revised in 1976. Attempts to justify the contention that a greater understanding of South African history is available if the rock paintings are carefully examined. Points out the problems relating to dating the rock art, but notes that results of new dating methods suggest that the art dates back at least 2000 years. Looks at a number of distinguishing characteristics found at rock art sites all over southern Africa such as use of animal-headed masks, face and body paint, use of bows and arrows and weighted digging sticks. Shows that other common features relate to the hunting and gathering economy, activities and beliefs, events such as clashes with other groups, and the documentation of the arrival of cattle and the depiction of such foreign items as ships and wagons.
SOUTHERN AFRICA; CATTLE; CONFLICT; HISTORY; MATERIAL CULTURE; ROCK ART
PH 759.0113 WOO

0431 Woodhouse, H.C.
A REMARKABLE KNEELING POSTURE OF MANY FIGURES IN THE ROCK ART OF SOUTH AFRICA
South African Archaeological Bulletin, Vol.26, 1971. refs. pp.128–131.
The paper deals with rock paintings in the area between Newcastle on the north, Barkly East on the south, Ladybrand on the west and Matatiele on the east, all of which depict a kneeling human figure. Explains that some figures wear an animal-headed mask and all are shown in a kneeling posture with arms stretched backwards and fingers spread out. In some cases figures are grouped together and in others only one such figure is depicted while all are of the same size but are painted using varying techniques, such as monochrome or shaded polychrome. Provides a detailed description of the sites investigated.
SOUTH AFRICA; ARCHAEOLOGY; ROCK ART
P 930.105 SAA

0432 Woodhouse, H.C.
ROCK PAINTING OF MEAT-DRYING OR 'BILTONG'
South African Journal of Science, Vol.74 No.2, 1978. pp.71–78.
The article refers to a rock painting in the Harrismith District. Describes the painting which apparently depicts seated figures and an upright dancing figure behind whom are what the

author believes are strips of meat suspended from a framework. Notes that in several accounts by early travellers, there are descriptions of meat being dried by Bushmen. Observes that a demand for salt required in the drying process would stimulate trade in that commodity.
SOUTH AFRICA; FOOD; ROCK ART
P 505 SAJ

0433 Woodhouse, H.C.
INTERPRETATION OF CERTAIN ROCK PAINTINGS IN SOUTH AFRICA: A SECOND OPINION
South African Archaeological Bulletin, Vol.34 No.130, 1979. pp.133–137.
The paper examines interpretations by several writers on the meaning of particular rock paintings. Suggests alternatives to what the original authors believed they represented. Points out that the loss of white pigment on some paintings may change their appearance and confuse the viewer as to the meaning. Refers to the following books giving alternative suggestions for the meanings of particular paintings: Battiss, W. *Artists on the rocks* (1948), Vinnicombe, P. *People of the eland* (1976), Cooke, C.K. *Rock art of South Africa* (1969), Lee, D.N. and Woodhouse, H.C. *Art on the rocks of South Africa* (1970), Rudner, I. and J. *The hunter and his art* (1970), Pager, H. *Stone Age myth and magic* (1975).
SOUTHERN AFRICA; ROCK ART; RESEARCH
P 930.105 SAA

0434 Woodhouse, H.C.
LION KILLS: A PREVIOUSLY UNIDENTIFIED THEME IN THE BUSHMAN ART OF SOUTHERN AFRICA
South Africa Archaeological Bulletin, Vol.38, 1983, refs. pp.96–98.
The article describes paintings from six rock art sites from the following areas: Ladybrand District, Aliwal North District, Burgersdorp District, Ficksburg District and Concession District in Mashonaland, Zimbabwe. Considers that the paintings all deal with lion kills, and in several cases include scavengers such as vultures and jackals, and in others there are human figures. Notes ethnographic evidence of Kalahari Bushmen driving lions off a kill and believes that these paintings represent works of art created by artists for their own enjoyment.
SOUTH AFRICA; ZIMBABWE; ANIMALS; HUNTING; ROCK ART
P 930.105 SAA

0435 Woodhouse, H.C.
BEES AND HONEYCOMBS
South African Archaeological Bulletin, Vol.45 No.152, 1990 refs. p.120.
The article explains the interpretation of paintings as representing honeycombs and bees, and is based on the paper delivered to the Diamond Jubilee Symposium of the South African Federation of Beekeepers in 1986. Observes that it was supported by about 80 slides, many from Zimbabwe. Notes that although not all the oval designs in Zimbabwean rock paintings are bee-related, at least 157 are. Also, the oval designs are depicted at a number of sites in South Africa for example, Uitenhage and Calvinia.
SOUTH AFRICA; ZIMBABWE; ANTHROPOLOGY; ROCK ART
P 930.105 SAA

0436 Working Group of Indigenous Minorities in Southern Africa (WIMSA)
WORKING GROUP OF INDIGENOUS MINORITIES IN SOUTHERN AFRICA (WIMSA): REPORT ON ACTIVITIES, APRIL 1996 – MARCH 1997
Windhoek: Working Group of Indigenous Minorities in Southern Africa, 1997. 68pp.
The report covers the following activities carried out in the reporting period: education and training; development planning; control over tourism; access to and security of land; financial assistance to communities; networking. Appendices include the workplan and objectives for 1997, a bibliography and a list of WIMSA papers. Considers the highlight of the year to have been the San Conference at Gross Barmen in September when 19 delegates from the region were able to update themselves on the latest developments affecting their communities as well as being able to exchange views and identify the most pressing problems and steps towards addressing them. WIMSA's achievements and constraints were evaluated and its future tasks determined.
BOTSWANA; NAMIBIA; SOUTH AFRICA; ANNUAL REPORTS; COMMUNITY DEVELOPMENT; DEVELOPMENT PLANNING; EDUCATION; INDIGENOUS PEOPLES; NON-GOVERNMENTAL ORGANISATIONS; REGIONAL COOPERATION; SELF-DEVELOPMENT
98/1165

0437 Working Group of Indigenous Minorities in Southern Africa (WIMSA)
WORKING GROUP OF INDIGENOUS MINORITIES IN SOUTHERN AFRICA (WIMSA): REPORT ON ACTIVITIES, APRIL 1999 TO MARCH 2000
Windhoek: working Group of Indigenous Minorities In Southern Africa, 2000. ill., photos. 44pp.
The report provides an overview of WIMSA's activities during the period under review and outlines both the achievements and the continuing challenges. Notes that now, with the exception of those living in Angola, most of the estimated 100,000 San living in southern Africa are aware of the existence of WIMSA. Covers the following activities; education and training; institutional capacity-building; tourism; land and natural

resources; networking. Highlights of the year included: establishment of the San Cultural Centre 60km from Cape Town where the first trainees have undertaken practical courses; the publication of the report "Torn apart; San children as change agents in a process of acculturation"; a series of workshops for San traditional leaders on land and law issues; and the granting of a conservancy to the Ju/'hoansi community and recognition of their Traditional Authority. The Appendix reveals that WIMSA now has 20 member organizations in Botswana, South Africa and Namibia and that there are ten support organizations world-wide.

BOTSWANA; NAMIBIA; SOUTH AFRICA; ANNUAL REPORTS; COMMUNITY DEVELOPMENT; DEVELOPMENT PLANNING; EDUCATION; INDIGENOUS PEOPLES; NON-GOVERNMENTAL ORGANISATIONS; REGIONAL COOPERATION; SELF-DETERMINATION

PH/B 338.968 WOR

0438 Working Group of Indigenous Minorities in Southern Africa (WIMSA)
WORKING GROUP OF INDIGENOUS MINORITIES IN SOUTHERN AFRICA (WIMSA): REPORT ON ACTIVITIES, APRIL 2000 TO MARCH 2001
2001. 83pp.
The report outlines activities conducted by WIMSA in the period under review. Explains that WIMSA's key tasks are: a) to advocate and lobby for San rights; b) to support the network it helped to establish for information exchange among San communities and other concerned parties; and c) to provide ongoing training and advice to San communities on administrative procedures, development issues, land tenure and tourism. Covers the following activities: education and training; institutional capacity building; international co-ordination; HIV/AIDS; human rights, research; tourism; land and natural resources; networking. Appendices list: WIMSA member organizations; WIMSA support organizations; names of the members of the newly established Regional San Education and Language Committee; and the Regional San Heritage and Cultural Committee. Notes WIMSA's progress in assisting San to overcome their marginalization by enabling San individuals to acquire education and training, supporting them in raising cultural awareness, networking to enable the exchange of ideas and news of new developments among San communities in the region and support of communities whose human rights are violated.

BOTSWANA; NAMIBIA; SOUTH AFRICA; ANNUAL REPORTS; COMMUNITY DEVELOPMENT; DEVELOPMENT PLANNING; EDUCATION; INDIGENOUS PEOPLES; NON-GOVERNMENTAL ORGANISATIONS; REGIONAL COOPERATION; SELF-DETERMINATION

R/B 338.96872 WIM

0439 Wright, John B.
BUSHMAN RAIDERS OF THE DRAKENSBERG, 1840–1870: A STUDY OF THEIR CONFLICT WITH STOCK-KEEPING PEOPLES IN NATAL
Pietermaritzburg: University of Natal Press, 1971. ill., refs. ix, 235pp.
The book deals with the cattle raids carried out by Bushman groups, accompanied in some cases by Sotho. Notes that these raids took place during three distinct periods: from 1845 to around 1852, from 1856 to the early 1860's and lastly from 1863 to 1872, with the total number of raids recorded being about 64. Notes that their aim was to obtain cattle rather than being an attempt to drive out the white settlers and Bantu-speaking pastoralists, nor did these raiders attack and kill farmers as occurred in the Cape. Considers that the raids had the following causes: increasing pressure on available land; decimation of wildlife, the major food source of the Bushmen; use of cattle as a source of barter with surrounding tribes. Reflects on the attitudes of both white settlers and Bantu-speaking pastoralists and the official policies of the authorities towards the Bushmen which led to their eventual disappearance from the area.

DRAKENSBERG; KWAZULU-NATAL; SOUTH AFRICA; CONFLICT; HISTORY; INTERGROUP RELATIONS

968 WRI

0440 Wright, John B.
RETHINKING THE HISTORY OF THE BUSHMEN IN THE DRAKENSBERG REGION IN THE MID-NINETEENTH CENTURY
Texts and images of people, politics and power: representing the Bushman people of southern Africa. Johannesburg. 4th – 7th August, 1994. Johannesburg: University of the Witwatersrand, 1994. 28pp.
The paper presents a new approach to the history of the so-called "Bushmen" of the southern Drakensberg in the mid-nineteenth century. Comments on major changes in thinking by both historians and anthropologists since the appearance in 1971 of the book "Bushman raiders of the Drakensberg, 1840–1870: a study in conflict with stock-keeping peoples in Natal". Examines the historical works which were the first to question the long-established academic distinction between Bushman hunter-gatherers and Hottentot pastoralists and the debates which followed the publication of Wilmsen's *Land filled with flies*. Notes that in both disciplines the nature of relationships between hunter-gatherers and other groups is reconsidered. In view of these new insights, reviews the conclusions reached in "Raiders of the Drakensberg" and reports that the "raiders" were not traditional San but a mixture of Khoisan, Bantu-speakers and Dutch-Afrikaans speakers who in addition to hunting and gathering, hunted using guns, traded and owned horses and cattle. Suggests the need for a new

terminology to describe such groups.
DRAKENSBERG; KWAZULU-NATAL; SOUTH AFRICA; CONFLICT; HISTORY; INTERGROUP RELATIONS; KHOEKHOE
PH/B 968.4 WRI

0441 Wyckoff-Baird, B.
INDICATORS FROM JU/'HOAN BUSMHEN IN NAMIBIA
Cultural Survival Quarterly, Summer, 1996. pp.18–21.
The paper outlines the evolution of democratic practices within the Nyae Nyae Farmer's Cooperative in Eastern Bushmanland. Gives the history of the NNFC which implements activities including natural resource management, health promotion, a Village Schools Programme and the running of a shop. Relates stages through which the current structure moved from one based on foreign models to one based on the traditional decision-making by consensus and relating to the needs of the Ju/'hoansi themselves.
NAMIBIA; NYAE NYAE; COOPERATIVES; DEMOCRACY; EDUCATION; FARMING; JU/'HOANSI; NON-GOVERNMENTAL ORGANISATIONS; SELF-DEVELOPMENT
99/182

0442 Yates, Royden
SHAMANISM AND ROCK PAINTINGS: ASPECTS OF THE USE OF ROCK ART IN THE SOUTH-WESTERN CAPE, SOUTH AFRICA
South African Archaeological Bulletin, Vol.46 No.153, 1991. Refs. pp.3–11.
The article discusses evidence for the direct interaction with paintings by San hunter-gatherers in south-western Cape. Offers three observations: paintings of images, smearing of paint, and smoothing of areas of pigment. Notices that these practices are shown to be consistent with shamanistic ritual in general, as well as with accounts of southern San painting. Explains that potency associated with the rock paintings and the paint is assumed to be the reason behind these interactions with paintings. Concludes that in the south-western Cape at least, rock paintings served not only to depict trance metaphors and hallucinations but also served as tangible expressions of supernatural potency.
SOUTH AFRICA; SOUTH WESTEN CAPE; ANIMALS; CULTURE; DANCE; HEALING; HUNTING-GATHERING; ROCK ART; SHAMANISM; TRANCE
P 930.105 SAA

0443 Yates, Royden; Golson, Jo; Hall, Martin
TRANCE PERFORMANCE: THE ROCK ART OF BOONTJIESKLOOF AND SEVILLA
South African Archaeological Bulletin, Vol.40, 1985. refs. pp.70–80.
The paper analyses a sample of paintings from the south-western Cape for evidence of trance symbolism. Notes the existence of such symbols although they differ from those from the Drakensberg but deems the differences to be superficial. Considers the implications of these interpretations with respect to two image types, "group scenes" and "conflicts".
KWAZULU-NATAL; SOUTH AFRICA; DRAKENSBERG; ARCHAEOLOGY; BELIEFS; RELIGION; RESEARCH; ROCK ART; SHAMANISM; TRANCE
P 930.105 SAA

0444 ?Eichab, H.A.
NAMIB GAO/GÒAN
Windhoek: Gamsberg Macmillan, 1997. 103pp.
The book contains poetry in Khoekhoegowab and covers a number of themes: superstition, religion, nature, politics, discrimination, environmental awareness and national unity. It is intended for senior primary and secondary school pupils and is included to demonstrate the orthography used for the writing of Khoekhoegowab in Namibia.
NAMIBIA; KHOEKHOEGOWAB; LANGUAGES; LINGUISTICS; LITERATURE
R/B 496.1 ?EIC

0445 =Oma, Kxao Moses
DO THE SAN OF SOUTHERN AFRICA HAVE A SAY ON EDUCATION?
1998. 9pp.
The paper concentrates on the education of San children at primary level in Botswana, South Africa and Namibia and outlines the constraints that San communities face in achieving their educational and linguistic aspirations. Comments on the differing response of the respective education systems in the three countries to the needs of San pupils. Notes that while active participation of parents in school affairs is essential if their educational goals are to be achieved, the major responsibility lies with Governments. Points out that if the needs of marginalised minorities go unrecognised, then no relevant policies will be implemented. Concludes that the Ministry of Basic Education and Culture in Namibia is prepared to consider the recommendations of the San and to implement them with the help of NGOs, thus hopefully serving as a role model for educational authorities in other countries. Highlights the role of WIMSA in providing education and training in response to the requests by the communities for such assistance.
NAMIBIA; SOUTH AFRICA
PH/B 372.7096872 OMA

0446 /Uriseb, A.
//HÛISA !NUBU //GAE?HÒADI
Windhoek: Gamsberg, 1993.
This textbook in Khoekhoegowaib is included in the bibliography to demonstrate the orthography used for the writing of

Khoesan languages in Namibia.
NAMIBIA; KHOEKHOEGOWAB; LANGUAGES; LINGUISTICS;
LITERATURE
R/B 496.1 /URI

0447 /Useb, Joram
'ONE CHIEF IS ENOUGH!': UNDERSTANDING SAN TRADITIONAL AUTHORITIES IN THE NAMIBIAN CONTEXT
Barnard, Alan; Kenrick, Justin. Africa's Indigenous Peoples: 'First Peoples or Marginalised Minorities'? Edinburgh: University of Edinburgh, Centre of African Studies, 2001. refs. xv, 322pp. pp.15–29. ISBN 0952791757.
The chapter examines forms of chieftainship or traditional leadership existing among the following San communities in Namibia: Hai//om, Kxoe, !Xu, !Xoo and Ju/'hoansi. Shows that contrary to widely held opinions, all these groups had some forms of elected or inherited leadership and gives the relevant terms in the various languages denoting names for leaders. Looks at the demanding new roles for San leaders in independent Namibia as they attempt to represent the aspirations and plans of their communities to the central government. Looks at the role of women as leaders and the reasons for their general reluctance to take on such roles. Reports on training workshops for traditional leaders run by various organizations to give practical training in administrative tasks and exchange views and experiences. Looks at legislation relating to San leadership, but notes that only leaders recognised by Government can serve on Land Boards or advise the President on land matters. Points out that so far only two traditional San leaders have received Government recognition. Concludes with the hope that eventually the leaders of all six San communities will be given the opportunity to carry out their own leadership goals and motivate their communities.
NAMIBIA; !XOO; !XUN; CONFERENCE PAPERS; HAI//OM; JU/'HOANSI; LAND RIGHTS; LAW; LEGAL RIGHTS; POLITICAL LEADERSHIP; TRAINING
R/B 305.80968 AFR

0448 /Useb, Joram
INDIGENOUS PEOPLE AND DEVELOPMENT
United Nations 19th Working Group on Indigenous Populations. 23–27 July, 2001. Geneva, Switzerland. 2001. 2pp.
The brief paper reveals the severe problems which will be faced by the !Kung in Tsumkwe District West if the Namibian government's plan to resettle 20,000 refugees in their area is put into effect. Points out that the !Kung had applied to the Ministry of Empowerment and Tourism for a tourism conservancy covering an area of 8,550 sq. km. which would have assisted in securing the future of the !Kung and Ju/'hoansi of the district. Reports that no reply had been received after two and a half years. Appeals to the Namibian government to carry out an environmental and social impact assessment before finally deciding on the relocation of the refugees.
NAMIBIA; GOVERNMENT POLICY; LAND RIGHTS
PH/B 306 IND

0449 //Garoeb, I.F.H.
DÀUREB /AE//GÀUB
Windhoek: Gamsberg Macmillan, n.d. 70pp.
A story in Khoekhoegowab included in the bibliography to demonstrate the orthography employed for the writing of this language in Namibia.
NAMIBIA; KHOEKHOEGOWAB; LANGUAGES; LINGUISTICS;
LITERATURE
R/B 496.1 //GAR

INDEXES

Author Index

//Garoeb, I.F.H. 0449
/Uriseb, A. 0446
/Useb, Joram 0447, 0448
?Eichab, H.A. 0444
=Oma, Kxao Moses 0445
Adams, F. 0001
Akira, Takada 0002
Amadi, Elechi 0003
Amodeo, Chris 0417
Anon 0004
Argyle, W.J. 0005
Bain, Donald 0006
Bannister, Anthony 0223
Barnard, Alan 0007, 0008–0010
Bartram, Laurence E.C. Jr. 0156
Batibo, Herman M. 0011–0013
Beake, Lesley 0014
Beckman, L. 0274
Bennett, Bruce S. 0015
Berger, Dhyani J. 0414
Bertin, G. 0016
Beurden Van, J. 0182
Bible Society of Botswana, Gaborone 0017
Biesele, Megan 0018–0020
Bikeur, A.C. 0021–0022
Binford, L.R. 0023
Bird-David, Nurit 0024
Bjerre, Jens 0025
Bleek, Dorothea F. 0026–0038, 0041
Bleek, W.H.I. 0039–0041
Blundell, Geoffrey 0224
Blurton-Jones, Nicholas 0042
Boko, Duma Gideon 0043
Bolaane, Maitseo 0044
Botelle, A. 0045
Botswana Christian Council, Gaborone 0046–0048
Bowie, Hamish 0146
Brearley, J. 0049
Bredekamp, Henry C. Jatti 0050
Bregin, Elana 0051
Brenzinger, Matthias 0052–0053
Brown, David Maughan 0054
Brown, Duncan 0055
Brörmann, Magdalena 0056, 0119
Budack, K.F.R. 0057
Butler, F.G. 0058
Campbell, Alec 0073, 0083
Campbell, C. 0059
Carstens, P. 0060

Cassidy, Lin 0061, 0146
Chebanne, Anderson 0062–0063
Chumbo, Sefako 0064
Coetzee, C. 0065
Coetzee, J.M. 0066
Coetzee, Paulette 0067
Collins, Chris 0068
Commerce and Industry, Ministry of, Gaborone, Department of Wildlife and National Parks 0255
Conference on human rights and democracy, Gaborone, 17th – 19th November, 1998 0069
Cooke, C.K. 0070–0071
Corrington, Matt 0072
Coulson, David 0073
Cowley, Clive 0074
Crawhall, Nigel 0075
Crowder, Michael 0248
Cukiri, Tshau Frisca 0076
Daly, Richard Heywood 0208
Darkwah, R.K.H. 0077
Deacon, Janette 0078, 0079
Dedering, T. 0080
Deetz, James 0081
Denbow, James 0082, 0083
Dickens, Patrick 0084
Dintwa, Bathusi 0085
Ditshwanelo: The Botswana Centre for Human Rights 0086
Doke, Clement M. 0087
Douglas, Stuart 0088
Dowson, Thomas A. 0089, 0090
Draper, Patricia 0091, 0092, 0093
Duggan-Cronin, Alfred Martin 0094
Eastwood, Edward B. 0095
Ebert, James I. 0096
Ebert, Melinda 0096
Ehret, Christopher 0097
Eistein, A. 0098
Elbourne, Elizabeth 0099
Elderkin, E.D. 0100
Ellis, William 0101
Elphick, Richard 0102–0104
Endicott, Karen L. 0105
England, Nicholas M. 0106
English, Mark 0107
Erni, C. 0108
Fagan, Brian M. 0109
Farrington, E. 0329
Felton, Silke 0110
Fewster, Kathryn Jane 0111

Fischer, Jean 0112
Frolov, B.A. 0113
Gall, Sandy 0114
Garlake, Peter S. 0115–0117
Gaski, Harald 0118
Geingos, Victoria 0119
George, Kipi 0120
Glasser, Sylvia 0121
Godwin, Peter 0122
Golson, Jo 0443
Good, Kenneth 0061, 0123–0124
Gordon, Robert J. 0125–0126
Greenberg, Joseph H. 0127
Guelke, Leonard 0128
Guenther, Mathias 0129–0133
Haacke, W.H.G. 0134
Hallowes, D.P. 0198
Hall, Martin 0443
Hammond-Tooke, W.D. 0135, 0136
Hardbattle, John 0137
Hargrove, Thomas Henry 0138
Hasselbring, Sue 0139, 0140
Hauge, M. 0274
Hawkes, Kristen 0042
Hays, Jennifer 0141
Headland, D.T. 0142
Heine, Bernd 0143, 0196
Heinz, H-J. 0144, 0145
Hermans, Janet 0146, 0270, 0394, 0421
Hitchcock, Robert K. 0096, 0147–0157, 0399
Hoehn, G.C. 0158
Hoff, Ansie 0159
Holliday, Anne L. 0090
Hollmann, Jeremy 0160
Honken, Henry 0161–0162
Hovelmann, Wendy 0163
Hudson, Derek J. 0164
Humphreys, A.J.B. 0165–0166
Ikeya, Kazonubu 0167
Imamura-Hayaki, K. 0168–0169
Isaacson, Rupert 0170
Isaksen, Jan. 0164
James, Alan. 0171
Jean Milmine, M.S. 0172
Jeffreys, M.D.W. 0173
Jenkins, T. 0274
Jeursen, Belinda 0174
Jolly, Pieter. 0175
Jones, Neville, 0176
Judson, W.A. 0177
Kaashe, Tseeku 0179

Kagaya, Ryohei 0180
Kazombungo, Jerson 0181
Keineetse, Keitseope 0182
Kelly, R.L. 0183
Kenrick, Justin 0010
Kent, Susan 0184, 0185–0186
Kimura, K. 0338
Kinahan, John 0187–0188
Kirby, Percival R. 0189–0190
Kohler, Oswin von 0191
Koketso, Gaewetse 0192
Kuela, Kiema 0076
Kuru Development Trust 0193–0194
Kuru Development Trust. Bokamoso Preschool Programme 0195
König, Christa 0196
Lane, P. 0197, 0394
Lanham, L.W. 0198
Le Roux, Braam 0199
Le Roux, Willemien. 0200–0201
Lebotse, Kabelo Kenneth 0202
Lee, Richard B. 0203–0208
Legassick, Martin 0209
Lewis-Williams, James David 0210–0225
Liebenberg, Louis 0226
Lloyd, L.C. 0041
Louw, J.A. 0227
Lutheran World Federation 0228
MacGaddery, Pauline 0400
Macdonald, Dave 0229
Madzudzo, Elias 0230
Maingard, L.F. 0231–0236
Malherbe, C. 0104
Manhire, Anthony 0237
Marks, Shula 0238–0239
Marshall, Lorna 0240–0241
Mason, R.J. 0242
Matenge, B. 0258
Mazel, Aron 0243
Mazonde, Isaac N. 0061, 0244–0247
Mgadla, P.T. 0077
Miers, Suzanne 0248
Miller-Ockhuizen, A. 0249
Mmaba, Kotsi 0064
Moesi, M. 0250
Mogwe, A. 0251, 0252
Mokgothi, Archie 0253
Mokobane, Mosimaneotsile I. 0254
Molamu, Louis 0229, 0255
Molebatsi, Chadzimula 0256, 0394
Monageng, Stella 0257, 0421

Monu E. 0255
Motshabi, Kgosi W 0258
Mphinyane, Sethunya T. 0259
Myers, F.R. 0260
Namaseb, Levi 0261
Naro Language Team, Gantsi, Botswana 0262
Nawa, Karabo Vincent 0263
Nettleton, Anitra 0264
Ngakaeaja, Mathambo 0265
Nienaber, G.S. 0266–0268
Norborg, Ake 0269
Nteta, Doreen 0270
Nthomang, Keitseope 0271–0273
Nurse, G.T. 0274
Oabile, Malebogo 0096
Okhiro, Gary Y. 0276
Oussoren, Otto 0277
Ouzman, Sven 0278–0281
O'Connell, James 0042
Pager, Harald 0282–0284
Painter, M. 0255
Pakleppa, Richard 0285
Parkington, John 0286–0288
Parry, Elspeth 0289
Parsons, Neil 0290
Pfaffe, Joachim Friedrich 0291–0292
Phaladi, Salalenna G.G. 0293
Pisani, E. du 0358
Platvoet, Jan G. 0294
Prins, Frans 0295
Ramore, L. 0297
Rampadi, Mama 0298
Rankopo, M.J. 0273
Rasebotsa, Nobantu 0299
Reid, A. 0197
Reid, L. 0142
Reuning, Helmut 0300
Richard, Phanuel 0301
Riches, D. 0302
Richter, L.M. 0303
Ritchie, C. 0304
Rivers, Roberta 0061, 0305
Robins, Steven 0306–0309
Rogers David 0310
Rohde, R. 0045
Rosenberg, H.G. 0207
Ross, Robert 0311
Royal-/o/oo, Kxao 0020
Rudner, Ione 0314
Rudner, Jalmar 0312–0314
Sadler, Katherine 0316

Sadr, Karim 0317, 0318
Sampson, Clavil Garth 0319–0320
Sanders, A.J.G.M. 0321
Sands, Bonny E. 0322
Saugestad, Sidsel 0323–0325, 0421
Schadeberg, Jurgen 0326
Schapera, Isaac 0327–0329
Schladt, Mathias 0330–0331
Schmidt, Sigrid 0332–0334
Segatlhe, Thabiso 0140
Segobye, A. 0197
Shanefelt, Robert 0335
Shell, Robert 0128
Sholto-Douglas, Stuart 0126
Silberbauer, George B. 0336–0337
Singer, R. 0338
Sixpence, Hunter Qace 0339
Skotnes, Pippa 0340
Smith, Andrew B. 0341
Smith, A.B. 0342
Smits, Lucas 0343
Snyman, J.W. 0344–0349
Solomon, Anne 0350–0351
Solway, Jacqueline S. 0352
South West Africa. Department of National Education 0353
Spohr, Otto H. 0354
Steyn, H.P. 0355–0358
Story, R. 0359
Stow, George W. 0360
Strydom, J.L.C. 0361
Sugawara, Kazuyoshi 0373
Suzman, James 0362–0365
Sylvain, Renee 0366–0367
Szalay, Miklos 0368
Tagart, E.S.B. 0371
Tanaka, Jiro 0372–0373
Taylor, Michael 0374–0376
Thackeray, Francis 0377
Thackeray, J.F. 0378
Theal, George McCall 0360, 0379
Thoma, Axel 0096, 0199
Thupe, Gaolatlhe 0380
Tobias, Phillip V. 0381
Tomaselli, Keyan G. 0382–0384
Traill, Anthony 0084, 0385–0390
Tributsch, Helmut 0391
Tshireletso, Lucky 0392
Tsonope, Joseph 0011–0013
Tucker, A.N. 0393
University of Botswana 0394
University of Botswana, Research and Development Unit

0277
Van Rijssen, W.J. 0395
Van der Post, Laurens 0396–0398
Vierich, Helga 0399
Viljoen, Hans 0400
Viljoen, Russel 0401
Visser-Wiegel, Coby 0402
Visser, Hessel 0403–0404
Vossen, Rainer 0405–0406
Voss, A.E. 0407
Wadley, L. 0408
Waldman, Linda 0409
Walker, Nick 0410–0411
Ward, Valerie 0412
Weich, F. 0413
Weinberg, Paul 0414
Wendt, W.E. 0415
Werner, W. 0001
Wessels, Elizabeth 0416
Wheat, Sue 0417
Widlok, T. 0009
Willcox, A.R. 0418–0420
Willet, Shelagh 0421
Wilmsen, Edwin N. 0422–0424
Wilson, Monica 0425
Wily, Elizabeth 0426
Winkler, Danny 0427
Winter, J.C. 0428
Woodburn, James 0429
Woodhouse, H.C. 0430–0435
Working Group of Indigenous Minorities in Southern Africa (WIMSA) 0436–0438
Wortley, Wendy 0300
Wright, John B. 0439–0440
Wyckoff-Baird, B. 0441
Yates, Royden 0442, 0443
Yellen, John E. 0157

Subject Index

!kung 0018, 0024–0026, 0042, 0045, 0072, 009–0093, 0098, 0105, 0112, 0114, 0119, 0131, 0133, 0135, 0138, 0142, 0183, 0184, 0203–0204, 0240–0241, 0246, 0274, 0285, 0290, 0294, 0300, 0303, 0333, 0336, 0359
!ora 0189, 0234, 0236, 0425
!ui 0026
!xoo 0008, 0084, 0098, 0119, 0139, 0161–0162, 0233, 0246, 0269, 0274, 0322, 0327, 0345, 0356, 0365, 0381, 0385–0388, 0390, 0447
!xun 0002, 0052, 0122, 0161, 0196, 0200, 0308, 0322, 0349, 0389, 0413, 0428, 0447
//anikhwe 0074, 0405
//xegwi 0198
/'auni 0094, 0269, 0327, 0357
/'auo 0359
/xam 0019, 0026–0035, 0037, 0040–0041, 0055, 0094, 0131, 0135, 0159, 0162, 0171, 0236, 0278, 0327, 0335, 0340, 0354, 0428
||anikhwe 0064
'Auo 0198,
=hua 0008, 0068, 0084, 0161–0162
=khomani 0008, 0072, 0075, 0094, 0101, 0114, 0170, 0308, 0309, 0357, 0414
=kx'au//'ei 0428
Access to education 0141, 0181, 0245, 0253–0254, 0277, 0298, 0380, 0392
Acculturation 0422
Adult education 0244, 0402
Advocacy 0048, 0050, 0110, 0114, 0122, 0125, 0152, 0155, 0193, 0200, 0208, 0260, 0298, 0309, 0362, 0367, 0409
Afrikaners 0209, 0366
Aged 0093
Agriculture 0001, 0111, 0138, 0191, 0377
Alcohol 0205, 0229
Alcoholism 0362
Animals 0028, 0030–0032, 0034, 0058, 0081, 0090, 0095, 0116–0117, 0135–0136, 0160, 0217, 0222, 0224, 0226, 0242, 0278–0279, 0284, 0313, 0318, 0372, 0377–0378, 0391, 0420, 0434, 0442
Annual reports 0436–0438
Anthropologists 0383
Anthropology 0028–0031, 0034, 0035, 0042, 0074, 0077, 0082, 0090–0092, 0103, 0105, 0126, 0130–0131, 0135, 0142, 0156, 0183, 0186, 0214, 0216–0218, 0221–0223, 0231, 0241, 0246, 0259–0260, 0276, 0288, 0290, 0302, 0311, 0336, 0372–0373, 0378–379, 0382, 0408, 0423, 0435
Archaeology 0004, 0023, 0079, 0083, 0156, 0165, 0176, 0187, 0188, 0191, 0197, 0217, 0220, 0231, 0237, 0242–0243, 0286, 0288, 0293, 0312, 0314, 0316–0317, 0319–0320, 0351, 0377, 0381, 0408, 0410, 0415, 0431, 0443
Army 0112, 0276
Art 0177, 0280, 0340, 0350, 0411
Assimilation 0245
Attitudes 0054, 0125, 0141, 0230, 0244, 0259, 0272, 0305, 0309, 0342, 0364, 0380
Bakgalagadi 0107, 0154, 0352, 0355, 0424
Bakgatla 0301
Bands 0131, 0241
Bangwato 0111, 0156, 0247, 0248, 0301, 0371
Basotho 0175
Behaviour 0377
Beliefs 0007, 0018–0020, 0028–0035, 0037, 0041, 0049, 0053, 0058, 0073, 0078, 0081, 0095, 0106, 0116–0117, 0131–0133, 0135–0136, 0144, 0159, 0173, 0175–0176, 0205, 0208, 0210, 0212, 0214, 0216–0224, 0264, 0278, 0284, 0310, 0313, 0316, 0326, 0329, 033–0337, 0360, 0377, 0378, 0391, 0395, 0396–0398, 0410, 0443
Bible 0017, 0296, 0413
Bibliographies 0164, 0257, 0297, 0323, 0332, 0354, 0421
Blood 0274
Book reviews 0019, 0078, 0081, 0089, 0110, 0130, 0135, 0158, 0166, 0213, 0243, 0276, 0287, 0290, 0311, 0313, 0335, 0342, 0356, 0395, 0423
Botany 0331, 0359
Bugakhwe 0064, 0139, 0376
Care-giving 0144
Case studies 0158
Cattle 0112, 0124, 0172, 0182, 0206, 0317, 0341, 0430
Children 0146, 0237, 0303, 0416
Church 0047, 0048
Clicks 0005, 0026, 0037–0038, 0040, 0063, 0076, 0097, 0100, 0127, 0161, 0266, 0323, 0330, 0348–0349, 0353, 0387, 0388–0389, 0403
Colonialism 0051, 0055, 0065, 0103–0104, 0109, 0128, 0239, 0247, 0295, 0341, 0368
Communal land 0001
Communication 0126
Community development 0193–0194, 0273, 0308, 0339, 0436–0438
Conference papers 0008, 0015, 0044, 0050, 0063, 0076, 0077, 0085, 0101, 0118, 0145, 0147, 0179, 0181, 0192, 0199, 0202, 0253–0254, 0257–0259, 0261, 0263, 0272, 0298, 0309, 0323–0325, 0339, 0344, 0364, 0370, 0380, 0392, 0402, 0409, 0416, 0429, 0447
Conference reports 0010, 0069, 0247, 0277, 0394
Conflict 0051, 0059, 0072, 0080, 0099, 0104, 0126, 0128, 0160, 0207, 0238, 0241, 0276, 0368, 0401, 0425, 0430,

0439–0440
Conservation   0149, 0151, 0157, 0226, 0374, 0376, 0414
Constitutions   0015, 0062
Cooperatives   0001, 0441
Cosmology   0033, 0132–0133, 0136, 0222, 0351
Cultural change   0091, 0103, 0138, 0172, 0342, 0368, 0399
Culture   0006, 0008, 0019, 0025, 0036, 0038, 0040, 0057, 0060, 0064, 0073, 0075, 0088, 0094, 0105, 0113, 0121, 0129, 0131, 0144, 0155, 0178, 0184–0185, 0203–0205, 0207, 0211, 0240–0241, 0244, 0276, 0295, 0311, 0315–0316, 0319, 0328–0329, 0334, 0341–0342, 0351, 0355, 0360, 0362, 0373, 0422, 0426, 0428, 0442
Curriculum   0163
Customs   0333
Damara   0274, 0332, 0334, 0358, 0408
Dance   0006, 0025, 0049, 0058, 0059, 0081, 0090, 0098, 0106, 0115, 0117, 0121, 0132, 0136, 0160, 0190, 0214–0219, 0222, 0225, 0264, 0276, 0278, 0294, 0310, 0313, 0316, 0326, 0336, 0355, 0372, 0395–0396, 0398, 0419, 0442
Danisi   0140
Decision-making   0328, 0363
Democracy   0247, 0441
Demography   0093, 0265, 0363, 0422
Desalination   0228
Development aid   0047, 0069, 0182, 0228
Development planning   0045–0046, 0048, 0085, 0096, 0206, 0363, 0436–0438
Development policy   0044, 0244, 0271, 0376, 0426
Development projects   0315, 0367
Development strategy   0271
Dictionaries   0180, 0196, 0390, 0393, 0404
Diet   0182, 0274, 0328
Droughts   0046, 0047
Early iron age   0317
Ecobotany   0137
Ecology   0153, 0208, 0341, 0357, 0372–0373, 0420
Economic development   0193, 0245, 0255, 0272–0273, 0297, 0339
Economy   0020, 0045, 0113, 0153, 0164, 0318, 0373, 0399
Education   0047, 0056, 0061, 0076, 0096, 0139, 0141, 0163, 0179, 0182, 0192, 0195, 0253–0254, 0258, 0261, 0263, 0277, 0291–0292, 0298, 0315, 0362–0364, 0380, 0392, 0416, 0436–0438, 0441
Educational policy   0244, 0253–0254
Egalitarianism   0105, 0184, 0204
Eggshells   0156, 0177
Empowerment   0043, 0075, 0193–0194, 0271, 0273, 0292, 0309, 0325, 0414
Environment   0091, 0138, 0153, 0341
Ethnic groups   0247, 0269

Ethnicity   0015, 0247, 0376, 0424
Ethnoarchaeology   0111
Ethnobiology   0098
Ethnobotany   0098, 0168, 0242, 0331, 0357–0359, 0381, 0414
Ethnohistory   0082
Evolution   0356
Exploitation   0114, 0245, 0270, 0367, 0371
Farm workers   0009, 0126, 0181, 0270, 0277, 0366–0367
Farming   0001, 0092, 0096, 0101, 0111–0112, 0123, 0138, 0182, 0228, 0230, 0301, 0304, 0336, 0399, 0441
Fertility   0377
Films   0174, 0382, 0383–0384
Fishing   0057, 0074, 0283, 0286
Folklore   0016, 0018–0019, 0025, 0027–0035, 0040–0041, 0132, 0171, 0287, 0332, 0335, 0354, 0360, 0379, 0396, 0397
Folktales   0039
Food   0023, 0057, 0064, 0074, 0156, 0165–0169, 0230, 0320, 0336, 0357–0359, 0417, 0432
Food production   0138
Foraging   0009, 0042, 0057, 0077, 0082, 0091, 0107, 0138, 0156, 0165, 0168–0169, 0183–0185, 0326, 0357–0399, 0424
Game reserves   0001, 0072, 0086, 0108, 0114, 0120, 0122, 0150–0151, 0182, 0226, 0252, 0259, 0365, 0414
Gender issues   0067, 0092–0093, 0105, 0110, 0170, 0204, 0251, 0288, 0366
Genetics   0381
Government policy   0020, 0044–0045, 0061, 0069, 0075, 0077, 0085–0086, 0107–0108, 0120, 0124, 0147–0148, 0150–0152, 0157, 0167–0168, 0192, 0202, 0230, 0252–0253, 0259, 0271–0272, 0277, 0285, 0304–0305, 0352, 0362–0363, 0365, 0371, 0374, 0376, 0414, 0417, 0427, 0448
Grammar   0026, 0068, 0084, 0134, 0161, 0180, 0196, 0227, 0233, 0322, 0346–0347, 0385, 0388, 0390
Griqua   0050, 0209, 0409, 0425
G/ui   0007, 0008, 0012–0013, 0072, 0107, 0139, 0156–0157, 0167–0169, 0183, 0186, 0235, 0242, 0249, 0269, 0274, 0300, 0336–0337, 0359, 0372–0373, 0386–0387, 0414, 0417, 0427
G//ana   0008, 0072, 0107, 0139, 0156, 0167–0169, 0186, 0232, 0235, 0249, 0269, 0274, 0300, 0344, 0359, 0372–0373, 0414, 0417, 0427
Hadza   0042, 0097, 0127, 0161, 0231, 0322
Hai//om   0009, 0026, 0087, 0126, 0131, 0269, 0327, 0365, 0447
Handicrafts   0096
Healing   0034–0035, 0058, 0098, 0106, 0132, 0136, 0144, 0170, 0215, 0221, 0224, 0276, 0294, 0310, 0326, 0367,

0372, 0396, 0442
Health 0144, 0265, 0362
Herders 0070, 0197
Herding 0103–0104, 0238, 0318
Herero 0156, 0242, 0422
Hiechware 0235–0236, 0327
History 0004, 0015, 0020, 0041, 0050–0052, 0055, 0059, 0065–0066, 0073, 0075, 0079–0080, 0099, 0102–0103, 0109, 0114–0115, 0125–0126, 0128, 0152, 0165, 0182, 0187, 0209, 0216, 0231, 0238–0239, 0245, 0247–0248, 0268–0269, 0280–0281, 0286, 0288–0290, 0301, 0307, 0311, 0314, 0326, 0329, 0340–0341, 0351, 0358, 0360, 0366, 0368, 0371, 0379, 0401, 0422, 0425, 0430, 0439–0440
Hostels 0146, 0253–0254
Human rights 0062, 0069, 0118, 0202, 0245, 0251, 0362, 0364, 0429
Hunting 0030, 0147, 0151, 0156–0157, 0284, 0333–0334, 0356, 0373, 0376, 0378, 0434
Hunting-gathering 0020, 0024, 0064, 0075, 0077, 0092, 0101, 0138, 0142, 0147, 0152, 0158, 0172, 0185–0187, 0238–0239, 0241–0242, 0246, 0260, 0274, 0279–0280, 0286, 0293, 0302, 0316, 0318–0319, 0326, 0336, 0355, 0357–0358, 0360, 0368, 0372, 0429, 0442
Indigenous peoples 0010, 0050, 0075, 0088, 0103–0104, 0118, 0145, 0147, 0154, 0178, 0238, 0272, 0306, 0325, 0337, 0364, 0382, 0409, 0417, 0424, 0427, 0429, 0436–0438
Inequality 0392, 0424
Initiation 0049, 0060, 0132, 0144
Integration 0426
Interaction 0010, 0042, 0051, 0091, 0107, 0109, 0111, 0114, 0126, 0129, 0165, 0175, 0195, 0201, 0244, 0259, 0278, 0293, 0301, 0305, 0311, 0355, 0363–0364, 0371, 0383, 0409, 0429
Intergroup relations 0011, 0041, 0052, 0082, 0099, 0101–0104, 0128, 0136, 0152, 0204, 0209, 0230, 0238, 0276, 0286, 0290, 0299, 0401, 0425–0426, 0439, 0440
Iron age 0318, 0377
Ju 0026–0327, 0346
Ju/'hoan 0020, 0119, 0353
Ju/'hoansi 0013, 0087, 0106, 0122, 0126, 0139, 0155, 0157, 0161–0163, 0205–0206, 0232, 0249, 0269, 0285, 0294, 0304, 0346–0349, 0365–0367, 0369, 0393, 0414, 0441, 0447
Kalanga 0230
Khoe 0026, 0100, 0235, 0346, 0405–0406
Khoekhoe 0039, 0050, 0065–0066, 0074, 0099, 0102–0104, 0109, 0114, 0128, 0130, 0159, 0188–0189, 0238–0239, 0266, 0268, 0274, 0286, 0329, 0332, 0338, 0341, 0368, 0425, 0428, 0440

Khoekhoegowab 0003, 0011, 0021–0022, 0026, 0039, 0057, 0087, 0127, 0134, 0140, 0227, 0231, 0261, 0266, 0268, 0322, 0327, 0334, 0346, 0348, 0354, 0361, 0369, 0379, 0400, 0403, 0405, 0444, 0446, 0449
Khoesan 0005, 0050, 0075, 0097, 0099, 0103–0104, 0127, 0130, 0138, 0178, 0189, 0238–0239, 0257, 0274, 0311, 0322, 0323, 0352, 0370, 0379, 0421, 0423–0425, 0428
Khomani 0306
Khwe 0052–0053, 0072, 0120, 0122, 0191, 0200, 0284, 0303, 0308, 0331, 0369
Khwedam 0013, 0053, 0100, 0143, 0315, 0330, 0331, 0369
Kinship 0007, 0138, 0241, 0372, 0423–0424, 0428
Kua 0013, 0063, 0140, 0156, 0186, 0399
Labour 0181, 0371
Labour relations 0181
Land ownership 0077
Land reforms 0148
Land rights 0001, 0043, 0045, 0061, 0069, 0072, 0101, 0108, 0119–0120, 0123, 0145, 0148, 0154, 0156, 0170, 0172, 0178, 0192, 0202, 0252, 0285, 0298, 0305–0306, 0308–0309, 0337, 0362–0365, 0376, 0414, 0417, 0427, 0429, 0447–0448
Land use 0001, 0045, 0096, 0104, 0126, 0152–0153, 0156, 0326, 0373–0374, 0422
Languages 0003, 0005, 0011–0013, 0016–0017, 0021–0022, 0026, 0028–0035, 0037–0040, 0053, 0062–0063, 0068, 0075, 0083–0084, 0087, 0097, 0100, 0102, 0127, 0134, 0140, 0143, 0161–0163, 0173, 0180, 0185, 0190–0191, 0196, 0198, 0227, 0231–0236, 0249, 0261–0262, 0266, 0268, 0296, 0306, 0322–0323, 0327–0330, 0344–0349, 0353–0354, 0359, 0361, 0377, 0379, 0381, 0385–0390, 0393, 0400, 0402–0406, 0413, 0421, 0424–0425, 0428, 0444, 0446, 0449
Law 0285, 0321–0352, 0447
Leadership 0204, 0306
Legal rights 0045, 0147, 0252, 0285, 0364, 0447
Life stories 0036, 0040, 0065, 0304, 0354, 0398
Linguistics 0003, 0005, 0011–0013, 0016–0017, 0021–0022, 0026, 0028–0035, 0037–0040, 0053, 0063, 0068, 0075, 0083–0084, 0087, 0097, 0100, 0102, 0127, 0134, 0140, 0143, 0161–0163, 0173, 0180, 0185, 0190–0191, 0196, 0198, 0227, 0231–0236, 0249, 0261–0262, 0266, 0268, 0296, 0322–0323, 0327, 0329–0330, 0344–0349, 0353–0354, 0359, 0361, 0377, 0379, 0381, 0385–0390, 0393, 0402–0406, 0413, 0421, 0425, 0428, 0444, 0446, 0449
Literacy 0061, 0076, 0139, 0163, 0291, 0402
Literature 0003, 0014, 0021–0022, 0051, 0054–0055, 0067, 0171, 0201, 0299, 0384, 0397–0398, 0400, 0407, 0444, 0446, 0449
Livestock 0101, 0103, 0128, 0138, 0246, 0250, 0265

Living conditions 0023, 0167, 0265, 0383
Local government 0061, 0192, 0265, 0305, 0365
Marginalization 0119, 0247, 0259, 0325, 0364–0365, 0367
Marriage 0240–0241
Matabele 0230
Material culture 0038, 0094, 0129, 0312, 0319, 0360, 0430
Medical research 0274, 0303, 0338, 0381
Migration 0297, 0377
Minority groups 0365
Minority rights 0015, 0062, 0075, 0154, 0247, 0251, 0352
Missionaries 0002, 0050, 0080, 0099, 0132, 0209, 0248, 0401, 0413
Morphology 0231, 0233, 0235–0236
Music 0106, 0189–0190, 0269
Mythology 0040, 0078, 0132, 0136, 0159, 0176, 0210, 0214, 0216, 0218, 0225, 0264, 0287, 0351, 0384, 0391, 0398, 0419
Nama 0007, 0060, 0080, 0087, 0100, 0131, 0161–0162, 0269, 0274, 0322, 0327, 0333–0334
Namaqua 0102
Naro 0007–0009, 0012, 0017, 0019, 0026, 0049, 0076, 0129, 0133, 0139–0140, 0186, 0195, 0201, 0235–0236, 0249, 0262, 0269, 0274, 0296, 0300, 0327, 0335, 0355, 0359, 0402, 0403, 0404, 0428
Natural resources 0044–0045, 0120, 0154, 0164, 0230, 0255, 0285, 0305, 0363, 0374, 0376
Nature conservation 0044, 0304
Non-governmental organisations 0002, 0020, 0046–0048, 0056, 0069, 0110, 0114, 0122, 0147, 0149, 0152, 0154–0155, 0167, 0182, 0193–0195, 0199, 0273, 0277, 0291, 0298, 0305, 0308–0309, 0325, 0362, 0367, 0369, 0409, 0436–0438, 0441
N/u 0038, 0198, 0369
Oral history 0064, 0137, 0171, 0307, 0402
Orthography 0013, 0076, 0163, 0249, 0323, 0330, 0353, 0390, 0393, 0402, 0403
Ovambo 0002
Pastoralism 0083, 0115, 0128, 0166, 0187–0188, 0197, 0274, 0293, 0312, 0317, 0341, 0368, 0408
Phonetics 0087, 0349, 0353, 0388–0389
Phonology 0063, 0180, 0196, 0232–0233, 0236, 0344, 0346, 0393
Photos 0006, 0036, 0094, 0223, 0326, 0414
Physical anthropology 0103
Physical planning 0422
Plant ecology 0372
Political leadership 0050, 0061, 0123, 0131, 0238, 0305, 0363, 0409, 0447
Political systems 0015, 0318
Politics 0010, 0014, 0061, 0062, 0072, 0088, 0099, 0119, 0184, 0208, 0243, 0305, 0308, 0407, 0429

Poverty 0002, 0043, 0046, 0069, 0075, 0101, 0107, 0119, 0124, 0149, 0185, 0201, 0229, 0301, 0306, 0309, 0325, 0362–0365, 0367, 0383, 0416, 0426
Prehistory 0023, 0070, 0111, 0138, 0158, 0176, 0187, 0197, 0288, 0293, 0312, 0319, 0411
Pre-school education 0181, 0195, 0253, 0258, 0263, 0380
Primary education 0146, 0179, 0380
Psychology 0274, 0300, 0381
Regional cooperation 0056, 0110, 0163, 0230, 0308, 0436–438
Religion 0007, 0018, 0020, 0027, 0034, 0058, 0073, 0078, 0081, 0090, 0095, 0099, 0106, 0116–0117, 0121, 0131, 0133, 0135–0136, 0159, 0173, 0175, 0205, 0208, 0210, 0212, 0215–0225, 0264, 0278–0279, 0284, 0294, 0310, 0313, 0316, 0326, 0329, 0335–337, 0360, 0378, 0391, 0395–0396, 0398, 0410, 0443
Remote area development 0043, 0061, 0085, 0107, 0124, 0146, 0192, 0202, 0244–0245, 0250, 0253, 0256, 0258, 0263, 0265, 0271, 0273, 0298
Research 0007, 0008, 0013, 0016, 0023–0024, 0026, 0028–0035, 0039–0040, 0068, 0073, 0078, 0081–0083, 0085, 0089, 0100, 0106, 0113, 0115–0118, 0130–0131, 0135, 0137, 0142, 0159–0160, 0174–0175, 0183, 0186, 0188–0190, 0197, 0205, 0211, 021–0215, 0217–0222, 0224–0225, 0232, 0234, 0237, 0242–0243, 0246, 0256–0260, 0275, 0280, 0282, 0290, 0300, 0302, 0310–0311, 0314, 0323–0324, 0330–0332, 0343, 0345, 0349–0351, 0354, 0370, 0385, 0391, 0394, 0408, 0411–0412, 0415, 0418–0421, 0433, 0443
Resettlement 0072, 0086, 0108, 0123, 0150–0151, 0167, 0200, 0321, 0427
Resources management 0044, 0061, 0157, 0255
Resources utilization 0206
Revisionism 0010, 0130–0131, 0317
Rituals 0049, 0106, 0133, 0170, 0212, 0284, 0316
River bushmen 0074, 0153
Rock art 0016, 0018, 0034, 0058, 0070–0071, 0073, 0078–0079, 0081–0082, 0089–0090, 0095, 0113, 0116–0117, 0135, 0158–0160, 0174–0175, 0197, 0210, 0212–0225, 0237, 0264, 0279–0284, 0287–0289, 0294–0295, 0310, 0313–0314, 0316, 0318, 0343, 0350–0351, 0360, 0378, 0391, 0395, 0411–0412, 0415, 0418–0420, 0430–0435, 0442–0443
Rural development 0192–0193, 0255–0256, 0363, 0376
Sandawe 0097, 0100, 0127, 0161, 0180, 0231
School drop outs 0141, 0179, 0181, 0254, 0277, 0416
School enrolment 0181, 0277
Schools 0179, 0392
Sedentism 0009, 0020, 0092, 0168–0169, 0184, 0242, 0265, 0336, 0355, 0373, 0414, 0426
Sekgalgadi 0012

Self-determination 0001, 0014, 0044, 0061, 0112, 0114, 0193–0194, 0200, 0202, 0208, 0230, 0298, 0308–0309, 0315, 0339, 0363, 0437–0438
Self-development 0020, 0047, 0056, 0147, 0149, 0152, 0155, 0199, 0206, 0228, 0250, 0271, 0325, 0436, 0441
Serfdom 0114, 0147, 0248, 0371
Setswana 0011–0012, 0062
Settlement policy 0043, 0107, 0202, 0252
Settlements 0009, 0020, 0205, 0244, 0250, 0276, 0373
Sex roles 0144, 0205
Shamanism 0058, 0081, 0090, 0106, 0115, 0121, 0132–0133, 0135, 0160, 0170, 0214–0225, 0264, 0278, 0294, 0310, 0313, 0350, 0372, 0396, 0419, 0442, 0443
Sheep 0070
Social change 0002, 0025, 0077, 0153, 0185, 0205, 0265, 0295, 0309, 0321, 0373, 0399, 0426
Social organisation 0006–0007, 0038, 0103, 0196, 0204, 0207, 0240, 0276, 0302–0321, 0329, 0336, 0355, 0372, 0379
Social organization 0009, 0023, 0025, 0042, 0064, 0105, 0132, 0153, 0183, 0208, 0211, 0224, 0241, 0246, 0328, 0360
Social structure 0131, 0423, 0425
Southern 0026, 0038, 0198, 0327, 0346, 0390
Stone age 0176
Surveys 0254
Sustainable development 0255
Teacher training 0380, 0392
Teaching 0292, 0380, 0392
Terminology 0050, 0323
Territoriality 0008, 0145, 0156, 0337
Teti 0140
Tourism 0101, 0147, 0202, 0295, 0305, 0376
Tracking 0226
Training 0056, 0061, 0192–0194, 0226, 0263, 0292, 0315, 0447
Trance 0025, 0058–0059, 0081, 0090, 0098, 0106, 0115, 0117, 0121, 0132–0133, 0135, 0160, 0170, 0214–0225, 0264, 0294, 0313, 0316, 0326, 0336, 0372, 0396, 0398, 0419, 0442, 0443
Tshwa 0013, 0139–0140
Tsua 0140, 0344
Ts'ixa 0376
Tyua 0153
Violence 0207
Visual perception 0158, 0279
Wages 0061, 0270
Water 0047–0048, 0108, 0422
Water supply 0228, 0417
Wildlife 0044, 0151, 0157
Women 0067, 0092, 0110, 0240, 0251, 0297, 0316

Women's role 0170
Work 0066
Xhosa 0060, 0227, 0231

Geographic Index

/Xai/Xai 0157
Africa 0289, 0377
Angola 0052, 0073, 0106, 0191, 0235, 0274, 0307, 0314, 0327, 0362
Australia 0337
Bambara 0377
Bere 0195
Botswana 0006–0013, 0015, 0017–0020, 0024, 0026, 0042– 0044, 0046–0049, 0056, 0061–0064, 0067–0069, 0071–0077, 0084, 0085, 0086, 0091, 0092–0094, 0096, 0098, 0105–0108, 0110–0111, 0114, 0118, 0122, 0124, 0129, 0131– 0133, 0135, 0137–0142, 0144–0151, 0153–0154, 0156–0157, 0161, 0164, 0167–0170, 0172, 0177–0179, 0181–0186, 0192–0195, 0197, 0199, 0201–0207, 0219, 0223, 0228– 0229, 0232–0233, 0235, 0242, 0244–0259, 0262–0263, 0265, 0269–0277, 0282, 0287, 0290, 0293– 0294, 0297–0302, 0305, 0312, 0314, 0317–0318, 0321, 0323–0328, 033–0337, 0339, 0341, 0344–0345, 0347, 0352, 0355, 0359, 0362, 0364, 0370–0371, 0372–0376, 0380–0381, 0385–0387, 0390, 0392– 0394, 0399, 0402–0404, 0410–0411, 0413– 0414, 0416–0417, 0421–0422, 0424, 0426–0427, 0429, 0436–0438
Bulilimamangwe 0230
Cape 0004, 0019, 0027–0035, 0037, 0040–0041, 0065–0066, 0099, 0102–0104, 0109, 0128, 0135–0136, 0160, 0171, 0209, 0214, 0236, 0237–0239, 0267– 0268, 0286, 0288, 0329, 0335, 0340–0341, 0368, 0401, 0425
Caprivi 0414
Central Africa 0082
Central District 0061
Central Kalahari Game Reserve 0072, 0086, 0107–0108, 0114, 0122–0123, 0137, 0150– 0151, 0154, 0156, 0167, 0169, 0252, 0259, 0372–0373, 0414, 0417, 0427
Chobe District 0061
Chobokwane 0228
Dobe 0020, 0203, 0205–0206, 0242
Drakensberg 0034, 0210 , 0215, 0295, 0310, 0412, 0419-0420, 0439-0440, 0443
D'kar 0046, 0048, 0182, 0193–0195, 0201, 0273, 0339, 0402
East Africa 0082
East Hanahai 0182
Eastern Cape 0050
Europe 0220
Free State 0090, 0279
Gemsbok National Park 0414
Ghanzi 0046, 0416
Ghanzi District 0047, 0061, 0094, 0123, 0129, 0147, 0179, 0181, 0193–0195, 0229, 0305, 0380

Hanahai 0195
Inalego 0265
Kacgae 0046, 0182
Kagga Kamma 0114
Kalahari 0075
Kalahari Desert 0147, 0156, 0168, 0170, 0276, 0290, 0357
Kalahari Gemsbok National Park 0101, 0114, 0170, 0309
Kang 0046
Kaudwane 0167
Kgalagadi District 0061, 0229, 0254
Kgatleng District 0061, 0301
Kgomodiatshaba 0301
Khwa 0228
Khwai 0044
Korfshoek 0280
Kutse 0184, 0185
Kwazulu-Natal 0136, 0210, 0295, 0310, 0412, 0420, 0439, 0440, 0443
Kweneng District 0061, 0301
Lesotho 0175, 0214, 0219, 0282, 0314, 0327, 0343, 0377
Lone Tree 0381
Maake 0263, 0265
Mali 0377
Marulamantse 0111
Matopos 0176
Matsieng 0410
Monong 0228, 0263, 0265
Motokwe 0048
Namib Desert 0187
Namibia 0001–0003, 0007–0009, 0013–0014, 0020–0022, 0025–0026, 0045, 0053, 0056–0057, 0072–0073, 0080, 0087, 0089, 0091, 0094, 0100, 0106, 0110, 0112, 0114, 0119–0120, 0122, 0126, 0131, 0134–0135, 0143, 0147, 0155, 0157–0159, 0161, 0163, 0170, 0178, 0187– 0188, 0196, 0199, 0205, 0240–0241, 0249, 0261, 0269, 0274, 0276, 0284– 0285, 0291–0292, 0294, 0303–0304, 0311–0312, 0314, 0316, 0325, 0327–328, 0330–0334, 0338, 0341– 0342, 0349, 0353, 0355, 0358– 0359, 0361–0367, 0369, 0383, 0389, 0400, 0403, 0408, 0413–0415, 0421, 0429, 0436–0438, 0441, 0444—0449
Nata 0184
Ncaang 0263
New Xade 0072, 0108, 0114, 0167
Ngamiland 0044, 0061, 0157, 0172, 0185, 0374–0376, 0422
Ngwatle 0265
Northern Cape 0036, 0050, 0101, 0165, 0306, 0319
Norway 0118
Nxai Nxai 0422

Nyae Nyae 0001, 0020, 0106, 0122, 0155, 0241, 0291, 0292, 0304, 0414, 0441
N!Oma 0293
Okavango Delta 0044, 0064, 0074, 0374
Omaheke District 0367
Omaheke South 0119
Otjozondupa 0045
Qabo 0228
Qwa Qwa National Park 0280, 0281, 0289
Schmidtsdrift 0088, 0122, 0200, 0308
Serowe 0111, 0371
South Africa 0004–0005, 0016, 0019, 0026–0041, 0050–0051, 0054– 0056, 0065–0067, 0073, 0075, 0079–0080–0081, 0083, 0088, 0090, 0094–0095, 0099, 0101– 0104, 0109–0110, 0114, 0121– 0122, 0125, 0127–0128, 0135, 0147, 0159–0161, 0165, 0170–0171, 0174, 0178, 0198, 0200, 0209–210, 0212–0216, 0219, 0221, 0224–0226, 0234–235, 0237–0239, 0243, 0264, 0266–0268, 0278–0283, 0286, 0288, 0295, 0306–0310, 0314– 0315, 0319–0320, 0322, 0327–0329, 0338, 0340–0341, 0354, 0357, 0362, 0364, 0368, 0379, 0382, 0384, 0391, 0395, 0401, 0407, 0409, 0412, 0414, 0418–0420, 0425, 0431– 0432, 0434–0440, 0442–0443, 0445
South Westen Cape 0442
Southern Africa 0010, 0058–0060, 0078, 0082, 0097, 0113, 0130, 0152, 0158, 0166, 0190, 0211, 0217– 0218, 0220, 0222, 0274, 0311, 0313, 0315–0316, 0346, 0356, 0360, 0378–0379, 0396, 0421, 0423, 0428, 0430, 0433
Southern District 0061
Takatokwane 0381
Tanzania 0042, 0097, 0100, 0127, 0147, 0161, 0180, 0231, 0322
Thaba Sione 0278
Tshabong 0011
Tsholotsho 0230
Tshumkwe 0014, 0155, 0276, 0304, 0383
Tsodilo Hills 0018, 0071, 0293, 0317, 0318, 0411
Ukhwi 0228, 0263, 0265
West Africa 0377
West Caprivi 0119, 0120
Western Cape 0050
Western Caprivi 0331
Xade 0072, 0108, 0336, 0372–0373
Xhabo 0250
Zambia 0052, 0073, 0307, 0314, 0362
Zimbabwe 0059, 0070– 0071, 0073, 0095, 0115–0117, 0153, 0176, 0230, 0282, 0307, 0362, 0410, 0434– 0435
Zulu 0005
Zutshwa 0185, 0228, 0255, 0263, 0265, 0273